משנה

ArtScroll Mesorah Series®

Rabbi Nosson Scherman / Rabbi Meir Zlotowitz
General Editors

הגדה של פסח

Chassidic Masters

by

Rabbi Shalom Meir Wallach

Haggadah of the

Published by

Mesorah Publications, ltd

in conjunction with

ArtScroll / ארטסקרול/ירושלים בע"מ Jerusalem, Ltd.

A TVUNAH PUBLICATION

FIRST EDITION
First Impression . . . February, 1990

Published and Distributed by
MESORAH PUBLICATIONS, Ltd.
Brooklyn, New York 11232

Distributed in Israel by
MESORAH MAFITZIM / J. GROSSMAN
Rechov Harav Uziel 117
Jerusalem, Israel

Distributed in Europe by
J. LEHMANN HEBREW BOOKSELLERS
20 Cambridge Terrace
Gateshead, Tyne and Wear
England NE8 1RP

Distributed in Australia & New Zealand by
GOLD'S BOOK & GIFT CO.
36 William Street
Balaclava 3183, Vic., Australia

Distributed in South Africa by
KOLLEL BOOKSHOP
22 Muller Street
Yeoville 2198
South Africa

ISBN:
0-89906-222-9 (hard cover)
0-89906-223-7 (paperback)

Typography by CompuScribe at ArtScroll Studios, Ltd.
4401 Second Avenue / Brooklyn, N.Y. 11232 / (718) 921-9000

Printed in the United States of America by Moriah Offset
Bound by Sefercraft, Quality Bookbinders, Ltd. Brooklyn, N.Y.

בחר ה׳ ביעקב

This volume is dedicated
in memory of

הרב יעקב ב״ר אליעזר קיפפעל זצ״ל

Rabbi Jacob Kiffel זצ״ל

נפטר במוצאי שבת קודש ט״ו סיון תשמ״ט / June 18, 1989

He was a 'brand rescued from fire' —
but the flame of his soul was never extinguished.

Orphaned and alone from the age of twelve,
he wandered from Poland through Siberia to France.
Always determined to be near Torah and its scholars,
and longing to become a talmid chochom himself.

He succeeded.

He came to America to learn, but by personal example
he became a rosh yeshiva of inspiration.
He taught joy, faith, fulfillment in Torah,
devotion to rebbayim, loyalty to friends.

All his life his smile and wit illuminated his surroundings
and inspired his comrades. A profoundly devoted husband
and father, he raised a generation of b'nei Torah
who are worthy of his hopes.

Snuffed out suddenly while still bright and vibrant,
his memory remains the light of his stricken family
and a model for all who knew him.

תנצב״ה

Publisher's Preface

The chassidic story and the chassidic insight into a verse or commandment have become staples of Jewish life and thought. scores of Chassidism's great leaders have become household words, and their stories and parables have given new dimensions to our understanding of life and our mission as Jews. This book mines that rich treasury of literature and tradition, and applies it to the *Haggadah*.

From an almost infinite library of commentary and tales, Rabbi Shalom Meir Wallach has assembled a new commentary on the *Haggadah*. As the Talmud teaches, one who exerts himself in the study of Torah will find success. Rabbi Wallach has exerted himself and he has found the material to create an enlightening and fascinating book that is not only a commentary on the *Haggadah,* but makes interesting and informative reading all year round.

In addition, this book offers an essay that explains and illustrates the major significance of stories in Chassidic teaching and life. And, not surprisingly, the essay itself is filled with meaningful stories.

The art of anthology is a delicate and demanding one. It demands taste, breadth, and writing skill. Rabbi Wallach has all three, and that is why this book was a runaway success in its original Hebrew edition in Israel. We are grateful to him for making this work available to the English-reading Jewish public. To Yaakov Petroll, who translated, is a scholar of consummate skill whose work has become familiar to ArtScroll readers. So is Rabbi Shlomo Fox-Ashrei, who edited. It is our privilege to make their work available to the English-reading Torah public. They have all rendered a valuable service to tens of thousands of people.

Once more it is our pleasure to acknowledge the Director of ArtScroll Jerusalem, Reb Shmuel Blitz for coordinating this major project in the same efficient, dedicated manner that he brings to all of ArtScroll's book from Israel. He is a major force in the field of Torah Judaica and we are proud that he has been a key factor in the ArtScroll Series since its earliest Years.

Introduction
Chasidim and the Chasidic Tale

The movement of Chasidus was founded some two hundred and fifty years ago by the sainted Ba'al Shem Tov, R' Yisrael of Mezhibuz. In a short period it conquered by storm most of greater Poland and Galitzia, and wide areas of Russia and Lithuania. Thereafter it spread to Rumania and Hungary. The disciples of the Ba'al Shem, and their disciples after them, founded dynasties of rebbes (*admorim*) who led tens of thousands of chasidim and created chasidic courts by the hundreds, each unique, each with its traditions and character, each with its teachings and its tales.

What was the message which the Ba'al Shem brought to the world? What was original in Chasidus?

The standard answer is that it turned to the masses, to the simple folk, who felt neglected and rejected. By placing emphasis on the heart and its intentions, by stressing the elements of joy and devotion, it made the common people stand up tall. In practice, this led to purposeful intention (כַּוָּנָה) in prayer, to song and dance, to the cohesion of the group and the all-inclusive embrace of all orders of society. Taken as a whole, it was a novel application of the remark of *Chazal*:

> The one who does more, and the one who does less, are equal, provided that each directs his heart towards Heaven (*Berachos* 5b).

"A Jew preoccupied on a market day, running about here and there, buying and selling, of a sudden might raise his eyes heavenward and, heart all atwitter, cry out, 'Oh my! The sun will soon set and I have not yet offered up my *minchah* prayer.' He seeks a secluded corner and prays in haste and confusion. And, nevertheless," the Ba'al Shem Tov would say, "angels and seraphim tremble before this prayer!"

And there is the well-known story of the *Ne'ilah* (Concluding Prayer) on a particular Yom Kippur. The Ba'al Shem prayed at great length and strove mightily to do away with an accusation brought in the court of heaven, an accusation which would lead to the passing of a terrible decree. His disciples, too, felt what was happening and joined their prayers to his in moving plea. Tears fell from their eyes in full rivulets and the cries echoed and re-echoed from the vault of the *beis midrash* — but went unanswered. The heavenly charge, as yet, stood ground; the gates of compassion were sealed.

Among those present was a villager, who could barely pray, and his son, who did not know how to read or write. The lad looked and looked at the congregation pouring its heart out to the Creator. His heart groaned within him; he longed to share in the prayer, but could not. "Yet there is something I can do, Master of the world," said the youngster. Out of his pocket came a reed pipe. He put it to his lips and let loose a sharp, high, shrill whistle.

All stood shocked and silent. And then the Ba'al Shem Tov broke out in song with a happy melody. That piercing note which came by way of a shepherd's pipe from the innermost recesses of a youngster's heart had torn through the barriers on high, drawing up all the prayers in its wake. The prosecution was silenced; the impending decree dismissed.

❦ ❦ ❦

The foregoing is all true. But we will be distorting and oversimplifying the picture if we say that it represents the total message of Chasidus.

Not for this alone did the Ba'al Shem receive Torah from Achiah of Shiloh, the teacher of Eliyahu HaNavi (as his disciple, the author of the *Toledos Yaakov Yosef* of Polno'e, bears witness; *Parashas Balak*). Not for this alone was he found worthy of the hidden light of Torah which enabled him to see from one end of the world to the other (by witness of his grandson, author of *Degel Machaneh Efraim*; *Parashas Bereishis*). Not for this alone did he realize tremendous achievements when his soul rose to heaven, night after night (as the Gaon of Vilna bears witness in *Keser Rosh*). Once, indeed, he remarked to his grandson in explaining the verse: "It (the Torah) is not in the heavens . . . nor on the far side of the ocean" (*Devarim* 30:12-13), "I swear to you that there is one who learns the Torah from the Holy One, Himself — not from an angel or a seraph — *in the heavens*. And he is not certain at any time that he will not be banished in the next moment to the abyss — *on the far side of the ocean*" (concluding passage of *Degel Machaneh Efraim*).

Chasidus is, essentially, a two-sided coin. On the one hand it turns to the masses. It encourages them; it presents a face of joy to them. But on the other hand it seeks out the exceptional among men, opening before them deep and hidden treasures of the mind. Upon them it makes limitless demands. The Ba'al Shem claimed that the snatched and hurried prayer of the preoccupied few shook the angels and seraphim. Yet, his disciple the Maggid of Zlotchov would say, "My *sin* of praying three times a day is more than enough. For is *that* how one prays to his Creator?" And R' Elimelech of Lizensk was convinced that it would be necessary to fashion a new *Gehinnom* for him; the existing one, he thought, was insufficient for someone of his failings. He once was asked, "Does the Rebbe truly believe that? We see his acts of devotion. 'If flame befalls the cedars, what fate awaits the moss clinging to the walls?' What awaits us?"

"The fates are not comparable," said the Rebbe. "A man hit by a large club receives a blow, but nothing more. If, however, he is pierced by a sharp needle, it penetrates farther and farther within."

How was Chasidus able to maneuver between, or embrace, both of these positions; to appeal to the masses and make demands of an elite; to be simple and joyous, yet profound and severe? There were schools of Chasidus that found a road of the golden mean. The Ba'al Shem attracted the common folk, but also gave guidance to superior disciples — the Maggid of Mezritch, R' Pinchas of Kuritz, the authors of the *Hafla'ah*, of *Meir Nesivim*, the Maggid of Ostraha and others. His successor, the Maggid of Mezritch, followed in his footsteps. He concentrated a group of the great about himself, among whom were to be found R' Elimelech of Lizensk, R' Zusha of Hanipoli, R' Shmelke of Nikolsburg, R' Pinchas of Frankfurt, R' Levi Yitzchak of Berdichev, and the author of the *Tanya*, R' Shneur Zalman of Liadi. Yet, at one and the same time, he threw open his doors to the masses. So, too, his disciple, R' Elimelech of Lizensk, who counted the Chozeh of Lublin, the Maggid of Kuzhnitz, the Rebbe of Apta and R' Menachem Mendel of Riminov among his disciples. And after him, the Chozeh of Lublin at whose 'table' sat four hundred 'wearers of the white' (that was the dress of rebbes of those days) and along with them, the common folk streamed to him to receive his blessing and be delivered from their ordeals.

But there were schools of chasidic thought, great and well known, who tended to follow one of the two paths and did not walk in both. Pshischa split off from Lublin. The Yehudi of Pshischa, disciple though he was of the Chozeh of Lublin, drew about himself a circle of the elite, dove down to the depths of the soul and brought them up to the heights of the spirit. R' Bunim of Pshischa, who succeeded him, refined his approach. His way brought upon itself the anger of the other courts which attempted to denounce it at the great wedding in Ostilla, attended by hundreds of *admorim*. Only the wisdom of the disciples of Pshischa, with the Chidushei HaRim of Gur at their head, saved the day and repelled the charges of the accusation. This school of thought reached its zenith under the fierce guidance of the Rebbe (Fiery Angel) of Kotzk, who asked that forty men follow him into the forest. They would call out, "Hashem is God," and He would rain down *manna* for them.

And in contrast there were those courts which found it proper to descend to the masses, to lead them and aid them. By the nature of things, there were clashes between the two philosophies; between the piercing brilliance of Kotzk and the innumerable, clearly visible miracles of the sainted Zaide of Radoshitz; between the profundities and the mystical ways of Breslav and the amazing acts of marvel of the Shpole Zaide.

When the picture is taken as a whole, however, chasidism was multi-faceted. Elevated minds could be found side by side with simple folk at every chasidic court. Each found his place therein; each rose to the heights he could scale, led and directed by the rebbe in the light of the philosophy of his particular school of thought and the traditions of his dynasty — be it the world of pensive thought of Chabad or the world of images and "aspects" (בְּחִינוֹת) of Breslav; the world of allusions (רְמָזִים) of Ruzhin, or that of the penetrating remark of Kotzk; that of the biting satire of Ropshitz, or the world of fiery enthusiasm of Karlin.

❦ ❦ ❦

The two-sided character of Chasidus is also reflected in its creative works, both written and oral. The profound words of Torah, the lofty thoughts which are a full treasure-house of the mind are to be found in hundreds of works of Chasidus over the generations; they are directed to the intellectual elite. Some were, right from the start, unintelligible to, and not meant for, a broader, general audience; the contents of *Heichal HaBrachah* of Komarna and *Toras Avraham* of Slonim fall into such a category.

Others read easily, as if they could be understood without effort. It is their like that the Rebbe of Polno'e had in mind when he remarked of the sayings of the Ba'al Shem quoted in his work, "They are like the stars in heaven which seem so tiny and are really, each in itself, a world and its entirety." When R' Nachman of Breslav first received his great disciple-to-be, R' Nasan, he told him about a disciple of the Ba'al HaTanya who heard one saying from his master and expounded upon it for eight years. Indeed, this was what R' Nasan, himself, did in composing the *Likutei Halachos* on the teachings of his own master. The introduction to *Noam Elimelech* promises that everyone will understand what is written in it at his particular level. So it appears. Yet his disciple, the Rebbe of Riminov, claimed, "Angels and seraphim labor to the point of exhaustion, before they comprehend a passage in this work." Such are the seemingly simple.

Men of intellect refresh themselves, then, from wells of thought which are bottomless. What of the masses, the simple folk? On the surface, it would seem that the tales were fashioned for them. They passed from mouth to mouth, from father to son. They were told and retold at gatherings of friends, at *kiddushim* and *melavei malkah*. They often tell of the miracles brought about by the *tzaddikim*, showing their powers, fostering belief in them, and they encourage the listeners themselves to achieve greater heights.

At times this was clearly expressed:

Nor is such an attitude limited to chasidic circles only. The pre-eminent sage, the *Aderes* (R' Eliahu David Rabinowitz-Te'omim, Rabbi of Yerushalayim and before then of Ponoviezh and Mir), of Lithuanian stock, wrote a warm approbation in particular to *Eser Kedushos*, a work on the miraculous deeds of ten rebbes. There, he lists the stories of the wondrous acts of the *Tanna'im* and *Amora'im* which are mentioned in the *gemara* — the *Tanna'im* and *Amora'im* of whom it is said, "The least among them could revive the dead" (*Avodah Zara* 10b); "If the *tzaddikim* wished to do so, they could create the world" (*Sanhedrin* 65b).

Such an attitude is also reflected in *Chazal* when they say that there is no age that does not have *tzaddikim* of the stature of our forefather *Avraham* (*Succah* 54b); that a man must declare, "When will my deeds approach those of my forefathers, Avraham, Yitzchak and Yaakov?" (*Tanna D'vei Eliahu* 24). From this perspective, it could be said that the first "chasidic tales" are those related in *Bereishis*.

But we will err greatly if we see the tale of the *tzaddik* as folklore only, even if we view it as folklore with an ethical purpose. If its sole reason for being were to instill and strengthen our belief in *tzaddikim*, that would be sufficient. As the Rebbe of Sanz, the Divrei Chaim said, "I do not know whether or not the tales of wonders are true. But this I do know. The *tzaddikim* had it within their power to accomplish such wonders" (*Mekor Chaim*). True or make-believe, they have a moral force. The chasidic tale, however, goes far beyond this.

It must! For the young Menachem Mendel, who was to become the Rebbe of Kotzk, was first drawn to Chasidus by the stories. The Kotzker symbolizes trenchant genius and opposition to tales of the miraculous.

David HaMelech said : "Our forefathers in Egypt did not pay attention to understand (לֹא הִשְׂכִּילוּ) Your wonders" (*Tehillim* 106:7). The Fiery Angel of Kotzk interpreted the verse as saying that Israel in Egypt did not reach their heights of understanding by contemplating the miracles (he treated wonders — נִפְלְאוֹתֶיךָ — as the subject, and forefathers — אֲבוֹתֵינוּ — as the object): "Your wonders did not make our forefathers in Egypt understand." Yet it was he who said, "I became a chasid because of an old man in my town. He told tales of *tzaddikim*. He told and told, and I listened and listened."

It was not the wondrous which spoke to the heart of the keen youth. He paid scant attention to such matters. When he arrived in Lublin, he bought a small pocketknife before entering the presence of the Chozeh of Lublin for the first time. "Did you come to Lublin to buy a pocketknife?" asked the Chozeh with a smile.

Then and there he answered, "Rebbe, you will not win me over with your holy sight (*ruach hakodesh*). I have come to learn, not to be impressed!"

No! It was not the wondrous which drew him. But the old man knew how to tell the stories and Menachem Mendel knew how to listen. For there is something to hear in the chasidic tale. One must bend an ear and know how to listen. In the town of Yaritchov there was a well-known fool called Peretz. One day R' Shalom of Kaminka teasingly asked him, "Why don't you get married?"

"Why should a man marry?" said Peretz.

"What a question!" said R' Shalom. "To have children."

"If I want children, I'll travel to the Rebbe of Belz and ask that he bless me with children," declared the fool.

When he told the story over, R' Chaim of Sanz would say, "Do you think that R' Shalom wished to mock the fool? Certainly not! He wished to teach us that just as the *tzaddik's* blessing for children will not take effect unless one has a wife, so too, the chasid, who comes to the rebbe to draw up the spiritual by the bucketful, should know that he will gain nothing if he does not himself become involved in the study of Torah and in devotion to *Hashem* (*Rabbenu HaKadosh MiSanz* III 86).

The story was to be seen on at least two levels. It entered the mind as well as the ears.

The chasidic tale must be examined closely. It has not been transmitted from generation to generation without reason. The outer form, which makes it attractive, is designed to preserve its contents and message. Nor is that lesson and inner meaning always evident.

It is told that someone once wished to repeat a saying of R' David of

Lelov to the Chiddushei HaRim of Gur. "Don't tell me," said the Rebbe, "what they said, we are unable to comprehend."

The tales present uplifting examples; they have an appeal to the mind. But there is something more.

They have a special force; they awaken remembrance of the merit of the *tzaddikim* and bring about deliverance by sheer faith. "Through the words and through the recollection of the miracle the very force of the miracle is aroused and continues to have effect. That is why it is a *mitzvah* to tell over the story of the Exodus from Egypt" (The Rebbe of Lutzk in his *Divros Shlomo* on the Book of *Esther*).

The following story told by the Rebbe of Ruzhin shows us that this is the way *tzaddikim* themselves viewed the stories:

> Once a matter of life-or-death came before the Ba'al Shem Tov. The Rebbe ordered that a wax candle be made. He went to the forest with it, affixed it to a tree, appealed to the Holy One with special prayers and names, and brought forth deliverance. Years passed and a similar incident presented itself to his disciple, my grandfather, the Maggid of Mezritch, who followed in the Ba'al Shem's path. He, too, had a candle made, went into the forest near the very same tree and said, "I do not know what thoughts and purposeful intentions (כַּוָּנוֹת) the Ba'al Shem had. But I affix this candle, relying on those intentions." His act was accepted in Heaven and salvation followed. Years later, when R' Moshe Leib of Sasov faced a like problem he said, "I don't know where the forest or the tree is, but I will retell the tale and may Hashem help." And help came (*Knesses Yisrael* 23).

The tale presents uplifting examples; it provides food for thought; it has an ongoing life of its own.

Even when the true meaning escapes us, the story works its magic. R' Nachman of Breslav once said, "I see that my words of Torah are not affecting you. I shall start to tell you stories." Stories affect us all. The *Haggadah* says: "Even if we were all men of wisdom (חֲכָמִים), understanding (נְבוֹנִים), experience (זְקֵנִים), and knowledge of the Torah (יוֹדְעִים אֶת הַתּוֹרָה), it would still be an obligation upon us to tell about the Exodus from Egypt." For, as the Tzemach Tzedek of Lubavitch says, wisdom (חָכְמָה), understanding (בִּינָה), and knowledge (דַּעַת) do not and can not reach places which the story enters. It makes its way by another path, indirectly, into the innermost recesses of the soul.

The chasidic tale is not only the legacy of the simple; it belongs to all. Each one understands it at his own level. As the Rebbe of Radomsk puts it:

> *Chazal* say that the common talk of the servants of the Patriarchs is more important than the Torah of their children (*Bereishis Rabbah* 60; Eliezer tells his story to Rivkah's family at length and it is a repeated version, whereas many *mitzvos* and *halachos* are written in brief, or only alluded to in the Torah). They are important because the tales of the servants of the Patriarchs become Torah for the sons (*Tiferes Shlomo, Chanukah*).

Haggadah of the Chassidic Masters

בדיקת חמץ

The *chametz* search is initiated with the recitation of the following:

הֲרֵינִי מוּכָן וּמְזוּמָן לְקַיֵּם מִצְוַת עֲשֵׂה וְלֹא תַעֲשֶׂה שֶׁל בְּעוּר חָמֵץ. לְשֵׁם יִחוּד קֻדְשָׁא בְּרִיךְ הוּא וּשְׁכִינְתֵּהּ, עַל יְדֵי הַהוּא טָמִיר וְנֶעְלָם, בְּשֵׁם כָּל יִשְׂרָאֵל. וִיהִי נֹעַם אֲדֹנָי אֱלֹהֵינוּ עָלֵינוּ, וּמַעֲשֵׂה יָדֵינוּ כּוֹנְנָה עָלֵינוּ, וּמַעֲשֵׂה יָדֵינוּ כּוֹנְנֵהוּ:

בָּרוּךְ אַתָּה יהוה אֱלֹהֵינוּ מֶלֶךְ הָעוֹלָם, אֲשֶׁר קִדְּשָׁנוּ בְּמִצְוֹתָיו, וְצִוָּנוּ עַל בִּעוּר חָמֵץ.

Upon completion of the *chametz* search, the *chametz* is wrapped well and set aside to be burned the next morning and the following declaration is made. The declaration must be understood in order to take effect; one who does not understand the Aramaic text may recite it in English, Yiddish or any other language. Any *chametz* that will be used for that evening's supper or the next day's breakfast or for any other purpose prior to the final removal of *chametz* the next morning is not included in this declaration.

כָּל חֲמִירָא וַחֲמִיעָא דְּאִכָּא בִרְשׁוּתִי, דְּלָא חֲמִתֵּהּ וּדְלָא בִעַרְתֵּהּ וּדְלָא יְדַעְנָא לֵהּ, לִבָּטֵל וְלֶהֱוֵי הֶפְקֵר כְּעַפְרָא דְאַרְעָא.

יְהִי רָצוֹן מִלְּפָנֶיךָ, יהוה אֱלֹהֵינוּ וֵאלֹהֵי אֲבוֹתֵינוּ, שֶׁתְּזַכֵּנוּ לָתוּר וּלְחַפֵּשׂ בְּנִגְעֵי בָּתֵּי הַנֶּפֶשׁ, אֲשֶׁר נוֹאַלְנוּ בַּעֲצַת יִצְרֵנוּ הָרָע, וּתְזַכֵּנוּ לָשׁוּב בִּתְשׁוּבָה שְׁלֵמָה לְפָנֶיךָ, וְאַתָּה בְּטוּבְךָ הַגָּדוֹל תְּרַחֵם עָלֵינוּ. עָזְרֵנוּ אֱלֹהֵי יִשְׁעֵנוּ עַל דְּבַר כְּבוֹד שְׁמֶךָ, וְתַצִּילֵנוּ מֵאִסּוּר חָמֵץ, אֲפִילוּ בְּכָל שֶׁהוּא, בְּשָׁנָה זוּ וּבְכָל שָׁנָה כָּל יְמֵי חַיֵּינוּ. אָמֵן, כֵּן יְהִי רָצוֹן:

ביעור חמץ

יְהִי רָצוֹן מִלְּפָנֶיךָ, יהוה אֱלֹהֵינוּ וֵאלֹהֵי אֲבוֹתֵינוּ, כְּשֵׁם שֶׁאֲנִי מְבַעֵר הֶחָמֵץ מִבֵּיתִי וּמֵרְשׁוּתִי, כַּךְ יהוה אֱלֹהֵינוּ וֵאלֹהֵי אֲבוֹתֵינוּ תְּבַעֵר כָּל הַחִיצוֹנִים וְאֶת רוּחַ הַטֻּמְאָה תְּבַעֵר מִן הָאָרֶץ, וְאֶת יִצְרֵנוּ הָרָע תַּעֲבִירֵהוּ מֵאִתָּנוּ, וְתִתֶּן לָנוּ לֵב בָּשָׂר לְעָבְדְךָ בֶּאֱמֶת, וְכָל הַסִּטְרָא אַחְרָא וְכָל הָרִשְׁעָה כֻּלָּהּ כֶּעָשָׁן תִּכְלֶה, וְתַעֲבִיר מֶמְשֶׁלֶת זָדוֹן מִן הָאָרֶץ, וְכָל הַמְּעִיקִים לַשְּׁכִינָה תְּבַעֲרֵם בְּרוּחַ מִשְׁפָּט, כְּשֵׁם שֶׁהֶעֱבַרְתָּ אֶת מִצְרַיִם וְאֶת אֱלֹהֵיהֶם בַּיָּמִים הָהֵם וּבִזְּמַן הַזֶּה. אָמֵן:

The following declaration, which includes all *chametz* without exception, is to be made after the burning of leftover *chametz*. It should be recited in a language which one understands. When *Pesach* begins on *Motzaei Shabbos,* this declaration is made on *Shabbos* morning. Any *chametz* remaining from the *Shabbos* morning meal is flushed down the drain before the declaration is made.

SEARCH FOR CHAMETZ

The *chametz* search is initiated with the recitation of the following:

Behold, I am prepared and ready to perform the positive and negative commandments of removing chametz. For the sake of the unification of the Holy One, Blessed is He, and His Presence, through Him Who is hidden and inscrutable – [I pray] in the name of all Israel. May the pleasantness of my Lord, our God, be upon us – may He establish our handiwork for us; our handiwork may He establish.

Blessed are You, HASHEM, our God, King of the universe, Who has sanctified us by His commandments, and commanded us concerning the removal of chametz.

Upon completion of the *chametz* search, the *chametz* is wrapped well and set aside to be burned the next morning and the following declaration is made. The declaration must be understood in order to take effect; one who does not understand the Aramaic text may recite it in English, Yiddish or any other language. Any *chametz* that will be used for that evening's supper or the next day's breakfast or for any other purpose prior to the final removal of chametz the next morning is not included in this declaration.

Any chametz which is in my possession which I did not see, and remove, nor know about, shall be nullified and become ownerless, like the dust of the earth.

May it be Your will, HASHEM, our God and the God of our forefathers, that You enable us to explore and search out our spiritual maladies, which we have acquired by following the advice of our Evil Inclination; that You enable us to return in complete repentance before You; and may You, in Your abundant beneficence have mercy upon us. Assist us, O God of our salvation, for the sake of Your Name's glory, and rescue us from transgressing the prohibition of chametz in the slightest degree, this year and every year, for all the days of our lives. Amen. So may it be.

BURNING THE CHAMETZ

May it be Your will, HASHEM, our God and the God of our forefathers, that just as I have removed the chametz from my house and my property, so may You, HASHEM, our God and the God of our forefathers, remove all the external influences, and the spirit of defilement from the earth; cause our Evil Inclination to leave us, and give us a heart of flesh to serve You with sincerity; may all the forces of the "Other Side" and all evil evaporate like smoke; may the realm of wantonness pass from the earth; and may You remove, in the spirit of justice, all that impede the Divine Presence; just as You removed Egypt and its idols in those days at this season. Amen.

The following declaration, which includes all *chametz* without exception, is to be made after the burning of leftover *chametz*. It should be recited in a language which one understands. When *Pesach* begins on *Motzaei Shabbos,* this declaration is made on *Shabbos* morning. Any *chametz* remaining from the *Shabbos* morning meal is flushed down the drain before the declaration is made.

כָּל חֲמִירָא וַחֲמִיעָא דְּאִכָּא בִרְשׁוּתִי, דַּחֲזִתֵּהּ וּדְלָא חֲזִתֵּהּ, דַּחֲמִתֵּהּ וּדְלָא חֲמִתֵּהּ, דְּבִעַרְתֵּהּ וּדְלָא בִעַרְתֵּהּ, לִבָּטֵל וְלֶהֱוֵי הֶפְקֵר כְּעַפְרָא דְאַרְעָא.

יְהִי רָצוֹן מִלְּפָנֶיךָ, יהוה אֱלֹהֵינוּ וֵאלֹהֵי אֲבוֹתֵינוּ, שֶׁתְּרַחֵם עָלֵינוּ וְתַצִּילֵנוּ מֵאִסּוּר חָמֵץ, אֲפִילוּ מִכָּל שֶׁהוּא, לָנוּ וּלְכָל בְּנֵי בֵיתֵנוּ וּלְכָל יִשְׂרָאֵל, בְּשָׁנָה זוּ וּבְכָל שָׁנָה וְשָׁנָה כָּל יְמֵי חַיֵּינוּ. וּכְשֵׁם שֶׁבִּיעַרְנוּ הֶחָמֵץ מִבָּתֵּינוּ וְשְׂרַפְנוּהוּ, כֵּךְ תְּזַכֵּנוּ לְבַעֵר הַיֵּצֶר הָרָע מִקִּרְבֵּנוּ תָּמִיד כָּל יְמֵי חַיֵּינוּ, וּתְזַכֵּנוּ לְדַבֵּק בְּךָ וּבְתוֹרָתְךָ וְאַהֲבָתְךָ וּלְדַבֵּק בְּיֵצֶר הַטּוֹב תָּמִיד, אֲנַחְנוּ וְזַרְעֵנוּ וְזֶרַע זַרְעֵנוּ מֵעַתָּה וְעַד עוֹלָם. כֵּן יְהִי רָצוֹן, אָמֵן:

עירוב תבשילין

It is forbidden to prepare on *Yom Tov* for the next day even if that day is the Sabbath. If, however, Sabbath preparations were started before *Yom Tov* began, they may be continued on *Yom Tov*. *Eruv tavshilin* constitutes this preparation. A matzah and any cooked food (such as fish, meat or an egg) are set aside on the day before *Yom Tov* to be used on the Sabbath and the blessing is recited followed by the declaration [made in a language understood by the one making the *eruv*]. If the first days *of Pesach* fall on Thursday and Friday, an *eruv tavshilin* must be made on Wednesday. [In *Eretz Yisrael,* where only one day *Yom Tov* is in effect, the *eruv* is omitted.]

בָּרוּךְ אַתָּה יהוה אֱלֹהֵינוּ מֶלֶךְ הָעוֹלָם, אֲשֶׁר קִדְּשָׁנוּ בְּמִצְוֹתָיו, וְצִוָּנוּ עַל מִצְוַת עֵרוּב.

בְּהָדֵין עֵרוּבָא יְהֵא שָׁרֵא לָנָא לַאֲפוּיֵי וּלְבַשּׁוּלֵי וּלְאַצְלוּיֵי וּלְאַטְמוּנֵי וּלְאַדְלוּקֵי שְׁרָגָא וּלְתַקָּנָא וּלְמֶעְבַּד כָּל צָרְכָּנָא, מִיּוֹמָא טָבָא לְשַׁבְּתָא לָנָא וּלְכָל יִשְׂרָאֵל הַדָּרִים בָּעִיר הַזֹּאת.

הדלקת נרות

The candles are lit and the following blessings are recited.
When *Yom Tov* falls on *Shabbos,* the words in parentheses are added.

בָּרוּךְ אַתָּה יהוה אֱלֹהֵינוּ מֶלֶךְ הָעוֹלָם, אֲשֶׁר קִדְּשָׁנוּ בְּמִצְוֹתָיו, וְצִוָּנוּ לְהַדְלִיק נֵר שֶׁל [שַׁבָּת וְשֶׁל] יוֹם טוֹב.

בָּרוּךְ אַתָּה יהוה אֱלֹהֵינוּ מֶלֶךְ הָעוֹלָם, שֶׁהֶחֱיָנוּ וְקִיְּמָנוּ וְהִגִּיעָנוּ לַזְּמַן הַזֶּה.

Any chametz which is in my possession which I did or did not see, which I did or did not remove, shall be nullified and become ownerless, like the dust of the earth.

May it be Your will, HASHEM, our God and the God of our forefathers, that You be merciful with us and rescue us from transgressing the prohibition of chametz even in the slightest degree – us, our entire household, and all of Israel – this year and every year, for all the days of our lives. And just as we have removed the chametz from our houses and burnt it, so may You enable us to remove the Evil Inclination from within us eternally, all the days of our lives; may You enable us to cleave to You, to Your Torah, and to Your love, and to cleave to the Good Inclination eternally – us, our children, and our children's children – from now and forever. So may it be. Amen.

ERUV TAVSHILIN

It is forbidden to prepare on *Yom Tov* for the next day even if that day is the Sabbath. If, however, Sabbath preparations were started before *Yom Tov* began, they may be continued on *Yom Tov. Eruv tavshilin* constitutes this preparation. A matzah and any cooked food (such as fish, meat or an egg) are set aside on the day before *Yom Tov* to be used on the Sabbath and the blessing is recited followed by the declaration [made in a language understood by the one making the *eruv*]. If the first days *of Pesach* fall on Thursday and Friday, an *eruv tavshilin* must be made on Wednesday. [In *Eretz Yisrael,* where only one day *Yom Tov* is in effect, the *eruv* is omitted.]

Blessed are You, HASHEM, our God, King of the universe, Who sanctified us by His commandments and commanded us concerning the commandment of eruv.

Through this eruv may we be permitted to bake, cook, fry, insulate, kindle flame, prepare for, and do anything necessary on the festival for the sake of the Sabbath – for ourselves and for all Jews who live in this city.

LIGHTING THE CANDLES

The candles are lit and the following blessings are recited.
When *Yom Tov* falls on *Shabbos,* the words in parentheses are added.

Blessed are You, HASHEM, our God, King of the universe, Who has sanctified us through HIs commandments, and commanded us to kindle the flame of the (Sabbath and the) festival.

Blessed are You HASHEM, our God, King of the universe, Who has kept us alive, sustained us, and brought us to this season.

Preparing for the Seder

The Seder preparations should be made in time for the Seder to begin as soon as the synagogue services are finished. It should not begin before nightfall, however. Matzah, bitter herbs and several other items of symbolic significance are placed on the Seder plate in the arrangement shown below.

Matzah – Three whole matzos are placed one atop the other, separated by a cloth or napkin. Matzah must be eaten three times during the Seder, by itself, with maror, and as the afikoman. Each time, the minimum portion of matzah for each person should have a volume equivalent to half an egg. Where many people are present, enough matzos should be available to enable each participant to receive a proper portion.

Maror and **Chazeres** – Bitter herbs are eaten twice during the Seder, once by themselves and a second time with matzah. Each time a minimum portion, equal to the volume of half an egg, should be eaten.

The Talmud lists several vegetables that qualify as maror, two of which are put on the Seder plate in the places marked Chazeres and maror. Most people use romaine lettuce (whole leaves or stalks) for Chazeres, and horseradish (whole or grated) for maror, although either may be used for the mitzvah of eating maror later in the Seder.

Charoses — The bitter herbs are dipped into charoses (a mixture of grated apples, nuts, other fruit, cinnamon and other spices, mixed with red wine). The charoses has the appearance of mortar to symbolize the lot of the Hebrew slaves, whose lives were embittered by hard labor with brick and mortar.

Z'roa [Roasted bone] and **Beitzah** [Roasted egg] — On the eve of Passover in the Holy Temple in Jerusalem, two sacrifices were offered and their meat roasted and eaten at the Seder feast. To commemorate these two sacrifices we place a roasted bone (with some meat on it) and a roasted hard-boiled egg on the Seder plate.

The egg, a symbol of mourning, is used in place of a second piece of meat as a reminder of our mourning at the destruction of the Temple — may it be rebuilt speedily in our day.

Karpas — A vegetable (celery, parsley, boiled potato) other than bitter herbs completes the Seder plate. It will be dipped in salt water and eaten. (The salt water is not put on the Seder plate, but it, too, should be prepared beforehand, and placed near the Seder plate.)

קדש

Kiddush should be recited and the Seder begun as soon after synagogue services as possible — however, not before nightfall. Each participant's cup should be poured by someone else to symbolize the majesty of the evening, as though each participant had a servant.

הֲרֵינִי מוּכָן וּמְזוּמָן לְקַדֵּשׁ עַל הַיַּיִן, וּלְקַיֵּם מִצְוַת כּוֹס רִאשׁוֹן מֵאַרְבַּע כּוֹסוֹת. לְשֵׁם יִחוּד קֻדְשָׁא בְּרִיךְ הוּא וּשְׁכִינְתֵּיהּ, עַל יְדֵי הַהוּא טָמִיר וְנֶעְלָם, בְּשֵׁם כָּל יִשְׂרָאֵל. וִיהִי נֹעַם אֲדֹנָי אֱלֹהֵינוּ עָלֵינוּ, וּמַעֲשֵׂה יָדֵינוּ כּוֹנְנָה עָלֵינוּ, וּמַעֲשֵׂה יָדֵינוּ כּוֹנְנֵהוּ:

קַדֵּשׁ / *Kaddesh*

Shpole Zaide

It is customary for teachers of the very young to have their tender pupils memorize the key words which give the order of the Seder (קַדֵּשׁ וּרְחַץ וְכוּ׳) along with their traditional interpretations.

Once, on the evening of the Seder, the *Shpole Zaide* asked his little son to recite the key aloud. The youngster began, "*Kaddesh* — when the father comes from the *beis knesses*, the synagogue, on the evening of the Seder, he must immediately recite *kiddush*."

His father waited for him to continue, but the child said that the teacher had not taught him anything further on this point. And so, his father taught him the conclusion: "so that the youngsters won't fall asleep, but will ask the *Ma Nishtannah* (the Four Questions)."

On the following day, the teacher was present at the Rebbe's *tish* (table) and the Rebbe asked him, "Why didn't you teach the children the concluding remarks?"

"I didn't want to have them go to the trouble," said the teacher, "especially since it isn't a very important reason. For even a man who has no children recites the *kiddush* immediately on his arrival from the *beis knesses*."

The Rebbe became angry, "Are you the one to judge which reason is important and which is not? Are you wiser than all the other teachers? How did you dare change the version that has been taught for generations? Let me tell you what those who lived before us alluded to with this statement.

"*When the father* — that is our Father in Heaven — *comes from the beis knesses on the evening of the Seder* and sees how his children, the people of Israel, have severed themselves from the life of the everyday and the darkness and troubles of the Exile, how they have come to the *beis knesses* to pray before Him and praise Him for their Redemption; when He sees this, *He must immediately say kiddush* — He must renew the *kiddushin*, the marriage bond between Himself and ourselves, and take us out of exile; *so that the youngsters won't fall asleep* — so that we don't sink into a deep slumber in our Exile; *but will ask the Ma Nishtannah, why is this night different from all other nights* — why is this night, this Exile, longer than all the other exiles."

When he had said this, the Zaide burst into torrential weeping and all

KADDESH

Kiddush should be recited and the Seder begun as soon after synagogue services as possible — however, not before nightfall. Each participant's cup should be poured by someone else to symbolize the majesty of the evening, as though each participant had a servant.

Behold, I am prepared and ready to recite the Kiddush over wine, and to fulfill the mitzvah of the first of the Four Cups. For the sake of the unification of the Holy One, Blessed is He, and His Presence, through Him Who is hidden and inscrutable — [I pray] in the name of all Israel. May the pleasantness of my Lord, our God, be upon us — may He establish our handiwork for us; our handiwork may He establish.

---

present wept along with him. The Zaide came to himself and said, "Now we must give our Father some joy; we must show Him that His child can dance in the darkness, too." And he ordered them to sing a melody and began to dance, as was his holy way (*Sipurei Chasidim*).

קַדֵּשׁ וּרְחַץ / *Kaddesh Urechatz*

Tiferes Shmuel

On the first *Pesach* after he had become Rebbe, the *Tiferes Shmuel of Alexander* remarked: "The order of the *seder* is *kaddesh urechatz* — say the *kiddush* (קִידוּשׁ) the prayer of sanctification of the Festival, and then wash hands. Should not the order have been the reverse? First wash — a man should wash himself clean of sin — and then rise and become holy (יִתְקַדֵּשׁ).

"If, however, we think in terms of a parable, we can understand the order. Not everyone is permitted to enter the palace of a king. Even those who have been invited to do so must make preparations, they must dress properly. And they can only go in at the appointed hour. If a man should enter without an invitation, without preparing himself — in sackcloth, or at an hour other than the one assigned — he would be severely punished.

"But if the man was fleeing from a band of murderous robbers, and would rush into the palace to save his life, no one would hold him blameworthy or punish him.

"On the evening of the first Seder in Egypt, Israel was sunk in the depths of impurity and corruption and was about to sink into the final depth and be completely assimilated. They were forced to leap up and out of the abyss into the palace of the King of kings to save themselves. They sanctified themselves (*kaddesh*) first, so to speak, and only afterwards went through stages of preparation; through the counting of the forty-nine days of the *omer*. That was the *urechatz*, the washing away of the sins" (*Eser Zechuyos* 20).

הֲרֵינִי מוּכָן / *Behold, I am prepared*

R' Chaim of Sanz

R' Chaim of Sanz was on his way to prayers. He reached the *beis midrash*, turned about, and retraced his steps. The *Rav of Barniv* followed him. R' Chaim returned home, remained

On Friday night begin here:

(וַיְהִי עֶרֶב וַיְהִי בֹקֶר)

יוֹם הַשִּׁשִּׁי: וַיְכֻלּוּ הַשָּׁמַיִם וְהָאָרֶץ וְכָל צְבָאָם. וַיְכַל אֱלֹהִים בַּיּוֹם הַשְּׁבִיעִי מְלַאכְתּוֹ אֲשֶׁר עָשָׂה, וַיִּשְׁבֹּת בַּיּוֹם הַשְּׁבִיעִי מִכָּל מְלַאכְתּוֹ אֲשֶׁר עָשָׂה. וַיְבָרֶךְ אֱלֹהִים אֶת יוֹם הַשְּׁבִיעִי וַיְקַדֵּשׁ אֹתוֹ, כִּי בוֹ שָׁבַת מִכָּל מְלַאכְתּוֹ אֲשֶׁר בָּרָא אֱלֹהִים לַעֲשׂוֹת.[1]

---

there for a brief period and, once more, started on his way to the *beis midrash*. When he noticed the *Rav of Barniv*, he said, "Do you know why I returned home? A man must mentally prepare himself before fulfilling any *mitzvah*. Walking to the *beis midrash* is itself a *mitzvah*. And because I was so concerned with preparing myself for prayer, I neglected to think that I was about to perform the *mitzvah* of walking to the *beis midrash*. That is why I returned home."

He raised his voice and added, "Now, behold, I am walking to the *beis midrash* to pray!" (*Otzar HaSipurim* VI:11).

וַיְכֻלּוּ / *(Thus the heaven and the earth) were finished*

R' Avraham Yaakov of Sadigur

Several free-thinking, 'enlightened' Jews (*maskilim*) had arranged among themselves to be present at the *tish* (table) of *R' Avraham Yaakov of Sadigur* to scoff and mock him when he would say *kiddush* over the wine.

When they arrived, the Rebbe's face lit up with pleasure. "How fitting it is to say *kiddush* now," he said. When we pronounce the passage of *vayechulu* (וַיְכֻלּוּ), we bear witness to the creation of the heaven and earth and the dominion of the Holy One over His world. Testimony is only relevant when doubts are cast and protest is raised. Let us stand before those who protest, and bear witness out loud."

And with that, he began the *kiddush* (*Imrei Tzaddikim* 4).

בָּרוּךְ אַתָּה ה' / *Blessed are You, Hashem*

R' Shlomo Leib of Lentchena

Once when *R' Shlomo Leib of Lentchena* uttered the name of Hashem in the blessing over the wine during *kiddush*, he was beset by fear. All his limbs trembled, the cup fell from his hand, and the wine spilled. The cup was refilled and he completed *kiddush* in a loud voice as was his custom.

Subsequently, he did not hold the cup in his free unsupported hand, but would place his hand on the arm rest of the chair and the cup would be placed within it (*Eser Ataros* 8).

On Friday night begin here:

(And there was evening and there was morning)

The sixth day. Thus the heaven and the earth were finished, and all their array. On the seventh day God completed His work which He had done, and He abstained on the seventh day from all His work which He had done. God blessed the seventh day and hallowed it, because on it He abstained from all His work which God created to make.[1]

1. *Bereishis* 1:31-2:3.

R' Aaron Leib of Premishlan

One of the chasidim of *R' Aaron Leib of Premishlan* begged of the Rebbe that he might behold Eliyahu HaNavi, at least in a dream. The Rebbe gave his promise.

Some time later, the chasid dreamt that Eliyahu had come to his home. In his great excitement and joy, he did not know how to receive Eliyahu or what to offer him. He asked his wife to serve cake for the Prophet's pleasure. Eliyahu looked at him and said, "Fie! Do you think I would pronounce the great and awesome name of Hashem in a blessing on mere physical goods?"

That short statement filled the chasid with such fear and dread, that, for the rest of his life, whenever he would open his mouth to make a blessing, his teeth chattered in terror (*Rachamei Av*).

מֶלֶךְ הָעוֹלָם / *King of the universe*

R' Chaim of Sanz

The *Rav of Barniv* very much wished to see how *R' Chaim of Sanz* awoke from sleep. He begged the Rebbe's *shammash* (personal attendant) to allow him to enter the Rebbe's bed chamber and was granted permission.

Towards morning, the Rebbe arose with a lion's roar* and cried out loudly, "I say praise before You (*Modeh Ani*), King." He repeated the word *King* several times until he said with a heartrending groan, "I don't yet feel the King's presence — " and he broke off and did not complete the *Modeh Ani*. He washed his hands, made the morning blessings and the blessings of the Torah — all while sitting on his bed — and instructed his *gabbai* to bring a *gemara*. He learned with fervor for some two hours, closed the *gemara*, ran his hand across his chest and said, "Ah! Now I know and feel that He is King," and he concluded the prayer, "*living and existing, Who has mercifully returned my soul to me, great is Your faithfulness*" (*Otzar HaSipurim* II:14).

[**lion's roar* — The opening words of the *Shulchan Aruch* are: He should be powerful like a lion to arise in the morning (*Orach Chaim* 1:1).]

On all nights other than Friday, begin here;
on Friday night include all passages in parentheses.

סַבְרִי מָרָנָן וְרַבָּנָן וְרַבּוֹתַי:

בָּרוּךְ אַתָּה יהוה אֱלֹהֵינוּ מֶלֶךְ הָעוֹלָם, בּוֹרֵא פְּרִי הַגָּפֶן:

בָּרוּךְ אַתָּה יהוה אֱלֹהֵינוּ מֶלֶךְ הָעוֹלָם, אֲשֶׁר בָּחַר בָּנוּ מִכָּל עָם, וְרוֹמְמָנוּ מִכָּל לָשׁוֹן, וְקִדְּשָׁנוּ בְּמִצְוֹתָיו. וַתִּתֶּן לָנוּ יהוה אֱלֹהֵינוּ בְּאַהֲבָה [שַׁבָּתוֹת לִמְנוּחָה וּ]מוֹעֲדִים לְשִׂמְחָה, חַגִּים וּזְמַנִּים לְשָׂשׂוֹן, אֶת יוֹם [הַשַּׁבָּת הַזֶּה וְאֶת יוֹם] חַג הַמַּצּוֹת הַזֶּה, זְמַן חֵרוּתֵנוּ [בְּאַהֲבָה] מִקְרָא קֹדֶשׁ, זֵכֶר לִיצִיאַת מִצְרָיִם, כִּי בָנוּ בָחַרְתָּ וְאוֹתָנוּ קִדַּשְׁתָּ מִכָּל הָעַמִּים, [וְשַׁבָּת] וּמוֹעֲדֵי קָדְשֶׁךָ [בְּאַהֲבָה וּבְרָצוֹן] בְּשִׂמְחָה וּבְשָׂשׂוֹן הִנְחַלְתָּנוּ. בָּרוּךְ אַתָּה יהוה, מְקַדֵּשׁ [הַשַּׁבָּת וְ]יִשְׂרָאֵל וְהַזְּמַנִּים.

On Saturday night, add the following two paragraphs:

בָּרוּךְ אַתָּה יהוה אֱלֹהֵינוּ מֶלֶךְ הָעוֹלָם, בּוֹרֵא מְאוֹרֵי הָאֵשׁ.

בָּרוּךְ אַתָּה יהוה אֱלֹהֵינוּ מֶלֶךְ הָעוֹלָם, הַמַּבְדִּיל בֵּין קֹדֶשׁ לְחוֹל, בֵּין אוֹר לְחֹשֶׁךְ, בֵּין יִשְׂרָאֵל לָעַמִּים, בֵּין יוֹם הַשְּׁבִיעִי לְשֵׁשֶׁת יְמֵי הַמַּעֲשֶׂה. בֵּין קְדֻשַּׁת שַׁבָּת לִקְדֻשַּׁת יוֹם טוֹב הִבְדַּלְתָּ, וְאֶת יוֹם הַשְּׁבִיעִי מִשֵּׁשֶׁת יְמֵי הַמַּעֲשֶׂה קִדַּשְׁתָּ, הִבְדַּלְתָּ וְקִדַּשְׁתָּ אֶת עַמְּךָ יִשְׂרָאֵל בִּקְדֻשָּׁתֶךָ. בָּרוּךְ אַתָּה יהוה, הַמַּבְדִּיל בֵּין קֹדֶשׁ לְקֹדֶשׁ.

מוֹעֲדִים לְשִׂמְחָה / *Appointed times for gladness*

R' Avraham Shalom of Stropkov

R' Avraham Shalom of Stropkov wondered how it was possible to rejoice in the midst of our bitter exile. He answered his question by way of a parable:

On all nights other than Friday, begin here;
on Friday night include all passages in parentheses.

By your leave, my masters and teachers:

Blessed are You, HASHEM, our God, King of the universe, Who creates the fruit of the vine.

Blessed are You, HASHEM, our God, King of the universe, Who has chosen us from all nations, exalted us above all tongues, and sanctified us with His commandments. And You, HASHEM, our God, have lovingly given us (Sabbaths for rest), appointed times for gladness, feasts and seasons for joy, (this Sabbath and) this Feast of Matzos, the season of our freedom (in love,) a holy convocation in memoriam of the Exodus from Egypt. For You have chosen and sanctified us above all peoples, (and the Sabbath) and Your holy festivals (in love and favor), in gladness and joy have You granted us as a heritage. Blessed are You, HASHEM, Who sanctifies (the Sabbath,) Israel, and the festive seasons.

On Saturday night, add the following two paragraphs:

Blessed are You, HASHEM, our God, King of the universe, Who creates the illumination of the fire.

Blessed are You, HASHEM, our God, King of the universe, Who distinguishes between sacred and secular, between light and darkness, between Israel and the nations, between the seventh day and the six days of activity. You have distinguished between the holiness of the Sabbath and the holiness of a Festival, and have sanctified the seventh day above the six days of activity. You distinguished and sanctified Your nation, Israel, with Your holiness. Blessed are You, HASHEM, who distinguishes between holiness and holiness.

A servant of a king was once suspected of treason and thrown into prison to await his sentence. While sitting in his dark cell, the door flew open and the king walked in. The king ordered a bountiful table set before the prisoner and ordered him to eat, sing, and be merry. The king, thereupon, left the cell and the door swung shut once more.

If the servant had been dull witted, he would have said to himself, "The

On all nights conclude here:

בָּרוּךְ אַתָּה יהוה אֱלֹהֵינוּ מֶלֶךְ הָעוֹלָם, שֶׁהֶחֱיָנוּ וְקִיְּמָנוּ וְהִגִּיעָנוּ לַזְּמַן הַזֶּה.

The wine should be drunk without delay while reclining on the left side.
It is preferable to drink the entire cup, but at the very least,
most of the cup should be drained.

ורחץ

The head of the household — according to many opinions, all participants in the Seder — washes his hands as if to eat bread, [pouring water from a cup, twice on the right hand and twice on the left] but without reciting a blessing.

כרפס

All participants take a vegetable other than maror and dip it into salt-water. A piece smaller in volume than half an egg should be used. The following blessing is recited [with the intention that it also applies to the maror which will be eaten during the meal] before the vegetable is eaten.

בָּרוּךְ אַתָּה יהוה אֱלֹהֵינוּ מֶלֶךְ הָעוֹלָם, בּוֹרֵא פְּרִי הָאֲדָמָה.

---

king is mocking me. He casts me into prison and commands me to rejoice! What cruelty! And if my king and judge is cruel, I am doubly miserable!''

But he was clever and thought, ''The king is wise and knows my state of mind. He is not in the habit of making sport of his subjects, certainly not of those pining away in prison. He wishes to see for himself if I am really one of his admirers and have been slandered. He is observing me through some slit to see if I have confidence in him and will obey his command and rejoice, trusting that I will be freed because I rely on his mercy.'' Then, he ate in joy and sang praises of the kindness of the king and his goodness.

The king witnessed this and summoned the judges, so that they, too, could see that the prisoner was among his admirers. And on the day of judgment the king raised him above all his ministers. Israel is the servant in prison . . . (*Divrei Shalom*).

כַּרְפַּס / *Karpas*

R' Yissachar Dov of Belz

The *Rebbe of Kretchnif* told the following story:

A chasid brought a sack of carrots to *R' Yissachar Dov of Belz* to be used as *karpas* during the Seder. He parted from the Rebbe and left for home. R' Yissachar Dov gave orders that the sack of carrots be burned with the *chametz*. Despite the astonishment of all

On all nights conclude here:

Blessed are You, HASHEM, our God, King of the universe, Who has kept us alive, sustained us, and brought us to this season.

The wine should be drunk without delay while reclining on the left side. It is preferable to drink the entire cup, but at the very least, most of the cup should be drained.

URECHATZ

The head of the household — according to many opinions, all participants in the Seder — washes his hands as if to eat bread, [pouring water from a cup, twice on the right hand and twice on the left] but without reciting a blessing.

KARPAS

All participants take a vegetable other than maror and dip it into salt-water. A piece smaller in volume than half an egg should be used. The following blessing is recited [with the intention that it also applies to the maror which will be eaten during the meal] before the vegetable is eaten.

Blessed are You, HASHEM, our God, King of the universe, Who creates the fruits of the earth.

---

present, no one questioned his instructions.

A few hours passed and the man who had brought the carrots appeared; he was very disturbed. His maidservant had asked him if he was pleased with the carrots, since they were large and appealing to the eye! She even revealed the secret of her success. She had, she said, watered the plants with beer.

Her master had been horrified. "Beer is *chametz*," he had thought. "The carrots are forbidden for *Pesach* and the Rebbe, heaven forbid, will use them for *karpas*." He had immediately saddled his horse and ridden full gallop to Belz. They calmed him and told him that the carrots had been burned with the *chametz*.

To the chasidim the incident seemed to be a miracle. But the Rebbe said, "I did not order the carrots burned because I knew that they had been watered with beer. How could I have known that? But I did know that it is forbidden to introduce changes which alter the ways of our fathers. When the carrots were brought for *karpas*, I thought to myself, 'When did the generations gone by ever use carrots for *karpas*? Something is not quite right here!' That is why I had them burned."

The Rebbe of Kretchnif concluded his narration with, "See how adherence to ancestral customs prevented a violation of eating *chametz* on *Pesach*" (*Arba'ah Arazin* 92).

יחץ

The head of the household breaks the middle matzah in two. He puts the smaller part back between the two whole matzos, and wraps up the larger part for later use as the afikoman. Some briefly place the afikoman portion on their shoulders, in accordance with the Biblical verse recounting that Israel left Egypt carrying their matzos on their shoulders, and say בְּבְהִלוּ יָצָאנוּ מִמִּצְרָיִם, *'In haste we went out of Egypt.'*

מגיד

The broken matzah is lifted for all to see as the head of the household begins with the following brief explanation of the proceedings.

הִנְנִי מוּכָן וּמְזוּמָן לְקַיֵּם הַמִּצְוָה לְסַפֵּר בִּיצִיאַת מִצְרָיִם. לְשֵׁם יִחוּד קֻדְשָׁא בְּרִיךְ הוּא וּשְׁכִינְתֵּיהּ, עַל יְדֵי הַהוּא טָמִיר וְנֶעְלָם, בְּשֵׁם כָּל יִשְׂרָאֵל. וִיהִי נֹעַם אֲדֹנָי אֱלֹהֵינוּ עָלֵינוּ, וּמַעֲשֵׂה יָדֵינוּ כּוֹנְנָה עָלֵינוּ, וּמַעֲשֵׂה יָדֵינוּ כּוֹנְנֵהוּ:

הָא לַחְמָא עַנְיָא דִּי אֲכָלוּ אַבְהָתָנָא בְּאַרְעָא דְמִצְרָיִם. כָּל דִּכְפִין יֵיתֵי וְיֵכוֹל, כָּל דִּצְרִיךְ יֵיתֵי וְיִפְסַח. הָשַׁתָּא הָכָא, לְשָׁנָה הַבָּאָה בְּאַרְעָא דְיִשְׂרָאֵל. הָשַׁתָּא עַבְדֵי, לְשָׁנָה הַבָּאָה בְּנֵי חוֹרִין.

יַחַץ / *Yachatz*

Tzemach Tzedek

At the Seder of the *Tzemach Tzedek*, the Rebbe of Lubavitch, one of those present, after breaking the middle matzah, measured the pieces against each other to see which was the bigger and would serve as *afikoman*. On seeing this, the Rebbe remarked,"If an object must be measured to determine whether it is great, then even something small may be greater than it" (*Sipurei Chasidim II 315*).

[The Rebbe was making a general statement about greatness and great men. Greatness which only can be determined in comparison with others is not true greatness.]

מַגִּיד / *Maggid*

Avnei Nezer

The *Rebbe of Sochachov*, author of *Avnei Nezer,* noted that the Aramaic translation of Onkelos renders וְהִגַּדְתָּ לְבִנְךָ – *you shall tell your son* (*Shemos* 13:8) as: וּתְחַוֵּי לִבְרָךְ, which may be understood as: *you should show your son*. We are to *show* him the Exodus, have him *see* it, in a sense, not merely tell him about it (*Neos Deshe* II p. 189).

[The usual translation of הַגֵּד in Aramaic is חַוִּי. The point is not that we have an unusual translation but that the Aramaic חַוִּי besides meaning *tell* also means *see*.]

YACHATZ

The head of the household breaks the middle matzah in two. He puts the smaller part back between the two whole matzos, and wraps up the larger part for later use as the afikoman. Some briefly place the afikoman portion on their shoulders, in accordance with the Biblical verse recounting that Israel left Egypt carrying their matzos on their shoulders, and say בִּבְהִלוּ יָצָאנוּ מִמִּצְרָיִם, *'In haste we went out of Egypt.'*

MAGGID

Behold, I am prepared and ready to fulfill the mitzvah of telling the story of the Exodus from Egypt. For the sake of the unification of the Holy One, Blessed is He, and His Presence, through Him Who is hidden and inscrutable – [I pray] in the name of all Israel. May the pleasantness of my Lord, our God, be upon us – may He establish our handiwork for us; our handiwork may He establish.

The broken matzah is lifted for all to see as the head of the household begins with the following brief explanation of the proceedings.

This is the bread of affliction that our fathers ate in the land of Egypt. Whoever is hungry – let him come and eat! Whoever is needy – let him come and celebrate Pesach! Now, we are here; next year may we be in the Land of Israel! Now, we are slaves; next year may we be free men!

יֵיתֵי וְיִפְסַח / *Let him come and celebrate Pesach*

R' Yissachar Ber of Radoshitz

Before the world recognized his greatness, *R' Yissachar Ber of Radoshitz* was very poor. One year, he did not even have a slice of bread to divide into the ten small pieces, customarily placed about the house prior to the Search for Leaven (בְּדִיקַת חָמֵץ), which the one who conducts the search seeks out while looking for *chametz* in general. To fulfill the *mitzvah* in the most proper fashion, he was forced to break his practice of not borrowing from another.

On the following morning, though he was able to perform the *mitzvah* of ridding his home of leaven in the full sense of the commandment, he was far from being able to look forward to "in the evening you shall eat matzos" (*Shemos* 12:18); his larder was completely bare.

In mid-afternoon two men arrived at his home in a magnificent carriage and asked for his whereabouts. His wife said that he was in the *beis midrash* and asked if she could be of help. They replied that they were from Germany and were here for the festival. Since they were meticulous in observing *Pesach* with all its strict rulings, and had heard that the rebbe was pious and God fearing, they would like to spend the festival with him. The rebbetzin sighed and said that there was no food in the house. She need not be concerned about that, they answered, as they had brought all that was

The Seder plate is removed and the second of the four cups of wine is poured. The youngest present asks the reasons for the unusual proceedings of the evening.

מַה נִּשְׁתַּנָּה הַלַּיְלָה הַזֶּה מִכָּל הַלֵּילוֹת?

שֶׁבְּכָל הַלֵּילוֹת אָנוּ אוֹכְלִין חָמֵץ וּמַצָּה, הַלַּיְלָה הַזֶּה – כֻּלּוֹ מַצָּה.

שֶׁבְּכָל הַלֵּילוֹת אָנוּ אוֹכְלִין שְׁאָר יְרָקוֹת, הַלַּיְלָה הַזֶּה – מָרוֹר.

---

necessary with them in the carriage. With that, they forthwith set the table in a grand manner and went off to pray.

At the end of the prayers, they turned to the Rebbe and asked that they be allowed to be his guests.

"You certainly may," said the Rebbe, "but I have prepared nothing."

"If we don't find anything, we won't eat," they said.

They walked home together and found light and joy in the house and a table set for a king. The Rebbe asked his wife if she had abided by his prohibition not to request alms from anyone. "Yes!" she said. "These guests brought all this with them." The Rebbe gave praise to Hashem and rejoiced in his guests whom he found to be exceptionally wise scholars of the Torah. They conducted the Seder in happiness and retold the story of the Exodus through the entire night. And, in a like manner, they spent the night of the second Seder, which is held in the lands of the Diaspora. After *havdalah*, at the close of *Yom Tov*, the guests went out — and failed to return. The Rebbe sought them everywhere in town but could not find them.

For *Shavuos*, the Rebbe of Radoshitz traveled to his master, the *Chozeh of Lublin*. The Chozeh asked him about his state of affairs and the Rebbe told him of his strained conditions and of the miracle which had occurred to him on *Pesach*.

"Do you know who your important guests were?" said the Chozeh. "They were the angels Michael and Gavriel! How fortunate you are. From now on, you will prosper and the years of want will pass away, never to return!"

And so it was. From that time forward, the name of the Rebbe of Radoshitz became known to the world and his fame spread afar (*Otzar HaSipurim* XVII:18).

יֵיתֵי / *Let him come*

R' Ze'ev Wolf of Strikov

R' Ze'ev Wolf of Strikov asked, "Why do we open the door when we say *Pour Your wrath* (שְׁפֹךְ חֲמָתְךָ) after the meal, and not before the meal when we recite the

The Seder plate is removed and the second of the four cups of wine is poured. The youngest present asks the reasons for the unusual proceedings of the evening.

Why is this night different from all other nights?

1. On all other nights we may eat chametz and matzah, but on this night — only matzah.

2. On all other nights we eat many vegetables, but on this night — we eat maror.

---

formula *whoever is hungry let him come and eat* (כָּל דִּכְפִין יֵיתֵי וְיֵכוֹל)? How can we invite guests, if the door is kept locked?"

And he answered, "*Whoever is hungry etc.* has a non-physical aspect. For, on the evening of the Seder, the gate to high spiritual attainments lies open. Not only can they be acquired, but we are invited to enter and receive them in overflowing measure — *whosoever is hungry let him come*! But there is a single prior condition which must be met. We must ourselves open the door. We must show that we are not lazy."

The *Rebbe of Kotzk* explained a *gemara* in a similar vein: Rabban Gamliel declared that if a man's inner spiritual self did not match his outward mode of behavior, he was to be barred from entering the *beis midrash*. And he posted a watchman to enforce his decree (*Berachos* 28a). Yet how could the watchman gauge a man's true personality?

In practice the watchman gave entry to no one. Whoever climbed the wall and entered via the window showed that his inner self complemented his outer one; he truly wished to learn (*Zer Zahav*).

מַה נִּשְׁתַּנָּה / Why [is this night] different

Ba'al HaHafla'ah

R' Pinchas, the author of the *Hafla'ah*, was asked why we pose questions on *Pesach* and not on *Succos*, when many changes are also introduced and we leave our permanent homes for the temporary structure of the *succah*.

"On *Pesach*," he answered, "when the ever-troubled, ever-pursued Jew sits down to his table, as if free, and sees the beautiful dishes set before him, as if he is a lord and master, he asks, in amazement, 'Why is this night different?'

"But on *Succos*, he enters a tottery *succah*. That is in keeping with, and normal to, the bitter life of Exile. There is no reason for amazement" (*Chasidim Mesaprim* I:525).

R' Yissachar Dov of Belz

R' Yissachar Dov of Belz did many things, out of the ordinary, on the evening of the Seder, so that his son (who later became R' Aharon of Belz) should be aroused to question him. But the youngster asked not a word.

"Don't my actions seem strange to you?" asked the father.

שֶׁבְּכָל הַלֵּילוֹת אֵין אָנוּ מַטְבִּילִין אֲפִילוּ פַּעַם אֶחָת, הַלַּיְלָה הַזֶּה – שְׁתֵּי פְעָמִים.

שֶׁבְּכָל הַלֵּילוֹת אָנוּ אוֹכְלִין בֵּין יוֹשְׁבִין וּבֵין מְסֻבִּין, הַלַּיְלָה הַזֶּה – כֻּלָּנוּ מְסֻבִּין.

The Seder plate is returned. The matzos are kept uncovered as the *Haggadah* is recited in unison. The *Haggadah* should be translated if necessary, and the story of the Exodus should be amplified upon.

עֲבָדִים הָיִינוּ לְפַרְעֹה בְּמִצְרָיִם, וַיּוֹצִיאֵנוּ יהוה אֱלֹהֵינוּ מִשָּׁם בְּיָד חֲזָקָה וּבִזְרוֹעַ נְטוּיָה. וְאִלּוּ לֹא הוֹצִיא הַקָּדוֹשׁ בָּרוּךְ הוּא אֶת אֲבוֹתֵינוּ מִמִּצְרָיִם, הֲרֵי אָנוּ וּבָנֵינוּ וּבְנֵי בָנֵינוּ מְשֻׁעְבָּדִים הָיִינוּ לְפַרְעֹה בְּמִצְרָיִם. וַאֲפִילוּ כֻּלָּנוּ חֲכָמִים, כֻּלָּנוּ נְבוֹנִים, כֻּלָּנוּ זְקֵנִים, כֻּלָּנוּ יוֹדְעִים אֶת הַתּוֹרָה, מִצְוָה עָלֵינוּ לְסַפֵּר בִּיצִיאַת מִצְרָיִם. וְכָל הַמַּרְבֶּה לְסַפֵּר בִּיצִיאַת מִצְרַיִם, הֲרֵי זֶה מְשֻׁבָּח.

מַעֲשֶׂה בְּרַבִּי אֱלִיעֶזֶר וְרַבִּי יְהוֹשֻׁעַ וְרַבִּי אֶלְעָזָר בֶּן עֲזַרְיָה וְרַבִּי עֲקִיבָא וְרַבִּי טַרְפוֹן שֶׁהָיוּ מְסֻבִּין בִּבְנֵי בְרַק, וְהָיוּ מְסַפְּרִים בִּיצִיאַת מִצְרַיִם כָּל אוֹתוֹ הַלַּיְלָה. עַד שֶׁבָּאוּ תַלְמִידֵיהֶם וְאָמְרוּ לָהֶם, רַבּוֹתֵינוּ הִגִּיעַ זְמַן קְרִיאַת שְׁמַע שֶׁל שַׁחֲרִית.

"Father, I don't question anything you do!" answered the boy (*Admorei Belz* IV:23).

כֻּלָּנוּ זְקֵנִים / *(If) we were all men of experience*

R' Nachman of Tulshin

R' Nachman of Tulshin was asked, "Why do the Sages say that the minds of the learned (*talmidei chachamim*) become more settled the older they become, and the minds of the ignorant become sillier and sillier with advancing age?"

"Once," he answered, "I traveled aboard the wagon of a gentile driver who stopped at every tavern along the way to have a drink. We once passed

3. On all other nights we do not dip even once, but on this night — twice.

4. On all other nights we eat either sitting or reclining, but on this night — we all recline.

The Seder plate is returned. The matzos are kept uncovered as the *Haggadah* is recited in unison. The *Haggadah* should be translated if necessary, and the story of the Exodus should be amplified upon.

We were slaves to Pharaoh in Egypt, but HASHEM our God took us out from there with a mighty hand and an outstretched arm. Had not the Holy One, Blessed is He, taken our fathers out from Egypt, then we, our children, and our children's children would have remained enslaved to Pharaoh in Egypt. Even if we were all men of wisdom, understanding, experience, and knowledge of the Torah, it would still be an obligation upon us to tell about the Exodus from Egypt. The more one tells about the Exodus, the more he is praiseworthy.

It happened that Rabbi Eliezer, Rabbi Yehoshua, Rabbi Elazar ben Azaryah, Rabbi Akiva, and Rabbi Tarfon were reclining (at the Seder) in Bnei Brak. They discussed the Exodus all that night until their students came and said to them: 'Our teachers, it is [daybreak] time for the reading of the morning Shema.'

---

the ruins of a one-time tavern. He halted, entered the broken-down building, and remained there for a long time. When he returned I asked him, 'All right! I can understand your wanting to visit a tavern for a drink, but why did you go into the ruins?'

" 'I went in,' said the driver, 'to think about the old days, when this tavern was full of life, and to remember the first-class, strong whiskey they sold here.'

"That story teaches us the difference between the wise *talmidei chachamim* and the ignorant. The ignorant waste their youth carousing and become addicted to following their desires. In old age, their bodies become 'ruins' and they cannot kick up their heels as they did in the past. Then it is that they spend their time in fruitless longing. The wise, however, in contrast, war against their desires while young, in order to serve Hashem. In old age, when the body is weak and the desires no longer have their former

אָמַר רַבִּי אֶלְעָזָר בֶּן עֲזַרְיָה, הֲרֵי אֲנִי כְּבֶן שִׁבְעִים שָׁנָה, וְלֹא זָכִיתִי שֶׁתֵּאָמֵר יְצִיאַת מִצְרַיִם בַּלֵּילוֹת, עַד שֶׁדְּרָשָׁהּ בֶּן זוֹמָא, שֶׁנֶּאֱמַר, לְמַעַן תִּזְכֹּר אֶת יוֹם צֵאתְךָ מֵאֶרֶץ מִצְרַיִם כֹּל יְמֵי חַיֶּיךָ.[1] יְמֵי חַיֶּיךָ הַיָּמִים, כֹּל יְמֵי חַיֶּיךָ הַלֵּילוֹת. וַחֲכָמִים אוֹמְרִים, יְמֵי חַיֶּיךָ הָעוֹלָם הַזֶּה, כֹּל יְמֵי חַיֶּיךָ לְהָבִיא לִימוֹת הַמָּשִׁיחַ.

בָּרוּךְ הַמָּקוֹם, בָּרוּךְ הוּא. בָּרוּךְ שֶׁנָּתַן תּוֹרָה לְעַמּוֹ יִשְׂרָאֵל, בָּרוּךְ הוּא. כְּנֶגֶד אַרְבָּעָה בָנִים דִּבְּרָה תוֹרָה: אֶחָד **חָכָם**, וְאֶחָד **רָשָׁע**, וְאֶחָד **תָּם**, וְאֶחָד **שֶׁאֵינוֹ יוֹדֵעַ לִשְׁאוֹל**.

---

force, they are able to serve Hashem in peace and quiet; nothing troubles them" (*Avaneha Barzel* 62).

לְמַעַן תִּזְכֹּר . . . כֹּל יְמֵי חַיֶּיךָ

That you may remember . . . all the days of your life

R' Elazar Menachem of Lelov

R' Elazar Menachem of Lelov: When a man peruses a book while at his table and, at the end of the meal, before returning it to its place, shakes off the crumbs which have fallen into it, [so that there will be no *chametz* in his books when *Pesach* comes,] he fulfills, in this way, in all the days of the year, the commandment *that you remember the day on which you went out of the land of Egypt all the days of your life* (Devarim 16:3) (*Likutei Divrei David* 29).

כֹּל יְמֵי חַיֶּיךָ הַלֵּילוֹת

The addition of the word "all" includes the nights as well

Lev Same'ach

The *Lev Same'ach of Alesk* showed exceptional devotion in his service to Hashem during *Succos* and, most particularly so, during the *hakafos*, when the Torah scrolls are carried about in dance. Even in old age, he did not change his conduct by a hair.

The local gentile judge was told about his wondrous behavior and came to the *beis knesses*. He remained until after the *hakafos*, witnessing the lengthy dancing. After accompanying the Rebbe home he said, "I was present during the dancing. Had I not seen it, I would not believe it. Your act of devotion

Rabbi Elazar ben Azaryah said: I am like a seventy-year-old man, but I could not succeed in having the Exodus from Egypt mentioned every night, until Ben Zoma expounded it: 'In order that you may remember the day you left Egypt all the days of your life.'[1] The phrase 'the days of your life' would have indicated only the days; the addition of the word 'all' includes the nights as well. But the Sages declare that 'the days of your life' would mean only the present world; the addition of 'all' includes the era of the Messiah.

Blessed is the Omnipresent; Blessed is He. Blessed is the One Who has given the Torah to His people Israel; Blessed is He. Concerning four sons does the Torah speak: a wise one, a wicked one, a simple one, and one who is unable to ask.

1. *Devarim* 16:3.

---

stands beyond the bounds of nature! I would suggest that, in your old age, you leave such tiring service to your sons, or at least, that of the evening, and that Your Honor should devote yourself to the service by day."

The Rebbe rose from his place and declared with great fervor: "In the presence of Hashem, one must show his devotion by day and by night, when one is young and when one is old!"

The judge was so overcome upon hearing this that he fell over backwards. With difficulty he stood up and said to those present, "I think you should leave the Rebbe; he is still under the effect of his devotions."

Such were the impressions of a non-Jew (*Or Chadash* ch. 6).

אֶחָד חָכָם / *A wise one*

R' Simchah Bunim

R' Simchah Bunim of Pshischa said:

Each one of the two hundred and forty-eight positive commandments of the Torah tells you, "Be a wise man." Each one of its three hundred and sixty-five prohibitions says, "Do not be a fool."

His disciple, *R' Menachem Mendel of Kotzk,* said:

I have evidence that it is possible to be a righteous fool. The *gemara* tells us that the angel who has been appointed to oversee pregnancy takes the soul and places it before the Holy One and asks, "What will happen to this soul? Will it be the soul of a poor man or a rich man; a wise man or a fool?" He does not ask whether it is destined for a righteous man or a wicked man, because that depends on the future free choice of the individual. Thus, it is entirely possible that a man will be born a fool, but by proper choice and self-development he will be righteous.

There you have it — the combination that makes up a righteous fool (*Siach Sarfei Kodesh* I:257).

R' Naftali Tzvi of Ropshitz

R' Naftali Tzvi of Ropshitz was very wise, very perceptive and keen witted. Once his master, the *Chozeh of Lublin,* said to him, "The Torah commands us: *You shall be innocent* (תָּמִים) *with Hashem, your God* (*Devarim* 18:13); it does not demand: you shall be wise!"

"True, Rebbe," said R' Naftali, "but one needs exceptional wisdom to reach such innocence" (*Or Yesharim* p.229).

אֶחָד חָכָם, וְאֶחָד רָשָׁע / *A wise one, a wicked one*

R' Tzvi Hirsch of Ziditchov

R' Michel of Sambur said in the name of his uncle *R' Tzvi Hirsch of Ziditchov*:

Why did the compiler of the *Haggadah* place the wicked son next to the wise son and not at the end of the list of four sons?

Had the wicked son stood next to and after the simple son or the one who is unable to ask, he would influence them and ruin them, before the wise man could foil his plans. But he is placed next to the wise son who can keep an eye on him and cut him down (*Eser Kedushos Tinyana* 34).

R' Tzvi Elimelech of Dinov

Once, on the evening of the Seder, *R' Tzvi Elimelech of Dinov* passed through the town to see how the common folk conducted the Seder. When he reached the window of one simple man, he heard him recite the paragraph of the Four Sons.

Each time he said the word *one* — a wise *one*, a wicked *one* — he read the word *one* (אֶחָד) in full voice and lengthened the final syllable, as is done when reading the *one* (אֶחָד) in *Hear O Israel, Hashem is our God, Hashem is One* of the *Shema*. The Rebbe was exceptionally pleased and said, "This man has turned the Four Sons into the declaration of faith of the *Shema*."

R' Yissachar Dov of Belz said that when his father, *R' Yehoshua of Belz*, heard the above, his face changed color several times.

"I understood," said R' Yissachar Dov, "that the tale reflected very important matters, indeed. Man, because of the physical aspect of his nature, is liable to sin. But he can overcome this side of himself by accepting the Majesty of Heaven. The Rebbe of Dinov meant that through the agency of the One (אֶחָד) of the *Shema*, all of the Four Sons can be corrected" (*Haggadah Imrei Kodesh Belz* p. 58).

Ba'al Shem Tov The *Yesod Ha'Avodah of Slonim* in the name of *R' Noach of Lechovitz*:

The *Ba'al Shem Tov* once told his disciples, "After all that I have gained in the upper realms in terms of spiritual understanding of the foundations of Torah and its *mitzvos*, and after all the pleasure I have derived from such understanding, I put it all aside and grasp onto simple faith; I am a simpleton and believe.

"And although it is stated: *The simpleton believes everything* (*Mishlei* 14:15), it is also stated: *Hashem guards the simpletons* (*Tehillim* 116:6) (*Yesod Ha'Avodah*).

R' Bunim of Pshischa The chasidus of Pshischa plumbed the depths of the soul. First and foremost, it demanded that a man not fool himself. Once the Rebbe asked his chasidim, "Tell me! Who is a chasid?"

"A chasid (literally a pious man)," they answered, "is one who goes beyond what is demanded by the letter of the law."

"Well then," said the Rebbe, "the law requires that you not fool your fellow man. And the chasid does not fool even himself; that goes beyond the letter of the law."

A young man was to be found in the town of Pshischa who did fool himself. He imagined that he had ascended far up the ladder of holiness and purity and was not far from the rung on which he would be thought worthy of Divine revelation and prophecy.

R' Chanoch Henoch of Alexander wished to teach him a lesson. One day the young man found a 'note from Heaven' on his seat, giving detailed practices of holiness and purity and asceticism on an impossibly high plane. It was signed by 'The Angel פילד.'

The young man was excited by the note and sought to know who the angel *Fild* was and what his position was in the heavenly hosts. He approached the Rebbe, *R' Bunim of Pshischa*, and showed him the note. The Rebbe understood who was behind the affair and summoned *R' Chanoch Henoch*. When he arrived, the Rebbe said, "This young man would like to know who the angel *Fild* is, the one who signed the note."

R' Chanoch answered, "His name is made up of the first letters of the words in the verse (*Mishlei* 14:15): פֶּתִי יַאֲמִין לְכׇל דָּבָר, *The fool believes everything*!" (*Siach Sarfei Kodesh* III:1; IV:152).

חָכָם, רָשָׁע, תָּם / *A wise one, a wicked one, a simple one*

Divrei Chaim One day, the *Divrei Chaim of Sanz* stood by the window looking out. A man passed by. The Rebbe tapped on the window and motioned him in. When he entered, the Rebbe asked, "Tell

חָכָם מָה הוּא אוֹמֵר? מָה הָעֵדֹת וְהַחֻקִּים וְהַמִּשְׁפָּטִים אֲשֶׁר צִוָּה יהוה אֱלֹהֵינוּ אֶתְכֶם?[1] וְאַף אַתָּה אֱמָר לוֹ כְּהִלְכוֹת הַפֶּסַח, אֵין מַפְטִירִין אַחַר הַפֶּסַח אֲפִיקוֹמָן.

רָשָׁע מָה הוּא אוֹמֵר? מָה הָעֲבֹדָה הַזֹּאת לָכֶם?[2] לָכֶם וְלֹא לוֹ, וּלְפִי שֶׁהוֹצִיא אֶת עַצְמוֹ מִן

---

me! If you found a purse filled with gold coins, would you return it to its owner?"

"Certainly, Rebbe," said the man. "I would return it immediately."

"You're a fool," said the Rebbe, and dismissed him.

Once more, he stood at the window and motioned to another passing man to enter. He put the same question to him.

"I'm not such a fool as to return a purse full of gold coins that fell into my hand," said the man.

"You are wicked," said the Rebbe, and sent him off.

Once again, he returned to the window, and beckoned to a third man to come in. And once again, he asked his question.

"How can I give an answer to the Rebbe?" said the man. "Do I know what will happen at such a moment? Will I have it in myself to suppress my evil desire (יֵצֶר הָרָע)? I hope that Hashem would help me overcome and help me return the lost object to its owner."

"You are a wise man," said the Rebbe, "that is how one should answer" (*Mekor Chaim* 166).

אֵין מַפְטִירִין . . . אֲפִיקוֹמָן / *One may not eat dessert*

R' Yissachar Dov of Belz

Just as it is not permitted to taste anything after eating the portion of the *Pesach* sacrifice, so that the aftertaste of the sacrifice remain in the mouth, in a like manner, speak to the wise son of matters which will leave a taste with him forever (*Admorei Belz III* 150).

רָשָׁע / *The wicked son*

R' Naftali Tzvi of Ropshitz

R' Naftali Tzvi of Ropshitz was asked why new *Haggados* are printed year in year out.

"The wicked son of last year," he replied, "seems to be a righteous man this year, in the light of the rapid decline of the generations" (*Chasidim Mesaprim* II:130).

The wise son — what does he say? 'What are the testimonies, decrees, and ordinances which HASHEM, our God, has commanded you?'[1] Therefore explain to him the laws of the Pesach offering: that one may not eat dessert after the final taste of the Pesach offering.

The wicked son — what does he say? 'Of what purpose is this work to you?'[2] He says, 'To you,' thereby excluding himself. By excluding himself

1. *Devarim* 6:20. 2. *Shemos* 12:26

מַה הָעֲבֹדָה הַזֹּאת לָכֶם? לָכֶם וְלֹא לוֹ

Of what purpose is this work to you? . . . thereby excluding himself

Akeidas Yitzchak

Chazal interpret the *to you* (לָכֶם) of the verse which speaks of work permitted on the festivals (*Shemos* 12:16) as referring 'to all your needs' (*Beitzah* 28b).

The wicked son throws out his *to you* in a like manner. He says, "All the eating that you engage in on the evening of the Seder is *to you* — to fill your bellies, and *not for Him* (וְלֹא לוֹ), for the Holy One."

In seeing things this way he 'denies the basic principle of Judaism' (כּפֵר בְּעִיקָר). For the basic principle is to "know Him in all your ways" and "let all your actions be for the sake of heaven." If he does not eat with a sense of sanctity, *blunt his teeth* (הַקְהֵה אֶת שִׁנָּיו). Why does he need teeth? After all, eating was not conceived except as a service in the name of Hashem (*Tiferes Rabboseinu Me'Alexander* 171).

Chida

The *Chida* (Chaim Yosef David Azulai) once met a man without a beard and asked him why he shaved.

"Just as I was born without a beard," said the man, "I continue to live without one."

"Now," said the Chida, "I understand what is meant by *therefore, blunt his teeth* which is found in the *Haggadah* with reference to the wicked son. Just as he was born without teeth, thus he should remain, without teeth" (*Otzar HaSipurim* VIII:14).

R' Yechezkel Michelson

An adherent of the freethinkers, the so-called enlightened ones (*maskilim*), complained to *R' Yechezkel Michelson of Plonsk*:

"Why does the compiler of the *Haggadah* tell us to blunt the teeth of the wicked son? The question of the wicked son appears in the Torah with an answer directly following: *And it will be when your sons will say to you,*

הַכְּלָל, כָּפַר בְּעִקָּר – וְאַף אַתָּה הַקְהֵה אֶת שִׁנָּיו וֶאֱמָר לוֹ, בַּעֲבוּר זֶה עָשָׂה יהוה לִי בְּצֵאתִי מִמִּצְרָיִם.[1] לִי וְלֹא לוֹ, אִלּוּ הָיָה שָׁם לֹא הָיָה נִגְאָל.

תָּם מָה הוּא אוֹמֵר? מַה זֹּאת? וְאָמַרְתָּ אֵלָיו, בְּחֹזֶק יָד הוֹצִיאָנוּ יהוה מִמִּצְרַיִם מִבֵּית עֲבָדִים.[2]

'What is this service to you?' And you will say, 'This is the Pesach sacrifice to Hashem' (*Shemos* 12:26-27)."

"You have ignored the great difference between the two questions," said R' Yechezkel. "The Torah put the question in the plural, in the mouths of a band of wicked men. Such a gang is dangerous and they must be answered with restraint.

"But the *Haggadah* speaks in the singular, of a lone wicked man who throws off the yoke of submission to Heaven. Concerning him, we are told, 'Rise and blunt his teeth' " (*Sichas Chulin Shel Talmidei Chachamim*, p.47).

R' Yisrael of Salant

R' Yisrael of Salant once arrived together with several Torah leaders of Lithuania to meet with the *Chidushei HaRim* and discuss how they might combat the plots of the free-thinking *maskilim*. Some suggested the gentle arts of persuasion. But the Gerer Rebbe, in contrast, pushed for a strong hand and open warfare.

"I wonder," said one of the rabbis with a smile, "why the *tzaddikim* of Poland don't direct their thoughts against the *maskilim* while pronouncing the blessing against the slanderers (וְלַמַּלְשִׁינִים) in the *Shemoneh Esrei*. Their prayer would bring the enemy down in defeat."

On the spot, the Rebbe answered, "If the *maskilim* would limit themselves to only thinking about us when they say the blessing which follows, *for the tzaddikim and the pious* etc. . . . (עַל הַצַּדִּיקִים), we would only need to think about them in the blessing against the slanderers. But now that they have arisen in battle against us, we must return their blows in double measure" (*Hamaor Hagadol*, p. 244).

כָּפַר בְּעִקָּר – הַקְהֵה אֶת שִׁנָּיו

He denies the basic principle of Judaism – blunt his teeth

R' Baruch of Mezhibuz

One of the chasidim once heard that the wife of *R' Baruch of Mezhibuz* was complaining about the family being in debt. He, together with a friend, made the rounds of the

from the community of believers, he denies the basic principle of Judaism. Therefore, blunt his teeth and tell him: 'It is because of this that HASHEM did so for me when I went out of Egypt.'[1] 'For me,' but not for him — had he been there, he would not have been redeemed.

The simple son — what does he say? 'What is this?' Tell him: 'With a strong hand did HASHEM take us out of Egypt, from the house of bondage.'[2]

1. *Shemos* 13:8. 2. 13:14.

---

neighboring villages and brought the *rebbetzin* a sum sufficient to cover the debts.

While they spent the *Shabbos* with the Rebbe, he remarked during the meal, "*Ribbono Shel Olam* (Master of the world), help this man who helped me pay my debts and give him so many and so many thousands of rubles.

"I suggest that You take the sum from someone whose actions are bad and give them to this man. But if You think that man will complain that You have caused him such great damage, I have a further suggestion. Take it from one who denies God's existence (כּוֹפֵר בְּעִיקָּר). Since he denies You, he won't complain to You."

And all things turned out according to the Rebbe's blessings. Throughout his life, the chasid never had less than the sum the Rebbe had specified (*Mekor Baruch* 7).

Seraph of Moglenitza

The *Fiery Angel (Seraph) of Moglenitza* told of a man who had come to him with a request that he speak to him and drive out thoughts of heresy.

"I cannot agree to speak of these matters, at all," said the Rebbe. "For we are warned by Shlomo HaMelech to stay at a distance from the doorstep of the house of heresy.

"Should you argue that I must speak of these things to save the soul of a member of Israel, I say that you cannot help him by violating a directive of the Sages!" (*Toledos HaNiflaos* 113).

לִי וְלֹא לוֹ / *For me, but not for him*

R' Avraham Yaakov of Sadigura

R' Moshe David Gutman, the personal attendant (*shammash*) of *R' Avraham Yaakov of Sadigura*, would stand at his post each evening until the Rebbe would bid him "good night" and go to bed. At times, when the Rebbe was buried in his thoughts and the hour was late, R' Moshe David would cause

וְשֶׁאֵינוֹ יוֹדֵעַ לִשְׁאוֹל, אַתְּ פְּתַח לוֹ. שֶׁנֶּאֱמַר, וְהִגַּדְתָּ לְבִנְךָ בַּיּוֹם הַהוּא לֵאמֹר, בַּעֲבוּר זֶה עָשָׂה יהוה לִי בְּצֵאתִי מִמִּצְרָיִם.[1]

יָכוֹל מֵרֹאשׁ חֹדֶשׁ, תַּלְמוּד לוֹמַר בַּיּוֹם הַהוּא. אִי בַּיּוֹם הַהוּא, יָכוֹל מִבְּעוֹד יוֹם, תַּלְמוּד לוֹמַר בַּעֲבוּר זֶה. בַּעֲבוּר זֶה לֹא אָמַרְתִּי אֶלָּא בְּשָׁעָה שֶׁיֵּשׁ מַצָּה וּמָרוֹר מֻנָּחִים לְפָנֶיךָ.

---

a slight noise, by moving a table or chair, to remind the Rebbe that he should take a brief rest.

One night, many hours had passed; the Rebbe paced back and forth, caught up in his thoughts. The attendant moved the chairs and tapped on the windows, without success. Finally, not long before dawn, he girded up his courage, approached the Rebbe and said, "Will the Rebbe please excuse me, but the sun will soon be up and you have not yet rested."

"For you it is easy," said the Rebbe. "You can sleep in peace. But what am I to do? I had a visitor today for whom my soul finds no solution. Should I include him as part of Israel? I find that bitter as gall; he is frightfully polluted. Shall I drive him out of Israel? I find that very difficult; after all, he is a Jew!" (*Eser Oros* 9).

אַתְּ פְּתַח לוֹ / *You must initiate for him*

Chozeh of Lublin

A man's mouth is called a door (פֶּתַח) as the prophet says: "Guard the doors of your mouth" (*Michah* 7:5). I and *R' Zusha of Hanipoli* once went in to see the *great Maggid of Mezritch*. The Maggid commented, "Yaakov Yitzchak, you forgot to lock the door." When I heard that, I took it upon myself to refrain from speech for seven years (*Or Haniflaos*, p.13).

וְהִגַּדְתָּ לְבִנְךָ / *You shall tell your son*

R' Yehoshua of Belz

The Torah has attached a precondition to the retelling of the story of the Exodus to children — "Words that flow from the heart enter the heart." In order to fix the story in the hearts of children, the fathers must first fix it in their own hearts. On this point the Torah says: "That you may tell in the ears of your son and the son of your son what I did in Egypt and of the signs which I put upon them — and you will know that I am Hashem" (*Shemos* 10:2). In order to tell over the story to your children, you must first know that I am Hashem! (*Ohel Yehoshua* 14).

As for the son who is unable to ask, you must initiate the subject for him, as it is stated: You shall tell your son on that day: 'It is because of this that HASHEM did so for me when I went out of Egypt.'[1]

One might think that the obligation to discuss the Exodus commences with the first day of the month of Nissan, but the Torah says: 'You shall tell your son on that day.' But the expression 'on that day' could be understood to mean only during the daytime; therefore the Torah adds: 'It is because of this that HASHEM did so for me when I went out of Egypt.' The pronoun 'this' implies something tangible, thus, 'You shall tell your son' applies only when matzah and maror lie before you — at the Seder.

1.*Shemos* 13:8.

מֻנָּחִים לְפָנֶיךָ *[When matzah and maror] lie before you*

R' Yissachar Dov of Belz

After *R' Yissachar Dov of Belz* had finished his Seder, he passed through the streets of town to hear how the common folk observed it. From one of the houses burst forth the voice of a householder calling out fervently:

"*This* (זֶה) implies only when matzah and *maror* are associated by marriage before you." (He mistakenly said מְחוּתָּנִים, *mechutanim,* rather than מֻנָּחִים, *munachim*.)

The Rebbe's attendant laughed, but the Rebbe nodded his head and said, "He's right! Matzah and *maror* are really associated by marriage.

"Imagine a rich man who has an accomplished daughter and wishes to marry her off. He finds an accomplished young man, but he is exceptionally poor. He buys him handsome clothes and wishes to have the marriage feast immediately. The young man asks for a delay so that he can make preparations for a proper wedding meal. The rich man is impatient and has the meal commence, using the dry bread in the young man's larder.

"With the passage of time, the young man acts impertinently towards his father-in-law. The rich man draws forth some of the rags which his son-in-law wore in the past and says, 'Do you remember from what state I saved you?' The young man in turn produces a piece of the dry bread and says, 'But you should remember that you wanted me and you couldn't wait.'

מִתְּחִלָּה, עוֹבְדֵי עֲבוֹדָה זָרָה הָיוּ אֲבוֹתֵינוּ, וְעַכְשָׁו קֵרְבָנוּ הַמָּקוֹם לַעֲבוֹדָתוֹ. שֶׁנֶּאֱמַר, וַיֹּאמֶר יְהוֹשֻׁעַ אֶל כָּל הָעָם, כֹּה אָמַר יהוה אֱלֹהֵי יִשְׂרָאֵל, בְּעֵבֶר הַנָּהָר יָשְׁבוּ אֲבוֹתֵיכֶם מֵעוֹלָם, תֶּרַח אֲבִי אַבְרָהָם וַאֲבִי נָחוֹר, וַיַּעַבְדוּ אֱלֹהִים אֲחֵרִים. וָאֶקַּח אֶת אֲבִיכֶם אֶת אַבְרָהָם מֵעֵבֶר הַנָּהָר, וָאוֹלֵךְ אוֹתוֹ בְּכָל אֶרֶץ כְּנָעַן, וָאַרְבֶּה אֶת זַרְעוֹ, וָאֶתֶּן לוֹ אֶת יִצְחָק. וָאֶתֵּן לְיִצְחָק אֶת יַעֲקֹב וְאֶת עֵשָׂו, וָאֶתֵּן לְעֵשָׂו אֶת הַר שֵׂעִיר לָרֶשֶׁת אוֹתוֹ, וְיַעֲקֹב וּבָנָיו יָרְדוּ מִצְרָיִם.[1]

בָּרוּךְ שׁוֹמֵר הַבְטָחָתוֹ לְיִשְׂרָאֵל, בָּרוּךְ הוּא. שֶׁהַקָּדוֹשׁ בָּרוּךְ הוּא חִשַּׁב אֶת הַקֵּץ, לַעֲשׂוֹת כְּמָה שֶׁאָמַר לְאַבְרָהָם אָבִינוּ בִּבְרִית בֵּין הַבְּתָרִים, שֶׁנֶּאֱמַר, וַיֹּאמֶר לְאַבְרָם, יָדֹעַ תֵּדַע כִּי גֵר יִהְיֶה זַרְעֲךָ בְּאֶרֶץ לֹא לָהֶם, וַעֲבָדוּם

"So, too, the Holy One shows us the *maror*, the bitter herbs, which remind us of the bitter servitude from which He delivered us. We, in turn, show Him the matzah, which did not have sufficient time to rise because He was in such a hurry to save us.

"Indeed the matzah and *maror* are *mechutanim*" (*Admorei Belz* III 209).

מַתְחִיל בִּגְנוּת וּמְסַיֵּם בְּשֶׁבַח

He begins with shame and concludes with the praiseworthy

R' Nachum of Slonim

[This is the mishnaic directive as to the format for telling the story of the Exodus; *Mishnah Pesachim* 10:4.]

R' Nachum of Slonim, one of the elders of the disciples of the *Zaide of Lechovitz*, told the following to the *Yesod Ha'Avodah of Slonim*:

While studying the *Avos D' R' Nasan* (Ch. 21), I came across the passage which states that R' Akiva, in teaching his students, recalled his childhood. I imagined that the passage would note that R' Akiva was saddened when he

Originally our ancestors were idol worshipers, but now the Omnipresent has brought us near to His service, as it is written: Joshua said to all the people, 'So says HASHEM, God of Israel: Your fathers always lived beyond the Euphrates River, Terach the father of Avraham and Nachor, and they served other gods. Then I took your father Avraham from beyond the river and led him through all the land of Canaan. I multiplied his offspring and gave him Yitzchak. To Yitzchak I gave Yaakov and Esav; to Esav I gave Mount Seir to inherit, but Yaakov and his children went down to Egypt.'[1]

Blessed is He Who keeps His pledge to Israel; Blessed is He! For the Holy One, Blessed is He, calculated the end of bondage in order to do as He said to our father Avraham at the Covenant between the Parts, as it is stated: He said to Avram, 'Know with certainty that your offspring will be aliens in a land not their own, they will serve them

1. *Yehoshua* 24:2-4.

---

remembered the years which had passed wastefully. But to my amazement, the recollection of the past caused R' Akiva to rejoice over his later years and he said, "I praise You, Hashem, my God, that You have given me, as my lot, to be among those who sit in the *beis midrash*."

This teaches us that whoever succeeds to improve later in life should not be saddened by his early days. On the contrary, he should rejoice and be encouraged by the good he has found in the end (*Ma'asei Avos*, ch. 4).

וָאוֹלֵךְ אוֹתוֹ בְּכָל אֶרֶץ כְּנָעַן / *I led him through all the land of Canaan*

Imrei Emes

When the *Imrei Emes of Gur* visited *Eretz Yisrael* in 5692 (1932), he traveled by land via Turkey, Syria and Lebanon. He arrived in the country by way of Rosh Hanikrah.

When asked if the journey had not been tiring, he answered tersely, as usual, "One must try all the ways" (*Perek Zichronos Lehagrash Ginzburg*).

[The everyday talk (שִׂיחַת חוּלִין) of the great serves as guidelines for behavior in, and attitudes to, life in general. The Rebbe meant to indicate that one must exhaust every possible approach, whatever the matter at hand.]

וְעִנּוּ אֹתָם, אַרְבַּע מֵאוֹת שָׁנָה. וְגַם אֶת הַגּוֹי אֲשֶׁר יַעֲבֹדוּ דָּן אָנֹכִי, וְאַחֲרֵי כֵן יֵצְאוּ בִּרְכֻשׁ גָּדוֹל.[1]

The matzos are covered and the cups lifted as the following paragraph is proclaimed joyously. Upon its conclusion, the cups are put down and the matzos are uncovered.

וְהִיא שֶׁעָמְדָה לַאֲבוֹתֵינוּ וְלָנוּ, שֶׁלֹּא אֶחָד בִּלְבָד עָמַד עָלֵינוּ לְכַלּוֹתֵנוּ. אֶלָּא שֶׁבְּכָל דּוֹר וָדוֹר עוֹמְדִים עָלֵינוּ לְכַלּוֹתֵנוּ, וְהַקָּדוֹשׁ בָּרוּךְ הוּא מַצִּילֵנוּ מִיָּדָם.

צֵא וּלְמַד מַה בִּקֵּשׁ לָבָן הָאֲרַמִּי לַעֲשׂוֹת לְיַעֲקֹב אָבִינוּ, שֶׁפַּרְעֹה לֹא גָזַר אֶלָּא עַל הַזְּכָרִים, וְלָבָן בִּקֵּשׁ לַעֲקוֹר אֶת הַכֹּל. שֶׁנֶּאֱמַר:

דָּן אָנֹכִי / *I execute judgment*

R' Abish of Tchernovitz

R' Abish of Tchernovitz was a simple, perfect soul. When his Rebbe, *R' Yisrael of Ruzhin,* escaped from a Russian jail and went into exile, R' Abish asked him, in all innocence, why he did not punish the czar for all that he had suffered, and have him dethroned.

"Do you believe that Hashem directs the world?" asked the Rebbe.

"Certainly!" said R' Abish.

"Do you believe in the miracle of the Exodus from Egypt and the Ten Plagues?"

"Without a doubt."

"Well, then, when I see that the all-powerful Holy One chooses to contain Himself, despite the evil behavior of the czar, I follow in His footsteps and control myself" (*Irin Kaddishin*, end of Part III).

וְאַחֲרֵי כֵן יֵצְאוּ בִּרְכֻשׁ גָּדוֹל

And afterwards they shall leave with great possessions

R' Meir of Premishlan

R' Meir of Premishlan was asked, "We place *maror* on the Seder plate in memory of the bondage; *charoses* in memory of the mortar; *matzah* in memory of the bread of poverty. Why do we not have a symbol to remind us of the great possessions with which we left Egypt?"

"It is only right that we do as we do," said the Rebbe. "The *maror* is a memento of the servitude and we still have traces of that today. But we place

and they will oppress them four hundred years; but also upon the nation which they shall serve will I execute judgment, and afterwards they shall leave with great possessions.'[1]

The matzos are covered and the cups lifted as the following paragraph is proclaimed joyously. Upon its conclusion, the cups are put down and the matzos are uncovered.

It is this that has stood by our fathers and us. For not only one has risen against us to annihilate us, but in every generation they rise against us to annihilate us. But the Holy One, Blessed is He, rescues us from their hand.

Go and learn what Lavan the Aramean attempted to do to our father Yaakov! For Pharaoh decreed only against the males, Lavan attempted to uproot everything, as it is said:

1. *Bereishis* 15:13-14.

---

no symbol of the great possessions because there is nothing left of them" (*Bircas Chaim* II, p.112).

צֵא וּלְמַד מַה בִּקֵּשׁ לָבָן הָאֲרַמִּי לַעֲשׂוֹת

Go and learn what Lavan the Aramean attempted to do

Tiferes Shlomo

A young man came before the *Tiferes Shlomo of Radomsk* and told him that he was at present occupied with the study of the Torah and supported by his father-in-law. But his father-in-law was trying to convince him to go into trade.

"*Go and learn* (צֵא וּלְמַד)," the Rebbe directed him. "Go to the *beis midrash* and continue to learn Torah. For your father-in-law is trying to do to you *what Lavan the Aramean attempted to do to our father Yaakov* (מַה בִּקֵּשׁ לָבָן הָאֲרַמִּי לַעֲשׂוֹת לְיַעֲקֹב אָבִינוּ). Lavan sent Yaakov to herd sheep rather than allow him to be a *dweller in tents** (יוֹשֵׁב אֹהָלִים) (*Ateres Shlomo,* p.95).

[**dweller in tents* — a student in the *beis midrash*.]

R' Hillel of Eibshutz

A son-in-law once summoned his father-in-law to a *din torah* (a rabbinical trial), because he refused to pay for his support and allow him to study, as he had promised.

The father-in-law argued that his son-in-law should support himself by the work of his own hands, following the dictum of the *Mishnah*: "Torah is good when it goes together with the way of the world" (that is, work — *Avos* 2:2).

אֲרַמִּי אֹבֵד אָבִי, וַיֵּרֶד מִצְרַיְמָה וַיָּגָר שָׁם בִּמְתֵי מְעָט, וַיְהִי שָׁם לְגוֹי, גָּדוֹל עָצוּם וָרָב.[1]

וַיֵּרֶד מִצְרַיְמָה – אָנוּס עַל פִּי הַדִּבּוּר.

וַיָּגָר שָׁם – מְלַמֵּד שֶׁלֹּא יָרַד יַעֲקֹב אָבִינוּ לְהִשְׁתַּקֵּעַ בְּמִצְרַיִם, אֶלָּא לָגוּר שָׁם. שֶׁנֶּאֱמַר, וַיֹּאמְרוּ אֶל פַּרְעֹה, לָגוּר בָּאָרֶץ בָּאנוּ, כִּי אֵין מִרְעֶה לַצֹּאן אֲשֶׁר לַעֲבָדֶיךָ, כִּי כָבֵד הָרָעָב בְּאֶרֶץ כְּנָעַן, וְעַתָּה יֵשְׁבוּ נָא עֲבָדֶיךָ בְּאֶרֶץ גֹּשֶׁן.[2]

בִּמְתֵי מְעָט – כְּמָה שֶׁנֶּאֱמַר, בְּשִׁבְעִים נֶפֶשׁ יָרְדוּ אֲבֹתֶיךָ מִצְרָיְמָה, וְעַתָּה שָׂמְךָ יהוה אֱלֹהֶיךָ כְּכוֹכְבֵי הַשָּׁמַיִם לָרֹב.[3]

They argued their case before *R' Hillel of Eibshutz* who said, "True, the *mishnah* is clear. But it is preferable that your son-in-law study and be learned in the entire Torah and be remiss in this one *mishnah*, rather than that he maintain this single *mishnah* and be ignorant in the entire Torah" (*Maskil el Dal* III 2).

וְלָבָן בִּקֵּשׁ לַעֲקוֹר אֶת הַכֹּל

Lavan attempted to uproot everything

R' Yaakov Aryeh

R' Aharon Menachem Mendel of Radzimin said:

When I was a little boy and we reached this part of the *Haggadah*, my sainted grandfather *R' Yaakov Aryeh* put me on his lap and said to me, "Know that there is a simple, direct, evil nature (יֵצֶר הָרָע) who pushes men to sin. His name is *Pharaoh*. We can hope to escape him, because he attacks openly. And even if we fail in our encounter, God forbid, there is hope that we will repent.

"But there is an evil nature whom we call *Lavan the Aramean* (אֲרַמִּי), because he fools us (מְרַמֶּה – treating אֲרַמִּי as if derived from the root רמה), and dresses up in white (לָבָן) like a righteous man, a *tzaddik*. He persuades a man that a particular sin is not a sin, but a *mitzvah*. We are liable to overlook the trap and, not seeing it as a sin, fail to repent.

"Of him, my child, it is said that he wishes to *uproot* everything" (*Chasidim Mesaprim* III 451).

An Aramean attempted to destroy my father. Then he descended to Egypt and sojourned there, with few people; and there he became a nation — great, mighty and numerous.[1]

Then he descended to Egypt — compelled by Divine decree.

He sojourned there — this teaches that our father Yaakov did not descend to Egypt to settle, but only to sojourn temporarily, as it says: They (the sons of Yaakov) said to Pharaoh: 'We have come to sojourn in this land because there is no pasture for the flocks of your servants, because the famine is severe in the land of Canaan. And now, please let your servants dwell in the land of Goshen.'[2]

With few people — as it is written: With seventy persons, your forefathers descended to Egypt, and now HASHEM, your God, has made you as numerous as the stars of heaven.[3]

1. *Devarim* 26:5. 2. *Bereishis* 47:4. 3. *Devarim* 10:22.

אֲרַמִּי אֹבֵד אָבִי

An Aramean attempted to destroy my father

Chidushei HaRim

Once, a grandson of one of the great *tzaddikim* visited Gur. He assumed that the Rebbe, the *Chidushei HaRim,* would show him great honor, because of his illustrious grandfather, and when he presented himself, he gave his family connections in full.

The Rebbe glared at him and thundered, "The Torah states: *an Aramean destroyed my father*!* If a man fools himself, in the end, he destroys the favorable account which exists through the merit of his father.

"Not only is this so, but that very merit becomes a stumbling block to him. At the end of the list of punishments for our sins in the Passage of Rebuke (תּוֹכֵחָה), it is said: *and I shall remember My covenant with Yaakov and also My covenant with Yitzchak, and also My covenant with Avraham (Vayikra* 26:42). The sainted *Sh'lah* interprets this as one of the reasons for punishment. The Holy One says, 'You had such ancestors and this is what you look like?'

"That is why in our prayers we say 'our God and the God of our fathers' (in the first paragraph of the *Shemoneh Esrei,* for example). If we ourselves

[**An Aramean etc.* The Gerer Rebbe interpreted *Arami* (ארמי) as if derived from רמה — to fool.]

וַיְהִי שָׁם לְגוֹי – מְלַמֵּד שֶׁהָיוּ יִשְׂרָאֵל מְצֻיָּנִים שָׁם.

גָּדוֹל עָצוּם – כְּמָה שֶׁנֶּאֱמַר, וּבְנֵי יִשְׂרָאֵל פָּרוּ וַיִּשְׁרְצוּ וַיִּרְבּוּ וַיַּעַצְמוּ בִּמְאֹד מְאֹד, וַתִּמָּלֵא הָאָרֶץ אֹתָם.[1]

---

are worthy, then, and only then, may we join the merits of our fathers to ourselves" (*HaMaor HaGadol* ch. 35).

מְצֻיָּנִים שָׁם / *(The Israelites were) distinctive there*

R' Simchah Bunim of Pshischa

Distinctive there: They did not change their names, language, or dress.

A freethinker, a *maskil*, wished to vex *R' Simchah Bunim of Pshischa* and said, "Did Avraham wear a *shtreimel* (the fur hat worn by the chasid on *Shabbos*) and a silk *kapote* (the caftan-like garb of the chasid)?"

"I don't know exactly what he wore," said the Rebbe. "But this I do know. He looked about to see what the gentiles wore and took up a different mode of dress" (*Siach Sarfei Kodesh*).

Chidushei HaRim

Rashi has written (in *parashas Chukas*) that the Amalekites who came to do battle with Israel spoke Canaanite, so that they would not be identified and Israel would not be able to pray for their downfall. And, indeed, when they saw this strange people, who spoke the tongue of Canaan and wore the dress of Amalek, Israel prayed without mentioning a specific nation but said: "If you give *this nation* into my hand, I will destroy their cities" (*Bamidbar* 21:2).

However, the Torah itself, as *R' Yehoshua of Belz* has noted, does not call them Amalekites, but Canaanites: "And the Canaanites heard . . . and did battle with Israel" (ibid. v. 1). This indicates, he said, how much a man changes his essential self when he changes his language.

The *Chidushei HaRim of Gur* wondered why the Amalekites did not change both their dress and speech. Had they done so, they would have fooled Israel completely.

This teaches us, he said, that had they adopted both the dress and speech of Canaan, they would have not only appeared, but would actually have become Canaanites (*Ohel Yehoshua* 25; *Siach Sarfei Kodesh* I 522).

Chidushei HaRim

When the government decreed that Jews were to learn the national language and were not to wear

There he became a nation — this teaches that the Israelites were distinctive there.

Great, mighty — as it says: And the Children of Israel were fruitful, increased greatly, multiplied, and became very, very mighty; and the land was filled with them.[1]

1. *Shemos* 1:7.

---

distinctive dress, the *Chidushei HaRim* saw this as an act of religious persecution which should be opposed even to the point of martyrdom.

At the time, Sir Moses Montefiore of England was passing through Poland on his way to Russia where he wished to confer with the czar on behalf of his fellow Jews. The Chidushei HaRim thought of meeting with Sir Moses to convince him to request that the decree be abolished.

When the *Rebbe of Kotzk* heard of the Gerer Rebbe's plans, he commented that he was certain that nothing would come of the meeting with Montefiore.

In Posen, he said, the freethinking *maskilim* had stirred up the feelings of the authorities against the longstanding, Orthodox form of Jewish education. The Orthodox wished to present a written defense of their traditional system of education, but could not find one of their own to pen it in elegant German. They turned to one of the *maskilim* and paid him to draft a letter.

R' Akiva Eiger, the Rabbi of Posen, however, thought that the letter would not be effective. He quoted the verse: "Do not put your trust in princes, in a man who does not possess salvation" (*Tehillim* 146:3), and interpreted it to mean 'in a man who is not himself saved through his action.' "The writer of the letter, the *maskil*, is an opponent of traditional education," said R' Akiva Eiger. "He is not trying to save himself. How could a letter written by him persuade the authorities to abolish the decree?"

Montefiore himself, said the Kotzker, wore modern dress and spoke foreign languages. Why should he agree to speak on behalf of traditional costume and Yiddish?

And when Montefiore did meet with the Chidushei HaRim he said, "I don't know why you stubbornly insist on wearing bear-fur hats. And as far as language is concerned, I have proof that Jews spoke foreign tongues. Mordechai understood the conversation of King Achashverosh's guards and was thus able to reveal their plot and deliver his people."

"But that, to the contrary," replied the Chidushei HaRim, "shows that Jews did not speak the language of the country. That is why the guards ignored Mordechai's presence. They knew that Jews spoke only their own language. They did not realize that Mordechai, because he was a member of the Sanhedrin, knew other languages."

"At least, you admit," said Montefiore, "that there is a need for someone to know foreign languages."

"Yes," said the Rebbe, "and my lord, you, with your mastery of languages, fill that need."

In the final analysis, Montefiore did not prove helpful. Deliverance from the decree came through the Chidushei HaRim's own strong opposition. The authorities imprisoned him. The Jews came out in stormy protest, so much so, that there was fear of revolt. The Rebbe was freed and the decree annulled (*Siach Sarfei Kodesh*).

R' Mordechai of Nadvornah

R' Mordechai of Nadvornah told the following story:

"I was once traveling to a particular place for *Shabbos* and sent a wagon with my baggage on ahead; I traveled separately, on Friday. Time rushed by, and I was forced to remain for *Shabbos* in a tiny village lacking my *Shabbos* outfit. I summoned a tailor and ordered him to fashion a *shtreimel*, immediately, from thirteen wide pieces of goat hide, since that was what was available in the hamlet.

"You can well imagine how I looked in that *shtreimel* and how everyone stared at me, but it was inconceivable to me that a Jew could go through a *Shabbos* without a *shtreimel* on his head."

At the time the Rebbe told the story, the Rabbi of Neupest was present in the audience. He and the members of his community had always followed the custom of German Jewry in their mode of dress. The Rebbe asked, "Rabbi of Neupest, did you understand [the significance of] my remark?"

When the Rabbi of Neupest returned home, he ordered a *shtreimel* and a chasidic coat to be made up for himself (*Sha'ar HaOsios*, p. 12).

R' Yissachar Dov of Belz

In Belz the chasidim would wear their shirts open at the collar, and their pants (breeches) gathered and tied at the knee, inserted into long socks. A chasid once came in a new style: shirt buttoned up to the neck; pants with legs open and down to the shoes.

R' Yissachar Dov of Belz smiled and said, "When a chasid comes to the rebbe, the rebbe tries to pass on to him the fear of Hashem. He can do so in plenty through the open shirt collar. And since the pants are fastened below, that feeling remains with the chasid. But with the new style of dress, it is very hard to instill the fear of God into the heart through the fastened collar. And if one succeeds in getting anything in, it tumbles down and out through the open pants' legs" (*Admorei Belz* III:311).

שֶׁלֹּא שִׁנּוּ אֶת שְׁמָם / *They did not change their name*

Ahavas Yisrael

In one of the communities near Kolmaya there was a rabbi called R' Meir of whom it was said that he gave his stamp of approval to products of doubtful *kashrus* in return for money. When the *Ahavas Yisrael of Vizhnitz* visited the town, members of the community lodged complaints against the rabbi and he promised to attend to matters, in his way.

When the rabbi appeared before him, the Rebbe said, "We all know that at the close of the *Shemoneh Esrei* prayer, we say a verse, the first and last letters of which correspond to the first and last letters of our names. This is to help us remember our names on the Final Judgment Day.

"I've often wondered, who is it that would not remember his name? Each of us hears his name tens of times a day. If someone should argue that in our fear and confusion before the Divine Judge we might forget our names, why would we not forget the verse, too?

"The verse is not meant for those who have taken non-Jewish names. Such Jews don't pray and don't say the verse.

"The verse is probably meant for rabbis. They don't usually hear their names, because they are addressed by their title — Rabbi — and they must be reminded of their names through a verse. Your verse is: מִפִּקּוּדֶיךָ אֶתְבּוֹנָן עַל כֵּן שָׂנֵאתִי כָּל אֹרַח שָׁקֶר, 'My contemplation of Your commands makes me hate every path of falsehood (*Tehillim* 119:104).' This verse will remind you of your name on the Final Day of Judgment, if you repeat it continually."

The rabbi, who was astute, caught the hint and stopped taking the bribes and lending his stamp of approval to invalid products (*Kedosh Yisrael* II).

Tzemach Tzedek

The Tzemach Tzedek of Lubavitch:

It is said that Israel had sunk to the forty-ninth, the all but final, depth of impurity in Egypt. Had they descended to the fiftieth, and bottom level, they could not have been saved.

The preservation of their distinctive name, language and dress prevented them from falling to the ultimate depth. But today, they have changed their name, language and dress; they are at the lowest state possible, that fiftieth depth. How can they be redeemed?

Fortunately, the present and the age of servitude in Egypt differ in one important factor. In Egypt, Israel had not yet received the Torah. They could have been assimilated completely. But after the Torah has been given, redemption is possible even from the abyss of the fiftieth depth of impurity (*Siach Sarfei Kodesh* IV 203).

וָרָב – כְּמָה שֶׁנֶּאֱמַר, רְבָבָה כְּצֶמַח הַשָּׂדֶה נְתַתִּיךְ, וַתִּרְבִּי וַתִּגְדְּלִי וַתָּבֹאִי בַּעֲדִי עֲדָיִים, שָׁדַיִם נָכֹנוּ וּשְׂעָרֵךְ צִמֵּחַ, וְאַתְּ עֵרֹם וְעֶרְיָה; וָאֶעֱבֹר עָלַיִךְ וָאֶרְאֵךְ מִתְבּוֹסֶסֶת בְּדָמָיִךְ, וָאֹמַר לָךְ, בְּדָמַיִךְ חֲיִי, וָאֹמַר לָךְ, בְּדָמַיִךְ חֲיִי.[1]

וַיָּרֵעוּ אֹתָנוּ הַמִּצְרִים, וַיְעַנּוּנוּ, וַיִּתְּנוּ עָלֵינוּ עֲבֹדָה קָשָׁה.[2]

וַיָּרֵעוּ אֹתָנוּ הַמִּצְרִים – כְּמָה שֶׁנֶּאֱמַר, הָבָה נִתְחַכְּמָה לוֹ, פֶּן יִרְבֶּה, וְהָיָה כִּי תִקְרֶאנָה מִלְחָמָה, וְנוֹסַף גַּם הוּא עַל שֹׂנְאֵינוּ, וְנִלְחַם בָּנוּ, וְעָלָה מִן הָאָרֶץ.[3]

רְבָבָה כְּצֶמַח הַשָּׂדֶה נְתַתִּיךְ
I made you as numerous as the plants of the field

R' Moshe of Kubrin

R' Moshe of Kubrin said:

The Holy One said, "I begged of you, Israel, that as you developed you should be 'as the plants of the field.' The more mature the stalks of grain are, the fuller and heavier are their heads, and the lower they bend under the weight. The heavier a tree is with fruit, the more bowed are its branches.

"But the opposite has occurred — וַתִּרְבִּי וַתִּגְדְּלִי, *you grew and developed* — you have stood overly erect with excessive pride; וְאַתְּ עֵרֹם וְעֶרְיָה, *and you were naked and bare* — you had no reason for the pride, for you were empty of fruit" (*Bircas Chaim* II, p. 131).

וַתִּרְבִּי / *You developed*

Divrei Chaim

The *Divrei Chaim of Sanz* said:

"A man imagines that he has grown (וַתִּרְבִּי — *you developed*); that he is worthy of being a rebbe. He convinces himself that he is a great man (וַתִּגְדְּלִי — *you have grown great*). He thinks he is adorned with *mitzvos* (וַתָּבֹאִי בַּעֲדִי עֲדָיִים — *you were bedecked with jewelry*); that he nurtures disciples with his words of Torah (שָׁדַיִם נָכֹנוּ — prepared to nurture). But in truth," he would say bitterly, "*you are naked and bare* (וְאַתְּ עֵרֹם וְעֶרְיָה) — he is bare of Torah, bare of *mitzvos*, hollow and empty. How far a man can lie to, and fool, himself!" (*Mekor Chaim* 100).

Numerous — as it says: I made you as numerous as the plants of the field; you developed and grew, and were bedecked with jewelry, beautiful of figure; and your hair grown long; but you were naked and bare. And I passed over you and saw you downtrodden in your blood and I said to you: 'Through your blood shall you live!' And I said to you: 'Through your blood shall you live!'[1]

The Egyptians did evil to us and afflicted us; and imposed hard labor upon us.[2]

The Egyptians did evil to us — as it says: Let us deal with them wisely lest they multiply and, if we happen to be at war, they may join our enemies and fight against us and then leave the country.[3]

1. *Yechezkel* 16:7,6. 2. *Devarim* 26:6. 3. *Shemos* 1:10.

בְּדָמַיִךְ חֲיִי / *Through your blood shall you live*

Divrei Chaim

The Divrei Chaim of Sanz said:

A man once usurped another's livelihood. He rented the tavern, which had been previously rented out to the other, from the local landlord.

The man who had lost his livelihood complained to R' Chaim, and the Rebbe summoned the one who had appropriated the rights to the tavern and reproached him.

But he tried to justify himself. "Rebbe," he said, "the previous tenant of the tavern is a sinner, a wicked, evil man. It is a good deed, a *mitzvah*, to bury him!"

The Rebbe smiled and replied, "And who told you that it is a *mitzvah* to bury the wicked? I'll bring you proof to the contrary.

"The *midrash* says that the wicked of Israel died in Egypt, during the three days of the plague of darkness, and were buried then, so that the Egyptians would not witness their death. After the plague had passed, Hashem took note that Israel was bare of *mitzvos*; they had nothing in their favor that would make them worthy of deliverance. And so He granted them two *mitzvos* involving blood — circumcision and the offering of the *pesach* sacrifice (with its placing of the blood on the doorposts and the lintel), as it is stated: *And I said to you, Through your blood you shall live! And I said to you, Through your blood you shall live!* (*Yechezkel* 16:6).

"But you would have it that it is a *mitzvah* to bury the wicked. If so, Israel would have had bundle upon bundle of *mitzvos*. There you have it, explicit proof that it is not a *mitzvah* to bury a wicked man.

וַיְעַנּוּנוּ – כְּמָה שֶׁנֶּאֱמַר, וַיָּשִׂימוּ עָלָיו שָׂרֵי מִסִּים, לְמַעַן עַנֹּתוֹ בְּסִבְלֹתָם, וַיִּבֶן עָרֵי מִסְכְּנוֹת לְפַרְעֹה, אֶת פִּתֹם וְאֶת רַעַמְסֵס.[1]

וַיִּתְּנוּ עָלֵינוּ עֲבֹדָה קָשָׁה – כְּמָה שֶׁנֶּאֱמַר, וַיַּעֲבִדוּ מִצְרַיִם אֶת בְּנֵי יִשְׂרָאֵל בְּפָרֶךְ.[2]

וַנִּצְעַק אֶל יהוה אֱלֹהֵי אֲבֹתֵינוּ, וַיִּשְׁמַע יהוה אֶת קֹלֵנוּ, וַיַּרְא אֶת עָנְיֵנוּ, וְאֶת עֲמָלֵנוּ, וְאֶת לַחֲצֵנוּ.[3]

וַנִּצְעַק אֶל יהוה אֱלֹהֵי אֲבֹתֵינוּ – כְּמָה שֶׁנֶּאֱמַר, וַיְהִי בַיָּמִים הָרַבִּים הָהֵם, וַיָּמָת מֶלֶךְ מִצְרַיִם, וַיֵּאָנְחוּ בְנֵי יִשְׂרָאֵל מִן הָעֲבֹדָה, וַיִּזְעָקוּ, וַתַּעַל שַׁוְעָתָם אֶל הָאֱלֹהִים מִן הָעֲבֹדָה.[4]

וַיִּשְׁמַע יהוה אֶת קֹלֵנוּ – כְּמָה שֶׁנֶּאֱמַר, וַיִּשְׁמַע אֱלֹהִים אֶת נַאֲקָתָם, וַיִּזְכֹּר אֱלֹהִים אֶת בְּרִיתוֹ אֶת אַבְרָהָם, אֶת יִצְחָק, וְאֶת יַעֲקֹב.[5]

וַיַּרְא אֶת עָנְיֵנוּ – זוֹ פְּרִישׁוּת דֶּרֶךְ אֶרֶץ, כְּמָה שֶׁנֶּאֱמַר, וַיַּרְא אֱלֹהִים אֶת בְּנֵי יִשְׂרָאֵל, וַיֵּדַע אֱלֹהִים.[6]

"Now, then, if you give the man back his livelihood, well and good. If you do not, yours will be a bitter end!" (*Mekor Chaim* 428).

מִן הָעֲבוֹדָה וַיִּזְעָקוּ / *(And the Children of Israel groaned) because of the servitude and cried*

R' Chanoch Henoch of Alexander

After the death of the *Chidushei HaRim of Gur*, his chasidim wished to crown R' Chanoch Henoch as their Rebbe, whereupon he told the following:

"A butcher was once butchering the carcass of an animal on Friday. Time passed as he cut and cut, until night fell. The butcher suddenly took note that *Shabbos* had arrived and dashed out of his shop at a run, to the *beis*

And afflicted us — as it says: They set taskmasters over them in order to oppress them with their burdens; and they built Pisom and Raamses as treasure cities for Pharaoh.[1]

They imposed hard labor upon us — as it says: The Egyptians subjugated the Children of Israel with hard labor.[2]

We cried out to HASHEM, the God of our fathers; and HASHEM heard our cry and saw our affliction, our burden and our oppression.[3]

We cried out to HASHEM, the God of our fathers — as it says: It happened in the course of those many days that the king of Egypt died; and the Children of Israel groaned because of the servitude and cried; their cry because of the servitude rose up to God.[4]

HASHEM heard our cry — as it says: God heard their groaning, and God recalled His covenant with Avraham, with Yitzchak, and with Yaacov.[5]

And saw our affliction — that is the disruption of family life, as it says: God saw the Children of Israel and God took note.[6]

1. *Shemos* 1:11. 2. 1:13. 3. *Devarim* 26:7. 4. *Shemos* 2:23. 5. 2:24. 6. 1:11.

---

knesses; the congregation was singing *Lecha Dodi*.* The butcher let loose a groan. It wasn't really the butcher's groan but a groan of the 'eternal Jew' within him.

"When the verse says, 'and the *Children of Israel* groaned because of the servitude,' it means to tell us that the 'child of Israel' within each of them groaned when he realize how deeply he had sunk into servitude. And then the Torah says: וַיֵּדַע אֱלֹקִים — *Elokim took note* (*Shemos* 2:25) — the Holy One filled them with knowledge (דַעַת).

"Only after the groan (וַיֵּאָנְחוּ), which showed an awareness of their involvement in the material, and only after they had acquired knowledge (וַיֵּדַע), can the Torah return to speak of Moshe: 'And Moshe was herding the flock of Yisro (ibid. 3:1)' — only then could He send the redeemer to them (*Siach Sarfei Kodesh*).

Lecha Dodi; The song composed by R' Shlomo Alkabetz, for the first part of the *Shabbos* evening prayer, *kabalas Shabbos*.

וְאֶת עֲמָלֵנוּ – אֵלּוּ הַבָּנִים, כְּמָה שֶׁנֶּאֱמַר, כָּל הַבֵּן הַיִּלּוֹד הַיְאֹרָה תַּשְׁלִיכֻהוּ, וְכָל הַבַּת תְּחַיּוּן.[1]

וְאֶת לַחֲצֵנוּ – זוֹ הַדְּחַק, כְּמָה שֶׁנֶּאֱמַר, וְגַם רָאִיתִי אֶת הַלַּחַץ אֲשֶׁר מִצְרַיִם לֹחֲצִים אֹתָם.[2]

וַיּוֹצִאֵנוּ יהוה מִמִּצְרַיִם בְּיָד חֲזָקָה, וּבִזְרֹעַ נְטוּיָה, וּבְמֹרָא גָּדֹל, וּבְאֹתוֹת וּבְמֹפְתִים.[3]

וַיּוֹצִאֵנוּ יהוה מִמִּצְרַיִם – לֹא עַל יְדֵי מַלְאָךְ, וְלֹא עַל יְדֵי שָׂרָף, וְלֹא עַל יְדֵי שָׁלִיחַ, אֶלָּא הַקָּדוֹשׁ בָּרוּךְ הוּא בִּכְבוֹדוֹ וּבְעַצְמוֹ. שֶׁנֶּאֱמַר, וְעָבַרְתִּי בְאֶרֶץ מִצְרַיִם בַּלַּיְלָה הַזֶּה, וְהִכֵּיתִי כָל בְּכוֹר

עֲמָלֵנוּ, אֵלּוּ הַבָּנִים* / *Our burden — refers to the children

R' Yisrael of Ruzhin

When *R' Yisrael of Ruzhin* was in prison, he sent his mother a message saying that she was responsible for his detention.

Her son, she explained, had once told her that Heaven informed him that it was within his power to bring an elevated soul into the world, a soul so elevated that its like had not existed for a thousand years. But he would have to accept suffering to do so. He had asked her whether he should agree to the condition.

"What does a father not do for his children?" she had answered.

He had agreed to accept the suffering and the future *Rebbe of Hosyatin* had been born. Now that he was in prison, he wished to remind his mother of her advice, so that she not be grieved (*Sha'ar HaOsios*, p. 8).

Yehudi Hakadosh of Pshischa

In the way of the world, a man is involved in his occupation, in business, sunken into his concerns. He doesn't have a moment free for Torah and prayer. When he is questioned about it, he answers that all of his efforts are directed to making a livelihood and bringing up his son to Torah, *mitzvos* and good deeds. But that son when he grows up also throws himself into the whirlwind of livelihood and he, too, doesn't have a moment to spare for himself, concerned as he is to raise his son up to Torah.

How I would love to meet that son, the end product of the chain of generations, for whom all his forebears toiled to raise him up to Torah!

The Torah alludes to this process: "These are the offspring of Noach; Noach was a righteous man; pure in his generation" (*Bereishis* 6:9). Noach decided

Our burden — refers to the children, as it says: *Every son that is born you shall cast into the river, but every daughter you shall let live.*[1]

Our oppression — refers to the pressure expressed in the words: *I have also seen how the Egyptians are oppressing them.*[2]

HASHEM brought us out of Egypt with a mighty hand and with an outstretched arm, with great awe, with signs and wonders.[3]

HASHEM brought us out of Egypt — not through an angel, not through a seraph, not through a messenger, but the Holy One, Blessed is He, in His glory, Himself, as it says: *I will pass through the land of Egypt on that night; I will slay all the firstborn in the*

1. *Shemos* 1:22. 2. 3:9. 3. *Devarim* 26:8.

---

that rather than labor on behalf of his children, who would then labor on behalf of their children, who would labor on behalf of their children, he would labor for himself; he himself would be righteous (*Nifleos HaYehudi* 33a).

This seems to be a development of *Rashi* based on the *midrash*: *"These are the offspring of Noach etc.* This teaches you that the important offspring of the righteous are their good deeds" (*Rashi* to *Bereishis* 6:9).

כָּל הַבֵּן הַיִּלּוֹד / *Every son that is born*

R' Yissachar Ber of Radoshitz

There was once a large crowd at the house of *R' Yissachar Ber of Radoshitz*, and they caused a considerable commotion. The Rebbe, concerned about their disturbing his wife's rest, hushed them up.

"You should know," he said, "that she has a large share in my Torah and my devotion to Hashem.

"When I was a young man, I found that I could not make ends meet. I gathered some goods and made the rounds from town to town to earn a livelihood. But I thought to myself, 'Is this the purpose for my existence? Was I born into the world to spend the time on the roads going from town to town?' And then the verse 'Every son that is born you shall cast into the river' (*Shemos* 1:22) came to mind. As *Chazal* say, 'Water can only mean Torah' — every man should be in the water, preoccupied with the water of Torah.

"You will ask, perhaps, 'What will we eat?' The Torah itself gives us the answer in the last part of the verse: 'but every daughter, you should let live. — the woman will busy herself in providing the livelihood.

"Immediately, I turned about and made my way home. Upon arrival, I

בְּאֶרֶץ מִצְרַיִם מֵאָדָם וְעַד בְּהֵמָה, וּבְכָל אֱלֹהֵי מִצְרַיִם אֶעֱשֶׂה שְׁפָטִים, אֲנִי יהוה.[1]

וְעָבַרְתִּי בְאֶרֶץ מִצְרַיִם בַּלַּיְלָה הַזֶּה – אֲנִי וְלֹא מַלְאָךְ. וְהִכֵּיתִי כָל בְּכוֹר בְּאֶרֶץ מִצְרַיִם – אֲנִי וְלֹא שָׂרָף. וּבְכָל אֱלֹהֵי מִצְרַיִם אֶעֱשֶׂה שְׁפָטִים – אֲנִי וְלֹא הַשָּׁלִיחַ. אֲנִי יהוה – אֲנִי הוּא, וְלֹא אַחֵר.

בְּיָד חֲזָקָה – זוֹ הַדֶּבֶר, כְּמָה שֶׁנֶּאֱמַר, הִנֵּה יַד יהוה הוֹיָה בְּמִקְנְךָ אֲשֶׁר בַּשָּׂדֶה, בַּסּוּסִים בַּחֲמֹרִים בַּגְּמַלִּים בַּבָּקָר וּבַצֹּאן, דֶּבֶר כָּבֵד מְאֹד.[2]

וּבִזְרֹעַ נְטוּיָה – זוֹ הַחֶרֶב, כְּמָה שֶׁנֶּאֱמַר, וְחַרְבּוֹ שְׁלוּפָה בְּיָדוֹ, נְטוּיָה עַל יְרוּשָׁלָיִם.[3]

וּבְמֹרָא גָּדֹל – זוֹ גִלּוּי שְׁכִינָה, כְּמָה שֶׁנֶּאֱמַר, אוֹ הֲנִסָּה אֱלֹהִים לָבוֹא לָקַחַת לוֹ גוֹי מִקֶּרֶב גּוֹי, בְּמַסֹּת, בְּאֹתֹת, וּבְמוֹפְתִים, וּבְמִלְחָמָה, וּבְיָד חֲזָקָה, וּבִזְרוֹעַ נְטוּיָה, וּבְמוֹרָאִים גְּדֹלִים, כְּכֹל אֲשֶׁר עָשָׂה לָכֶם יהוה אֱלֹהֵיכֶם בְּמִצְרַיִם לְעֵינֶיךָ.[4]

---

repeated my thoughts to my wife. She agreed to earn our living, to take up my route, going from town to town. I entered the *beis midrash* to sink myself into the Torah. Now you can understand how much I owe to her'' (*Nifleos HaSaba Kadisha* 12b).

אֲנִי ה' / I, Hashem

R' Yoel of Tshaploh

R' Yoel of Tshaploh was a disciple of *R' Menachem Mendel of Vitebsk* and *R' Shlomo of Karlin*. When they passed away, he became a disciple of *R' Mordechai of Lechovitz*. Once, he felt an overwhelming longing for his master, and saddling his horse, he rode off to Lechovitz. On arriving, he tied the horse to a peg and made his way to the Rebbe's study. He knocked on the door. The Rebbe asked, ''Who's there?'' To which R' Yoel answered, ''I.''

The Rebbe called out loudly, ''Who can allow himself to say *I*? *I, Hashem; it is I and no other*. It is only fitting for the Holy One to use *I*!''

R' Yoel immediately mounted his horse and returned home. He felt that he had received what he needed (*Ma'asei Avos* 97).

land of Egypt from man to beast; and upon all the gods of Egypt will I execute judgments; I, HASHEM.[1]

'I will pass through the land of Egypt on that night' — I and no angel; 'I will slay all the firstborn in the land of Egypt' — I and no seraph; 'And upon all the gods of Egypt will I execute judgments' — I and no messenger; 'I, HASHEM' — it is I and no other.

With a mighty hand — refers to the pestilence, as it is stated: Behold, the hand of HASHEM shall strike your cattle which are in the field, the horses, the donkeys, the camels, the herds, and the flocks — a very severe pestilence.[2]

With an outstretched arm — refers to the sword, as it says: His drawn sword in His hand, outstretched over Jerusalem.[3]

With great awe — alludes to the revelation of the Shechinah, as it says: Has God ever attempted to take unto Himself a nation from the midst of another nation by trials, miraculous signs, and wonders, by war and with a mighty hand and outstretched arm and by awesome revelations, as all that HASHEM your God did for you in Egypt, before your eyes?[4]

1. *Shemos* 12:12. 2. 9:3. 3. *I Divrei Hayamim* 21:16. 4. *Devarim* 4:34.

וּבְמֹרָא גָּדֹל / *With great awe*

R' Mordechai David of Dombrova

R' Mordechai David of Dombrova visited his master, the *Chozeh of Lublin,* and attended his Seder. The Chozeh looked at him when he said the passage: *with great awe alludes to the revelation of the Shechinah*. R' Mordechai was seized by a great fear; all his limbs shook, and, in his terror, he felt that his teeth were being shaken loose. He prayed to Hashem that his teeth remain in his mouth, so that he might eat the *matzah-of-mitzvah* and the afikoman (*Kerem HaChasidus* III 68).

בְּאֹתוֹת וּבְמֹפְתִים / *With signs and wonders*

R' Eliezer Ze'ev of Kretchnif

A *maskil* impertinently asked *R' Eliezer Ze'ev of Kretchnif*, "Why did Israel witness obvious signs and miracles during the Exodus and upon crossing the Red

וּבְאֹתוֹת – זֶה הַמַּטֶּה, כְּמָה שֶׁנֶּאֱמַר, וְאֶת הַמַּטֶּה הַזֶּה תִּקַּח בְּיָדֶךָ, אֲשֶׁר תַּעֲשֶׂה בּוֹ אֶת הָאֹתֹת.[1]

וּבְמֹפְתִים – זֶה הַדָּם, כְּמָה שֶׁנֶּאֱמַר, וְנָתַתִּי מוֹפְתִים בַּשָּׁמַיִם וּבָאָרֶץ

As each of the words דָּם, blood; אֵשׁ, fire; and עָשָׁן, smoke, is said, a bit of wine is removed from the cup, with the finger or by pouring.

דָּם וָאֵשׁ וְתִמְרוֹת עָשָׁן.[2]

דָּבָר אַחֵר – בְּיָד חֲזָקָה, שְׁתַּיִם. וּבִזְרֹעַ נְטוּיָה, שְׁתַּיִם. וּבְמֹרָא גָּדֹל, שְׁתַּיִם. וּבְאֹתוֹת, שְׁתַּיִם. וּבְמֹפְתִים, שְׁתַּיִם. אֵלּוּ עֶשֶׂר מַכּוֹת שֶׁהֵבִיא הַקָּדוֹשׁ בָּרוּךְ הוּא עַל הַמִּצְרִים בְּמִצְרַיִם, וְאֵלּוּ הֵן:

Sea, but today, we experience nothing of the sort?"

"I remember," said the Rebbe, "when the Rumanians conquered Siget, they had a victory parade to display their power — regiment upon regiment of troops and long columns of weapons, tanks and artillery. Twenty years have passed since then and no further parade has been staged. Why?

"At the time of the conquest, the government had to show its power to the people in order to impress its might upon them. But once they witnessed that power and strength, why should they march by, through the city streets, in their military masses?" (*Sha'ar HaOsios*, p. 118).

וְאֶת הַמַּטֶּה הַזֶּה תִּקַּח בְּיָדֶךָ / *Take this staff in your hand*

R' Nachman of Breslav

When *R' Nachman of Breslav* gave his discourse *Trust in Hashem* (*Likutei Maharan* 79), which explains that the staff of Moshe represents the freedom of choice which allows a man to turn to one side of an issue or the other, he walked about in his house, here and there, as was his custom, holding his staff in hand and said, *"And the staff of Elokim in my hand"* (*Shemos* 17:9). He emphasized *my hand*, as if to say that he was the master of his choice and had the staff in his hand, and could turn it in whatever direction he desired.

Fortunate is he who has gained such a state! (*Chayei Maharan* 36).

אֲשֶׁר תַּעֲשֶׂה בּוֹ אֶת הָאֹתֹת

That you may perform the miraculous signs with it

R' Shmuel Abba of Zichlin

The verse (*Shemos* 4:17) alludes to the role of the signs and wonders performed by the

With signs — refers to the miracles performed with the staff as it says: Take this staff in your hand, that you may perform the miraculous signs with it.[1]

With wonders — alludes to the blood, as it says: I will show wonders in the heavens and on the earth

As each of the words דָּם, blood; אֵשׁ, fire; and עָשָׁן, smoke, is said, a bit of wine is removed from the cup, with the finger or by pouring.

Blood, fire, and columns of smoke.[2]

Another explanation of the preceding verse: [Each phrase represents two plagues,] hence: mighty hand — two; outstretched arm — two; great awe — two; signs — two; wonders — two. These are the ten plagues which the Holy One, Blessed is He, brought upon the Egyptians in Egypt, namely:

1. *Shemos* 4:17. 2. *Yoel* 3:3.

---

tzaddik in order to arouse others to an awareness of Hashem and have them return to Him in *teshuvah*.

Think! Who needs a staff? The healthy do not need it. And it does not help a sick man confined to bed with suffering. But it does serve as an aid to the man who is not completely well and yet, not bound to a bed.

So too, signs and wonders will not bring the man who is mortally ill in spirit, who does not believe in God at all and denies His existence, to have faith. Nor does the man who is strong and healthy in his faith have need of the signs. It is the man of shaky faith who is helped by the wonders. They are the strong staff on which he can support his faith.

The verse alludes to this: *Take this staff in your hand* — take the nature of the staff into consideration when you are to *perform the miraculous signs with it* (*Lahav Esh* 30).

אֵלּוּ עֶשֶׂר מַכּוֹת

These are the ten plagues

R' Pesach Slonimski of Meitchet

When *R' Pesach Slonimski of Meitchet* came before *R' Avraham, the Zaide of Slonim* for the first time, he told him of the bitterness he felt, because he was troubled in matters of faith. He had presented his problems to several *tzaddikim* and they had given him satisfying answers. But as soon as he arrived home, the questions had resurfaced. He was unable to fix the ideas in his heart.

"Pharaoh of Egypt asked questions," said the Rebbe, " *'Who is Hashem*

As each of the plagues is mentioned, a bit of wine is removed from the cup.
The same is done by each word of Rabbi Yehudah's mnemonic.

דָּם. צְפַרְדֵּעַ. כִּנִּים. עָרוֹב. דֶּבֶר. שְׁחִין. בָּרָד.
אַרְבֶּה. חֹשֶׁךְ. מַכַּת בְּכוֹרוֹת.

רַבִּי יְהוּדָה הָיָה נוֹתֵן בָּהֶם סִמָּנִים:

דְּצַ״ךְ • עֲדַ״שׁ • בְּאַחַ״ב.

The cups are refilled. The wine that was removed is not used.

רַבִּי יוֹסֵי הַגְּלִילִי אוֹמֵר: מִנַּיִן אַתָּה אוֹמֵר שֶׁלָּקוּ הַמִּצְרִים בְּמִצְרַיִם עֶשֶׂר מַכּוֹת וְעַל הַיָּם לָקוּ חֲמִשִּׁים מַכּוֹת? בְּמִצְרַיִם מָה הוּא אוֹמֵר, וַיֹּאמְרוּ הַחַרְטֻמִּם אֶל פַּרְעֹה, אֶצְבַּע אֱלֹהִים הִוא.[1] וְעַל הַיָּם מָה הוּא אוֹמֵר, וַיַּרְא יִשְׂרָאֵל אֶת הַיָּד הַגְּדֹלָה אֲשֶׁר עָשָׂה יהוה בְּמִצְרַיִם, וַיִּירְאוּ הָעָם אֶת יהוה, וַיַּאֲמִינוּ בַּיהוה

---

that I must heed his voice?' Moshe's answers were the plagues — a plague after the first question; another plague after the second question."

And so it happened to R' Pesach. His body was afflicted with sores equal in number to his questions. Thereafter he was not troubled by questions and grew close in body and soul to his Rebbe (*Ma'asei Avos* 156).

דְּצַ״ךְ עֲדַ״שׁ בְּאַחַ״ב / *D'Tzach Adash B'Achav*

Chozeh of Lublin

Riaz heard the following from his master, the *Rabbi of Barniv,* who heard it from his grandfather, *R' Eliezer of Tzikov*, who had witnessed the incident when he accompanied his father, *R' Naftali of Ropshitz*, to spend *Pesach* with the *Chozeh of Lublin*:

When the Chozeh reached the abbreviations *D'tzach etc.*, he said, "*Dreit sich a Deitch b'Achav* (a German wanders about *Achav*)." The company present was astonished and the Rebbe of Ropshitz suggested, "The Rebbe should look into the *Haggadah* and go over the passage." The Chozeh looked into the *Haggadah* and said in a loud voice, "*Dreit sich a Deitch b'Achav,*" again, to the amazement of all present.

The first day of *Pesach* passed, and that evening (מוֹצָאֵי יוֹם טוֹב), *R' Shimon Oderberger of Germany*, known as R' Shimon Deitch (the German), arrived. When he descended the wagon and went to greet the Rebbe, the Chozeh

As each of the plagues is mentioned, a bit of wine is removed from the cup. The same is done by each word of Rabbi Yehudah's mnemonic.

1. Blood 2. Frogs 3. Vermin 4. Wild Beasts 5. Pestilence 6. Boils 7. Hail 8. Locusts 9. Darkness 10. Plague of the Firstborn.

Rabbi Yehudah abbreviated them by their Hebrew initials: D'TZACH, ADASH, B'ACHAV

The cups are refilled. The wine that was removed is not used.

Rabbi Yose the Galilean said: How does one derive that the Egyptians were struck with ten plagues in Egypt, but with fifty plagues at the Sea? — Concerning the plagues in Egypt the Torah states: The magicians said to Pharaoh, 'It is the finger of God.'[1] However, of those at the Sea, the Torah relates: Israel saw the great 'hand' which HASHEM laid upon the Egyptians, the people feared HASHEM and they believed in HASHEM and in His

1. *Shemos* 8:15.

---

said, "I felt, and shared in, your suffering while saying the *Haggadah*."

When R' Shimon left the Chozeh, they asked him, "What happened to you on the night of the Seder, and how did you get here so quickly from home?"

R' Shimon told them that he had been traveling to Lublin for *Pesach* and when he reached the hamlet of Achav, not far from Lublin, a wagon wheel broke. By the time it was repaired, it was too late to travel to Lublin and he was forced to remain in the village for *yom tov*. During the Seder, he thought of the Chozeh conducting the Seder with his pious company and how here he was in the village, unable to be among them. Overcome by his misery, he stopped his recitation of the *Haggadah*, went out, and wept greatly.

That was when the Rebbe could not contain himself and had said in pain, *"Dreit sich a Deitch b'Achav"* (*Otzar HaSipurim* V:5).

וַיַּרְא יִשְׂרָאֵל . . . וַיַּאֲמִינוּ / *Israel saw . . . and they believed*

Chidushei HaRim *Israel saw the great 'hand' which Hashem laid upon the Egyptians*. But even after they had seen, the Torah tells us: *and they believed in Hashem.* They had yet to reach the level of faith. This shows us that believing is greater than seeing (*Siach Sarfei Kodesh* I 406).

וּבְמֹשֶׁה עַבְדּוֹ.' כַּמָּה לָקוּ בְאֶצְבַּע? עֶשֶׂר מַכּוֹת. אֱמוֹר מֵעַתָּה, בְּמִצְרַיִם לָקוּ עֶשֶׂר מַכּוֹת, וְעַל הַיָּם לָקוּ חֲמִשִּׁים מַכּוֹת.

R' Mordechai of Lechovitz

One of the chasidim of *R' Mordechai of Lechovitz* was the business partner of a *misnaged* (opponent of chasidus). The chasid convinced his partner to accompany him to the Rebbe.

When they arrived, the Rebbe was in the middle of a meal. The *misnaged* looked on and was very impressed. When asked why he was so impressed, he said, "You can actually see how he eats in holiness — it is like the act of devotion of the *kohen gadol* (the High Priest) in the *Beis HaMikdash*!"

The chasid was taken aback by the answer. He entered the Rebbe's chamber and asked, "How is it that my friend was fortunate to see on his first visit that which I have as yet not seen?"

"Nothing to wonder at," said the Rebbe. "He is a *misnaged* and must be shown; you are a chasid and must believe!" (*Sipurei Chasidim, Mishpatim*)

וַיַּאֲמִינוּ / ***They believed***

R' Tzvi Elimelech of Dinov

I have been told by those who heard him that *R' Meshulam Zusha* said that he did not expect a reward in the world-to-come for the period in which he served Hashem after he already knew the truth of His greatness; he hoped for a reward for serving Hashem in faith, in the tradition which he received from his fathers (*Agra D'Pirka* 3).

R' Yitzchak Isaac of Komarna

The *Ba'al Shem* would tell the story that, when he was young, his teacher, the Prophet *Achiah HaShiloni,* taught him the Holy Names — their meaning, their use and how to teach them. Since he was as yet little, he wished to see if he could truly use them. He placed a cloth on the Dniester River and crossed the river on it by the power of a Holy Name. He had done *teshuvah* for this act all his days and fasted to correct the fault. He finally succeeded in correcting it in the following way. He was once forced to cross the Dniester to save his life from the Turkish army. He placed his prayer sash (*gartel*) on the river and crossed without using any Holy Name — but through great faith in God. He was thus favored because he had studied Torah for its own sake, and because his soul clung to the Creator at all times (*Notzer Chesed* ch. 86).

servant Moshe.[1] How many plagues did they receive with the finger? Ten! Then conclude that if they suffered ten plagues in Egypt [where they were struck with a finger], they must have been made to suffer fifty plagues at the sea [where they were struck with a whole hand].

1. *Shemos* 14:31.

R' Yitzchak of Neschiz

An epileptic once begged of *R' Yitzchak of Neschiz* that he be cured. The Rebbe refused to help him. The man placed all his money before him and said, "Take what you will for a *pidyon*."

"Believe me," said the Rebbe, "you can be cured, but you lack faith; that's what's missing. You heard that there is a rebbe in Neschiz who works wondrous cures, and you came. Yet, in all truth, it is Hashem alone Who brings redemption, not I. When you believe in Him, you shall be cured.

"I will tell you a story; listen and pay attention. A villager was once robbed. He came to the *Maggid of Koszhnitz* to ask for a blessing that he be delivered from his trouble.

" 'Believe me,' said the Maggid, 'I did not rob you. The members of my family can bear witness that I was home all that day.'

"The man and his wife begged the Maggid to bless them that the stolen goods be returned, and the husband gave a gold coin as a *pidyon*.

" 'I want more,' said the Maggid. The man put down three gold coins and the Maggid asked for more and more and finally he said, 'I want sixty gold coins.' They gave forty, then agreed to fifty, but the Maggid stood by his demand. 'Nothing less than sixty,' he said.

"At that, his wife scooped up the pile of coins from the table and said to her husband, 'Let's go. Hashem can bring us help, without our giving away all this!'

"When he heard this the Maggid said, 'You have already been helped. Know that it was difficult to fulfill your request, because you trusted in me and forgot Hashem. Now, that you have remembered Him, that in itself saves you. Leave only the single gold coin which you first gave me' " (*Zikaron Tov*, *Inyanei Tzedakah* 25).

וּבְמשֶׁה עַבְדּוֹ / *And in His servant Moshe*

Ba'al HaTanya

The *Ba'al HaTanya* once saw his son wearing expensive clothing. "How is it that a poor fellow like yourself can allow himself to have such an expensive outfit made up?" he asked.

"I am not poor," replied his son. "My dowry is safely deposited with a wealthy man and I am your son and eat at your table."

"My son, what a man does not have in his house cannot be taken into consideration. And though you eat at my table, one never knows what tomorrow will bring."

Not very long afterwards, the rich man, with whom the dowry was deposited, lost everything in his possession, including the young man's money. War broke out with France and the Rebbe and his household were forced to leave their place of residence. The Rebbe's son saw that all had been foreseen by his father and asked, "Why didn't you expressly tell me to ask for the return of the dowry?"

"Many years ago," said the Rebbe, "in my wanderings I came upon a tavern, where drunken gentiles were rolling about. I asked the tavern keeper, who was a Jew, for a room in which I might pray the evening prayer (*ma'ariv*).

"After I had prayed, the taverner said to me, 'Rebbe, I would like your advice.' I replied, 'Believe me! I am not a rebbe and I am lacking in advice!' To which he answered, 'As far as I am concerned you are a *tzaddik* like all the *tzaddikim* and I have confidence in your advice.'

"I thought to myself, 'True, I am not a rebbe, but perhaps I will be able to give him good advice.' I asked him what it was that troubled him.

"He told me that the tavern had been in the family for five generations. However, many of the villagers had left for other parts and his earnings had dwindled. He had, therefore, rented a tavern in a neighboring village. The establishment there was flourishing. Yet he had qualms about leaving his ancestral heritage, and he returned to it each night to sleep. On the other hand, he was concerned lest his newly founded establishment, uninhabited by night, might be liable to theft. Should he leave this tavern completely and move to the other, or continue to maintain both?

"I listened and answered that a man's place is where he finds his livelihood. Since it was in the other village, he ought to move there. He thanked me, and while I was as yet eating my evening meal, he packed all his belongings and loaded them onto a wagon. He wished to travel in the dead of night. But I was very weary, and begged of him that he wait until daylight. He agreed to stay the night and prepared a bed for me.

"When I rose in the morning, he brought me a hot drink and urged me to travel with them to the new tavern and bless him with prosperity.

"We started out. His wife glanced back and saw a column of smoke rising in the village. We turned about and retraced our steps and found the tavern being consumed by a raging fire.

"Heaven had decreed that all the belongings of the tavern keeper be destroyed. But, because of his hospitality and faith in *tzaddikim,* he had been given a reprieve. For the verse וְצַדִּיק בֶּאֱמוּנָתוֹ יִחְיֶה, 'the righteous man, in his faith shall live' (*Chavakuk* 2:4), may be interpreted, 'Through his faith in the *tzaddik* a man will live.'

"And you, my son, if you had put your faith in *tzaddikim*, like that tavern keeper, you would have run to ask for your dowry as soon as I dropped my hint."

The Yismach Yisrael of Alexander retold the story to his chasidim on the day before *Rosh Hashanah* and added the following:

"That is what is meant by the passage in the prayers on the Days of Awe, 'עֲצָתוֹ אֱמוּנָה, His advice is faith.' The advice of Hashem by which He saves a man is through faith in Hashem and His servant Moshe" (Introduction to *Tiferes Yisrael*).

Tiferes Shmuel of Alexander

I remember that when I was a youngster my sainted father was once teaching Torah to the townsmen of Turchin. He reached the verse: "And Yehoshua bin Nun was full of the spirit of wisdom because Moshe had placed his hands upon him and the Children of Israel hearkened to him" (*Devarim* 34:9). The wisdom of Yehoshua, he explained, flowed from two sources. There was a heavenly factor from above — "because Moshe had placed his hands upon him." And there was a human factor, from below — the belief in the wise (*emunas chachamim*) which the Children of Israel had with regard to him (*Tiferes Shlomo* 203).

R' Yisrael of Ruzhin

R' Yisrael of Ruzhin asked the chasid Reb Yaakovke of Yarishov, "Did you know *R' Baruch of Mezhibuz*?"

"I did not really *know* him, but I *believed* in his holiness," answered Reb Yaakovke, wisely.

The Rebbe was pleased by his answer and said, "That is, indeed, as it should be!

"When Israel went out of Egypt, they reached the heights of human understanding of Hashem. The maidservant who witnessed the crossing of the Red Sea saw that which the prophet Yechezkel did not see in his vision. It was then that the Evil Desire (יֵצֶר הָרָע) came upon them and tried to sway them and lead them into error. 'You have already seen everything,' he said. 'You have grasped it all. You have reached the limit of understanding.' But they were not led astray. They knew that much, as yet, lay hidden and that they were in need of simple faith. That is why the Torah tells us that, just at that point in time, 'They believed in Hashem.'

"And the verse continues: 'and in His servant Moshe.' For just as a man must realize that, as far as his belief in Hashem is concerned, no matter how much he grasps the greatness and lofty transcendence of the Creator, he has not reached an infinitesimal part of understanding, so he must know that he cannot grasp the exalted loftiness of the *tzaddik*. The more we understand the heights of his holiness, the more we must believe that he immeasurably surpasses our grasp" (*Sipurei Tzaddikim* 81).

רַבִּי אֱלִיעֶזֶר אוֹמֵר. מִנַּיִן שֶׁכָּל מַכָּה וּמַכָּה שֶׁהֵבִיא הַקָּדוֹשׁ בָּרוּךְ הוּא עַל הַמִּצְרִים בְּמִצְרַיִם הָיְתָה שֶׁל אַרְבַּע מַכּוֹת? שֶׁנֶּאֱמַר, יְשַׁלַּח בָּם חֲרוֹן אַפּוֹ – עֶבְרָה, וָזַעַם, וְצָרָה, מִשְׁלַחַת מַלְאֲכֵי רָעִים.[1] עֶבְרָה, אַחַת. וָזַעַם, שְׁתַּיִם. וְצָרָה, שָׁלֹשׁ. מִשְׁלַחַת מַלְאֲכֵי רָעִים, אַרְבַּע. אֱמוֹר מֵעַתָּה, בְּמִצְרַיִם לָקוּ אַרְבָּעִים מַכּוֹת, וְעַל הַיָּם לָקוּ מָאתַיִם מַכּוֹת.

רַבִּי עֲקִיבָא אוֹמֵר. מִנַּיִן שֶׁכָּל מַכָּה וּמַכָּה שֶׁהֵבִיא הַקָּדוֹשׁ בָּרוּךְ הוּא עַל הַמִּצְרִים בְּמִצְרַיִם הָיְתָה שֶׁל חָמֵשׁ מַכּוֹת? שֶׁנֶּאֱמַר, יְשַׁלַּח בָּם חֲרוֹן אַפּוֹ, עֶבְרָה, וָזַעַם, וְצָרָה, מִשְׁלַחַת מַלְאֲכֵי רָעִים.[1] חֲרוֹן אַפּוֹ, אַחַת. עֶבְרָה, שְׁתַּיִם. וָזַעַם, שָׁלֹשׁ. וְצָרָה, אַרְבַּע. מִשְׁלַחַת מַלְאֲכֵי רָעִים, חָמֵשׁ. אֱמוֹר מֵעַתָּה, בְּמִצְרַיִם לָקוּ חֲמִשִּׁים מַכּוֹת, וְעַל הַיָּם לָקוּ חֲמִשִּׁים וּמָאתַיִם מַכּוֹת.

כַּמָּה מַעֲלוֹת טוֹבוֹת לַמָּקוֹם עָלֵינוּ.

אִלּוּ הוֹצִיאָנוּ מִמִּצְרַיִם,
וְלֹא עָשָׂה בָהֶם שְׁפָטִים, דַּיֵּנוּ.
אִלּוּ עָשָׂה בָהֶם שְׁפָטִים,
וְלֹא עָשָׂה בֵאלֹהֵיהֶם, דַּיֵּנוּ.
אִלּוּ עָשָׂה בֵאלֹהֵיהֶם,
וְלֹא הָרַג אֶת בְּכוֹרֵיהֶם, דַּיֵּנוּ.
אִלּוּ הָרַג אֶת בְּכוֹרֵיהֶם,
וְלֹא נָתַן לָנוּ אֶת מָמוֹנָם, דַּיֵּנוּ.

Rabbi Eliezer said: How does one derive that every plague that the Holy One, Blessed is He, inflicted upon the Egyptians in Egypt was equal to four plagues? — for it is written: He sent upon them his fierce anger: wrath, fury, and trouble, a band of emissaries of evil.[1] [Since each plague in Egypt consisted of] 1) wrath, 2) fury, 3) trouble and 4) a band of emissaries of evil, therefore conclude that in Egypt they were struck by forty plagues and by the sea two hundred!

Rabbi Akiva said: How does one derive that each plague that the Holy One, Blessed is He, inflicted upon the Egyptians in Egypt was equal to five plagues? — For it is written: He sent upon them His fierce anger, wrath, fury, trouble, and a band of emissaries of evil.[1] [Since each plague in Egypt consisted of] 1) fierce anger, 2) wrath, 3) fury, 4) trouble and 5) a band of emissaries of evil, therefore conclude that in Egypt they were struck by fifty plagues and by the sea two hundred and fifty!

The Omnipresent has bestowed
so many favors upon us!

Had He brought us out of Egypt, but not executed judgments against the Egyptians,
it would have sufficed us.

Had He executed judgments against them, but not upon their gods, it would have sufficed us.

Had He executed judgments against their gods, but not slain their firstborn,
it would have sufficed us.

Had He slain their firstborn, but not given us their wealth, it would have sufficed us.

---

1. *Tehillim* 78:49.

אִלּוּ נָתַן לָנוּ אֶת מָמוֹנָם,
וְלֹא קָרַע לָנוּ אֶת הַיָּם, דַּיֵּנוּ.
אִלּוּ קָרַע לָנוּ אֶת הַיָּם,
וְלֹא הֶעֱבִירָנוּ בְתוֹכוֹ בֶּחָרָבָה, דַּיֵּנוּ.
אִלּוּ הֶעֱבִירָנוּ בְתוֹכוֹ בֶּחָרָבָה,
וְלֹא שִׁקַּע צָרֵינוּ בְּתוֹכוֹ, דַּיֵּנוּ.
אִלּוּ שִׁקַּע צָרֵינוּ בְּתוֹכוֹ,
וְלֹא סִפֵּק צָרְכֵּנוּ בַּמִּדְבָּר
אַרְבָּעִים שָׁנָה, דַּיֵּנוּ.

נָתַן לָנוּ אֶת מָמוֹנָם
(Had He) given us their wealth

Avnei Nezer

Once, on *Shabbos Shirah,* while the chasidim were drinking and toasting each other at the table (*tish*) of the *Avnei Nezer*, one of those present complained to the Rebbe of the difficulty he had in earning a living and commented that he would like to have *"the loot of the sea."

"Certainly, if you will be on the exalted plane of Israel as they stood on the shore of the Red Sea, after crossing through the parted waters, then you will also have the loot of the sea," replied the Rebbe (*Abir HaRoim* II 338).

סִפֵּק צָרְכֵּנוּ בַּמִּדְבָּר
(Had He) provided for our needs in the desert

R' Meir Shalom of Kalishin

R' Meir Shalom of Kalishin was asked what's involved when chasidim crown a rebbe to be their leader.

"We find in holy *sefarim*," he said, "that everything is to be classified as 'world' (עוֹלָם), 'year' (שָׁנָה) or 'soul' (נֶפֶשׁ). In other words, everything fits into a category of place (world), time (year), or personality (soul).

"The Children of Israel in the desert were in a dry and desolate place and yet drew the *Shechinah* (Divine Presence) to encamp there. That is with respect to *world* or place. As far as *year* or time is concerned, we find that the rabbinical court (בֵּית דִין) is appointed to sanctify the new moon. Heaven follows the court's decision and grants its sanctity.

[* *The loot of the sea* — the silver, gold, and other valuables of the Egyptian army drowned in the Red Sea, which the sea cast upon its shores to be gathered by Israel.]

Had He given us their wealth, but not split the Sea for us, it would have sufficed us.

Had He split the Sea for us, but not led us through it on dry land, it would have sufficed us.

Had He led us through on dry land, but not drowned our oppressors in it, it would have sufficed us.

Had He drowned our oppressors in it, but not provided for our needs in the desert for forty years, it would have sufficed us.

"And when Israel chooses a leader — that falls within the category of *soul* or personality. Then, too, Hashem allows his Divine Presence to rest upon that man" (*Gan Hadasim* 18).

R' Yitzchak Isaac of Komarna

The *Ba'al Shem Tov* and a disciple once, during a journey, found themselves in a desolate, dry area. Water was not to be found for many miles about. The disciple felt parched and said to his master, "I am very thirsty." The Ba'al Shem said not a word. When the disciple saw how dangerously thirsty he was, he said, "Master, I am thirsty to the point of collapse."

"Do you believe," said the Ba'al Shem, "that when the Holy One created the universe, He envisioned your dire straits and prepared water for you to drink?"

The disciple did not reply immediately, but pondered the matter. He, then, answered, "I truly believe that."

"Wait a while," said the Ba'al Shem.

They went on and came upon a non-Jew carrying two large pitchers of water on his shoulders. They gave him a few small coins and he gave them to drink.

"Why are you carrying water in this barren dessert?" asked the Ba'al Shem.

"My noble owner has gone mad," said the man, "and sent me to draw water from a distant well. I must carry the water three miles and have no idea why."

"Just contemplate Divine Providence," said the Ba'al Shem to his disciple. "Hashem, for your sake, created a nobleman who would go mad, so that you might have water. And Hashem ordained this in His providence at the moment the world was created" (*Nesiv Mitzvosecha; Nesiv HaYichud* 3:1).

אִלּוּ סִפֵּק צָרְכֵּנוּ בַּמִּדְבָּר
אַרְבָּעִים שָׁנָה,
וְלֹא הֶאֱכִילָנוּ אֶת הַמָּן, דַּיֵּנוּ.
אִלּוּ הֶאֱכִילָנוּ אֶת הַמָּן,
וְלֹא נָתַן לָנוּ אֶת הַשַּׁבָּת, דַּיֵּנוּ.
אִלּוּ נָתַן לָנוּ אֶת הַשַּׁבָּת,
וְלֹא קֵרְבָנוּ לִפְנֵי הַר סִינַי, דַּיֵּנוּ.

הַמָּן / *The Manna*

Chozeh of Lublin

The *Chozeh of Lublin* once taught, "The Torah tells us that the *Manna* (מָן) was given its name 'because they did not know what it was' (מָה הוּא — *Shemos* 16:15). And that was because it was spiritual food, food that the angels, who serve Hashem, eat. Those who ate it rose from day to day, higher and higher, so much so that a man could not recognize his friend from one day to the next and would ask, 'Who is he (מִי הוּא)?'

"Indeed, even today, there is a young man here who wanders among the trees and no one really knows him. Tomorrow all will ask, 'Who is he?'

R' David of Lelov, who was present, went out to see who it was that was wandering among the trees and found *R' Simchah Bunim of Pshischa* (*Siach Sarfei Kodesh* I 209).

R' Chanoch Henoch of Alexander

R' Chanoch Henoch of Alexander was asked why chasidim *snatch at and partake of the food of the dishes the rebbe tastes.

"Every man draws down food to himself in accordance with his spiritual essence (*shoresh*, lit. 'root')," said the Rebbe. "When Israel went up out of Egypt they reached a lofty, heavenly state and were found worthy of eating *Manna*, 'the bread of heaven.' The *tzaddik* is heavenly in nature and his food, too, is of the same sort as *Manna*" (*Siach Sarfei Kodesh* IV 83).

[**snatch at and partake of the food etc.* This is the practice of eating *she'irayim,* the 'leftovers', so to speak, of the rebbe. The comment of the Rebbe of Alexander is not a homiletic bon mot, pure and simple. It has halachic overtones. The Talmud says: Whosoever enjoys a meal in which a wise man (תַּלְמִיד חָכָם) participates is like one who enjoys the brightness of the *Shechinah* (*Berachos* 64a; see, too, the Rambam's positive instruction to endeavor to eat with *talmidei chachamim* — *Hilchos De'os* 6:2).]

Had He provided for our needs in the desert for forty years, but not fed us the Manna,
it would have sufficed us.

Had He fed us the Manna, but not given us the Shabbos, it would have sufficed us.

Had He given us the Shabbos, but not brought us before Mount Sinai, it would have sufficed us.

Chidushei HaRim

"Behold I will rain down for you bread from Heaven . . . that I might test them whether they will walk in My Torah, or not" (*Shemos* 16:4).

What test is involved with the eating of *Manna*?

Chazal tell us: "This is the way of Torah — you shall eat bread with salt, and drink water in small measure" (*Avos* 6:4). They have also said: "Before a man prays that the words of the Torah will enter his innards, he should first pray that delicacies will not enter his innards." For the pursuit of fine foods and pleasures runs counter to the life of Torah.

The *Manna* had a special characteristic; in eating it, one could taste any food he desired. This presented a great test. For those who wished to rise in the realm of Torah must not desire to taste anything, but only to sustain life (*Siach Sarfei Kodesh* IV 62).

נָתַן לָנוּ אֶת הַשַּׁבָּת / *(Had He) given us the Shabbos*

Akeidas Yitzchak of Alexander

The *mashgiach* (spiritual supervisor) of the *yeshiva* of Slobodka, *R' Avraham Grodzinski,* visited the *Akeidas Yitzchak* of Alexander. In the course of their conversation the Rebbe asked, "The *gemara* says: The Holy One said to Moshe, 'I have a fine gift in My treasure house called *Shabbos*. I would like to give it to Israel. Go and inform them!' What is there about *Shabbos* which make it a mystery that needs revelation?

"Once a poor man came to my sainted grandfather. My grandfather had nothing else to give him and so took the jewelry of the *rebbetzin* and gave that. When his wife heard of this, she ran after the man. After she had caught up to him, she said, 'The jewels are very valuable. Be aware of that, and don't sell them cheaply!'

"The Holy One sent Moshe to tell Israel, 'Be aware that *Shabbos* is a valuable gift; don't change it into nothing more than a steaming bowl of *cholent* and a slice of spicy *kugel*' " (*Vaya'al Moshe*).

Chidushei HaRim

The *Chidushei HaRim of Gur* reproached his chasidim regarding the sanctity of the Sabbath:

אִלּוּ קֵרְבָנוּ לִפְנֵי הַר סִינַי,
וְלֹא נָתַן לָנוּ אֶת הַתּוֹרָה, דַּיֵּנוּ.

The *Shabbos* is like a great rebbe, a great teacher. Just as Rabban Gamliel proclaimed that whoever had an inner self unlike his outer show, who thought one way and acted differently, was to be denied entry into the *beis midrash* to hear the Torah discourse, so too, he whose inner and outer self do not correspond to each other is not allowed to enter *Shabbos*.

I am also denied entry, but the difference between me and you is that I stand at the door and am aware that I am barred from coming in. You, however, stand from afar and do not even knock (*Or*, p. 46).

R' Chaim of Sanz

It was forbidden by law to cut down timber in the royal forest which grew about the city of Vienna. But a wealthy lumber dealer and some senior officials had made an illegal pact allowing him to fell trees there. As a result, he earned huge profits. But he gained the envy of his competitors who informed upon him to the authorities. His house was surrounded in the dark of night, a unit of police arrested him, and he was spirited off. His wife searched for him for four months, but learned nothing of his whereabouts.

In her misery, she traveled to *R' Chaim of Sanz*. The Rebbe said that if her husband would promise to observe *Shabbos* properly, he would be freed. The woman said she had no way of securing her husband's promise, for she had no idea where he was being held. But the Rebbe told her to go home in peace and, on the way home, she would find out where he was.

The woman boarded the train and bitterly bemoaned her fate. Opposite her sat a senior officer who asked her why she wept. After she told him her tale, he revealed that he was the commandant of the prison in which her husband was to be found. He arranged to have her meet with her husband and she told him of the Rebbe's condition. The man hesitated, for the lumberyards of all his rivals were open on *Shabbos*. Finally, he came to the conclusion that it was better to close his establishment once a week on *Shabbos* rather than languish in prison all seven days of the week.

His wife went and informed the Rebbe of her husband's decision and the Rebbe told her that she might return home untroubled. Her husband, he said, was already free and awaiting her (*Rabbeinu HaKadosh MiSanz* 295).

לִפְנֵי הַר סִינַי / *Before Mount Sinai*

R' Shlomo of Radomsk

R' Shlomo of Radomsk did not wish to be a rebbe. Once, just before *Shavuos*, when he saw large crowds of chasidim arriving, he rose and traveled to *R' Yechezkel of Kuzhmir* to spend the festival in his presence.

The *Rebbe of Kuzhmir* was surprised to see him and reproached him saying, "You cannot abandon an assembly of Hashem and leave them like a flock of sheep without a shepherd. The Torah tells us that Moshe Rabbenu 'descended from the mountain to the people.' This teaches us, says *Rashi*, that he did not occupy himself, after coming down from Sinai, with his private interests (*Shemos* 19:14).

"Now what private interests would Moshe have had in the desert? The answer is that each man of Israel was preparing himself to receive the Torah. In all likelihood, Moshe too would have wished to sanctify and purify himself like an angel. But he was a faithful shepherd and did not turn to his private interests of the spirit; he descended from the mountain to the people. You, however, left the people to attend to your own needs and to sanctify yourself."

The Rebbe of Radomsk heard the reproach and replied, then and there, "True! But Moshe even when he descended to the people was, as yet, at the foot of Mount Sinai. I also came here, to Mount Sinai" (*Nifleos HaTiferes Shlomo* 118).

סִינַי / *Mount Sinai*

R' Tzvi Hirsch Gidziler

R' Tzvi Hirsch Gidziler was exceptionally humble, truly insignificant in his own eyes. Once *R' Moshe of Lelov* visited him and found it difficult to remain indoors because of the smell of fresh hides which had been placed on the stove to dry.

"Why are these hides here?" he asked. "After all, you spend your time in learning and devotion to Hashem."

"True!" said R' Hirsch. "But my children earn their livelihood by the sale of hides and they find it more convenient to dry them here, in my house."

"*Chazal* tell us, indeed," said the Rebbe of Lelov, "that the Holy One gave the Torah on Mount Sinai, a *lowly* hill, so that we might learn from the act, the importance of modesty. But why then did He not give the Torah in a valley? The Torah shows us, thereby, that there is a limit to humility. A man must be something of a hill or mountain and not allow himself to be trampled upon by others" (*Likutei Divrei David* 49).

קֵרְבָנוּ לִפְנֵי הַר סִינַי . . . נָתַן לָנוּ אֶת הַתּוֹרָה / *(Had He) brought us before Mount Sinai . . . (Had He) given us the Torah*

R' Moshe Leib of Sasov

I was once in Lublin for *Succos*. The *Chozeh of Lublin* went to the *succah* to fulfill the *mitzvah* of *esrog* and *lulav*. All the chasidim followed, and I went along with them. For the space of a whole hour, he burned and trembled with visible enthusiasm. The chasidim followed suit in their excitement, moving to and fro, quaking

אִלּוּ נָתַן לָנוּ אֶת הַתּוֹרָה,
וְלֹא הִכְנִיסָנוּ לְאֶרֶץ יִשְׂרָאֵל, דַּיֵּנוּ.
אִלּוּ הִכְנִיסָנוּ לְאֶרֶץ יִשְׂרָאֵל,
וְלֹא בָנָה לָנוּ אֶת בֵּית הַבְּחִירָה, דַּיֵּנוּ.

---

in great fear. I, for my part, sat quietly on a bench, waiting for the Rebbe to end his preliminary preparations. I did not want to give preference to the secondary over the more important but wished to concentrate on the Rebbe as he pronounced the blessing. It is impossible to describe his exaltation then.

My attitude is alluded to in the Torah. "And the entire people saw the sounds and torches and the blast of the *shofar* and the smoking mountain" (*Shemos* 20:15). They saw the preliminaries to the giving of the Torah and were very excited by them: "And the people saw and moved" (ibid.). Moshe on the other hand, 'approached the fog where *Elokim* was' (ibid. 20:18); he was not overcome by the outward phenomena at Sinai, but reached towards the inner core of the Ten Commandments to receive the Torah itself (*Likutei Maharil, Yisro* s.v. וכל).

נָתַן לָנוּ אֶת הַתּוֹרָה / *(Had He) given us the Torah*

Chidushei HaRim

The Holy One gave us the Torah. By the Law (*halachah*) a giver should give in good measure, and whoever gives his fellow a field surrounded by other fields also grants him a path of entry to the field. If Hashem gave us the Torah, he most certainly granted each of us the path, the power and ability to reach the Torah (*Siach Sarfei Kodesh* I 407).

Divrei Chaim of Sanz

A descendant of *tzaddikim* once chanced to be in the presence of the *Divrei Chaim of Sanz* on *Shavuos*. This grandchild had nothing about him in the way of Torah learning nor the good manners (דֶּרֶךְ אֶרֶץ) which should surpass learning. He was full of pride and the demand for honor because of his family tree.

"Do you know," the Rebbe asked him, "why the days before *Shavuos* are called illustrious days (הַיָּמִים הַמְיוּחָסִים)?"

The grandchild of the illustrious did not know.

"Before the Torah was given," said the Rebbe, "the pedigreed, the wellborn, were important. After *Shavuos*, after the Torah had been given, however, the importance passed over to those who are learned in Torah and are graced with good manners (דֶּרֶךְ אֶרֶץ). Being wellborn is no longer sufficient" (*Kol Hakasuv LeChaim,* p. 126).

Had He given us the Torah, but not brought us into the Land of Israel, it would have sufficed us.

Had He brought us into the Land of Israel, but not built the Temple for us, it would have sufficed us.

לְאֶרֶץ יִשְׂרָאֵל / *Into the Land of Israel*

R' Binyamin David of Ostrowa

R' Binyamin David of Ostrowa was in charge of the monies collected for *Eretz Yisrael*. When he was once in the presence of *R' Yechezkel of Kuzhmir*, the Rebbe asked him, "Why is the Holy Land called *Eretz Yisrael*, the Land of Israel? After all, it was promised to all our forefathers, to Avraham and Yitzchak, as well as to Yisrael."

"Had it been named after Avraham and Yitzchak," said R' Binyamin David, "Yishmael and Esav would also have a share in it. That is why it has received the name of our forefather Yaakov only."

"No!" said the Rebbe. "It is named *Yisrael* because only one who acts like a *Yisraeli*, a Jew, and observes the *mitzvos* and upholds the Torah has a share in the Land" (*Siach Sarfei Kodesh* V, p. 8).

R' Yoel of Satmar

R' Yosef Tzvi Dushinsky, the Rav of *Yerushalayim,* told *R' Yoel of Satmar* that he had been questioned by a British board of inquiry about the immigration of non-observant Jews. He had said that one could not tell in advance who was non-observant. The answer had aroused the ire of the secular Zionists and the Mizrachi. For it implied that those who declared that they were non-observant should not be permitted to immigrate.

The Rebbe of Satmar smiled and said, "Perhaps they are of the same opinion as Rav Hai Gaon."

The conversation was cut short abruptly. Those who had been present, wishing to know to what the Rebbe had alluded, came and asked him. He showed them the *Aruch* under the entry *eser* (עֶשֶׂר — ten), which notes that the *mishnah* in *Keilim* (1:6-9) lists ten degrees of holiness of place which do not include the holiness of *Eretz Yisrael,* although it appears in the *mishnah* (it is the eleventh item). Rav Hai Gaon is cited by the *Aruch* as saying that *Eretz Yisrael* stands apart from the others. For all the other places, because of their holiness, deny entry to people bearing certain types of impurity. But *Eretz Yisrael*, though it is holy, is accessible to even the impure (*Olamos Shacharvu* 60).

הִכְנִיסָנוּ לְאֶרֶץ יִשְׂרָאֵל / *(Had He) brought us into the Land of Israel*

R' Avraham Dov of Avritch

A man who had been sent from Tzefas, in the Holy Land, to gather funds for his

עַל אַחַת כַּמָּה, וְכַמָּה טוֹבָה כְפוּלָה וּמְכֻפֶּלֶת לַמָּקוֹם עָלֵינוּ. שֶׁהוֹצִיאָנוּ מִמִּצְרַיִם, וְעָשָׂה בָהֶם שְׁפָטִים, וְעָשָׂה בֵאלֹהֵיהֶם, וְהָרַג אֶת בְּכוֹרֵיהֶם, וְנָתַן לָנוּ אֶת מָמוֹנָם, וְקָרַע לָנוּ אֶת הַיָּם, וְהֶעֱבִירָנוּ בְתוֹכוֹ בֶּחָרָבָה, וְשִׁקַּע צָרֵינוּ בְּתוֹכוֹ, וְסִפֵּק צָרְכֵּנוּ בַּמִּדְבָּר אַרְבָּעִים שָׁנָה, וְהֶאֱכִילָנוּ אֶת הַמָּן, וְנָתַן לָנוּ אֶת הַשַּׁבָּת, וְקֵרְבָנוּ לִפְנֵי הַר סִינַי, וְנָתַן לָנוּ אֶת הַתּוֹרָה, וְהִכְנִיסָנוּ לְאֶרֶץ יִשְׂרָאֵל, וּבָנָה לָנוּ אֶת בֵּית הַבְּחִירָה, לְכַפֵּר עַל כָּל עֲוֹנוֹתֵינוּ.

---

community visited the city of *R' Avraham Dov of Avritch* and spoke wonders in praise of *Eretz Yisrael*. He described the air, the landscape, flowers and fruits. In language rich in expression, he pictured the holy places and gravesites of the *tzaddikim*. His enthusiasm knew no bounds, until he finally bubbled over and said, "Rebbe, what can I say? Why should I go on? Even the rocks of *Eretz Yisrael* are pearls and precious stones of all sorts!"

The Rebbe who had already previously pined to go up to the Holy Land could no longer find peace. He left his city and his flock of chasidim, went up to Israel, and settled in Tzefas.

Sometime afterwards the funds gatherer returned home from his travels. He came before the Rebbe and asked with interest, "Well, then, has the Rebbe found what he hoped to see?"

"The land is, indeed, very, very, good," said the Rebbe. "The holy places, the graves of the *tzaddikim*, the Western Wall, the tomb of Rachel, the air — the air of *Eretz Yisrael* grants wisdom — everything is exceptional. But when you said the rocks were pearls, that was an exaggeration."

The man reacted strongly and said, "Rebbe, whoever is found worthy sees it!"

The Rebbe rose without a word, and closeted himself in his room. For an entire year he did not leave that room. For an entire year he secluded himself and devoted himself to his Maker, through study and prayer, cut off from the world. When the year drew to a close, he emerged and invited the residents of Tzefas to a feast of thanksgiving.

All sat, filled with curiosity, desirous to hear why the Rebbe had lived in enforced solitude and why he had called upon them to gather for this feast. The Rebbe proclaimed, "Indeed, the statement is correct. The rocks *are*

Thus, how much more so, should we be grateful to the Omnipresent for all the numerous favors He showered upon us: He brought us out of Egypt; executed judgments against the Egyptians; and against their gods; slew their firstborn; gave us their wealth; split the Sea for us; led us through it on dry land; drowned our oppressors in it; provided for our needs in the desert for forty years; fed us the Manna; gave us the Shabbos; brought us before Mount Sinai; gave us the Torah; brought us to the Land of Israel; and built us the Temple, to atone for our sins.

---

pearls; whoever is found worthy sees it."

Those present did not understand him and so he told them about the collector of funds and what the man had said. "In all my life," he said, "no one ever spoke to me with such force. I felt that Heaven had put the words on his lips in order to encourage me to reach such a state. I closed myself off in my room; I sanctified and purified myself. And, indeed, my eyes were opened. I bear true witness before you. The rocks of Israel are precious stones and shine with the luster of pearls" (*Pri Kodesh Hillulim* 111).

R' Mordechai Shlomo of Boyan

On his first visit to *Eretz Yisrael*, *R' Mordechai Shlomo of Boyan* was received by his chasidim in Haifa. Five of his followers entered the car that took him to Tel Aviv. During the two-hour ride, the Rebbe did not say a word, but looked out the window with great concentration.

One of the chasidim could not contain himself and asked, "Tell us, master, what is there to be seen from the window?"

To which the Rebbe replied, "Of *Eretz Yisrael* it is said that 'the eyes of Hashem, your God, are upon it' (*Devarim* 11:12). Certainly, then, *we* ought to look at it" (*Demu'ios Hod* III 252).

R' Yisrael of Ruzhin

A chasid wished to go up to the Holy Land.

"Know that *Eretz Yisrael* is like a feather bed, a down quilt," said his rebbe, *R' Yisrael of Ruzhin*. "In the cold of a winter night, a man crawls under the quilt. At first it is cold. Only with time does it grow warmer and warmer. For the quilt is not of itself warm; it gathers up the warmth of a man's body and warms him, in turn, all the more.

"So it is with the Holy Land. If a man of fire comes to live in her, she adds the heat of holiness to him in his devotion. But to the cold soul, she remains as cold as she was before" (*Ner Yisrael* I 164).

רַבָּן גַּמְלִיאֵל הָיָה אוֹמֵר. כָּל שֶׁלֹּא אָמַר שְׁלשָׁה דְּבָרִים אֵלּוּ בַּפֶּסַח, לֹא יָצָא יְדֵי חוֹבָתוֹ, וְאֵלּוּ הֵן,

פֶּסַח. מַצָּה. וּמָרוֹר.

פֶּסַח שֶׁהָיוּ אֲבוֹתֵינוּ אוֹכְלִים בִּזְמַן שֶׁבֵּית הַמִּקְדָּשׁ הָיָה קַיָּם, עַל שׁוּם מָה? עַל שׁוּם שֶׁפָּסַח הַקָּדוֹשׁ בָּרוּךְ הוּא עַל בָּתֵּי אֲבוֹתֵינוּ בְּמִצְרַיִם. שֶׁנֶּאֱמַר, וַאֲמַרְתֶּם, זֶבַח פֶּסַח הוּא לַיהוה, אֲשֶׁר פָּסַח עַל בָּתֵּי בְנֵי יִשְׂרָאֵל בְּמִצְרַיִם בְּנָגְפּוֹ אֶת מִצְרַיִם, וְאֶת בָּתֵּינוּ הִצִּיל, וַיִּקֹּד הָעָם וַיִּשְׁתַּחֲווּ.[1]

פֶּסַח מַצָּה וּמָרוֹר / *Pesach — the Pesach offering; matzah — the unleavened bread; maror — the bitter herbs*

Chidushei HaRim

Matzah is meant to remind us of freedom, while *maror* is meant to remind us of the bondage which preceded that freedom. Why, then, is *matzah* referred to before *maror*?

R' Simchah Bunim of Pshischa gave the following parable:

A king had an only son whom he loved and upon whom he lavished every favor. The son, however, was an ingrate and rebelled against his father who, forthwith, banished him. Years passed and the king was moved to pity for his son. He sent one of his ministers to seek him out and bring him back. The minister inquired and investigated. He found the prince in an out-of-the-way village, barefoot, dressed in tatters and drinking himself silly in the local tavern. The minister approached him and asked him how he was.

"Marvelous," answered the youth. "If I had a sheepskin jacket and a pair of boots no one could be happier."

The minister wept to hear to what depths the once-pampered prince had fallen.

Thus it is that David HaMelech in speaking of Egypt and the Exodus says: "And He saw in what straits they were — when He heard their song" (*Tehillim* 106:44). They were mired in the muck of bondage, and yet they sang. For the nadir of servitude is the coming to terms with the state of degradation.

We eat the *matzah* before the *maror*, because Israel was totally unaware

Rabban Gamliel used to say: Whoever has not explained the following three things on Passover has not fulfilled his duty, namely; PESACH – the Pesach offering; MATZAH – the unleavened bread; MAROR – the bitter herbs.

Pesach – Why did our fathers eat a Pesach offering during the period when the Temple stood? – Because the Holy One, Blessed is He, passed over the houses of our fathers in Egypt, as it is written: You shall say: 'It is a Pesach offering for HASHEM, Who passed over the houses of the Children of Israel in Egypt when He struck the Egyptians and spared our houses; and the people bowed down and prostrated themselves.'[1]

1. *Shemos* 12:27.

---

of the bitterness of servitude indicated by the *maror* until they were worthy of the light of deliverance alluded to by the *matzah*. They truly tasted redemption before they felt their bondage (*Siach Sarfei Kodesh* I 244).

אֲשֶׁר פָּסַח עַל בָּתֵּי בְנֵי יִשְׂרָאֵל / *Who passed over the houses of the Children of Israel*

R' Moshe Leib of Sasov

R' Moshe Leib of Sasov loved his fellow Jews and would often say to his chasidim, "Would that you would love the righteous man, the *tzaddik*, as much as the Holy One loves the least of those in Israel."

Once, when he visited his master, *R' Elimelech of Lizensk*, his rebbe gave him the honor of speaking.

"The Torah tells us," he said, "that *Hashem* 'passed over the houses of the Children of Israel in Egypt.' Are we to take this in a literal sense? How can we? His glory fills the entire world. We must rather imagine that when *Hashem* came upon the home of an Israelite living in an Egyptian neighborhood, He would skip (פָּסַח) and dance, so to speak, and say with joy, 'A Jew lives here! A Jew lives here!' " (*Chidushei HaRamal*).

אֲשֶׁר פָּסַח / *Who passed over*

R' Baruch of Mezhibuz

The Holy One demands of man that he make the greatest of efforts possible before He extends His help. As *Chazal* put it:

When a man sanctifies himself slightly, Heaven makes him very holy; he sanctifies himself on earth and Heaven above sanctifies him (*Yoma* 39a).

The middle matzah is lifted and displayed while the following paragraph is recited.

מַצָּה זוּ שֶׁאָנוּ אוֹכְלִים, עַל שׁוּם מָה? עַל שׁוּם שֶׁלֹּא הִסְפִּיק בְּצֵקָם שֶׁל אֲבוֹתֵינוּ לְהַחֲמִיץ, עַד שֶׁנִּגְלָה עֲלֵיהֶם מֶלֶךְ מַלְכֵי הַמְּלָכִים הַקָּדוֹשׁ בָּרוּךְ הוּא וּגְאָלָם. שֶׁנֶּאֱמַר, וַיֹּאפוּ אֶת הַבָּצֵק אֲשֶׁר הוֹצִיאוּ מִמִּצְרַיִם עֻגֹת מַצּוֹת כִּי לֹא חָמֵץ, כִּי גֹרְשׁוּ מִמִּצְרַיִם, וְלֹא יָכְלוּ לְהִתְמַהְמֵהַּ, וְגַם צֵדָה לֹא עָשׂוּ לָהֶם.[1]

The maror is lifted and displayed while the following paragraph is recited.

מָרוֹר זֶה שֶׁאָנוּ אוֹכְלִים, עַל שׁוּם מָה? עַל שׁוּם שֶׁמֵּרְרוּ הַמִּצְרִים אֶת חַיֵּי אֲבוֹתֵינוּ בְּמִצְרַיִם. שֶׁנֶּאֱמַר, וַיְמָרְרוּ אֶת חַיֵּיהֶם, בַּעֲבֹדָה קָשָׁה, בְּחֹמֶר וּבִלְבֵנִים, וּבְכָל עֲבֹדָה בַּשָּׂדֶה, אֵת כָּל עֲבֹדָתָם אֲשֶׁר עָבְדוּ בָהֶם בְּפָרֶךְ.[2]

בְּכָל דּוֹר וָדוֹר חַיָּב אָדָם לִרְאוֹת אֶת עַצְמוֹ כְּאִלּוּ הוּא יָצָא מִמִּצְרָיִם. שֶׁנֶּאֱמַר, וְהִגַּדְתָּ לְבִנְךָ בַּיּוֹם הַהוּא לֵאמֹר, בַּעֲבוּר זֶה עָשָׂה

If one works at it and makes the tiring effort, help will come from Heaven. The Holy One says to Israel, "Make for me a single crack of an opening with *teshuvah*, just the width of the point of a needle, and I will make an opening for you through which carts and wagons may pass" (*Shir HaShirim Rabba* 5:2 para. 2).

But in Egypt Israel had sunken to the forty-ninth depth of impurity and were falling lower and lower. They were almost at the point of complete assimilation. Therefore, Hashem hastened their redemption. He did not wait until they gave Him a crack of an opening the width of a needle point, lest He be too late.

And thus the verse says: "and Hashem passed over the doorway" (*Shemos* 12:23) — He waived the opening of the "door" on our part. The Redemption came about completely through His initiative (*Butzina Dinehora* 1).

The middle matzah is lifted and displayed while the following paragraph is recited.

Matzah – Why do we eat this unleavened bread? – Because the dough of our fathers did not have time to become leavened before the King of kings, the Holy One, Blessed is He, revealed Himself to them and redeemed them, as it is written: They baked the dough which they had brought out of Egypt into unleavened bread, for it had not fermented, because they were driven out of Egypt and could not delay, nor had they prepared any provisions for the way.[1]

The maror is lifted and displayed while the following paragraph is recited.

Maror – Why do we eat this bitter herb? – Because the Egyptians embittered the lives of our fathers in Egypt, as it says: They embittered their lives with hard labor, with mortar and bricks, and with all manner of labor in the field: whatever service they made them perform was with hard labor.[2]

In every generation it is one's duty to regard himself as though he personally had gone out of Egypt, as it is written: You shall tell your son on that day: 'It was because of this that HASHEM did

1. *Shemos* 12:39. 2. 1:14.

וְגַם צֵדָה לֹא עָשׂוּ לָהֶם

Nor had they prepared any provisions for the way

R' Simchah Bunim of Pshischa

R' Simchah Bunim of Pshischa: The condition for the Redemption from Egypt was that Israel leave their homes, abandon all their possessions and make their way into the desert. Such is not the practice which is in fashion today. But man must realize that that is the way of redemption, that is the way which leads to the receiving of the Torah (*Siach Sarfei Kodesh* I 48).

יהוה לִי, בְּצֵאתִי מִמִּצְרָיִם.[1] לֹא אֶת אֲבוֹתֵינוּ בִּלְבָד גָּאַל הַקָּדוֹשׁ בָּרוּךְ הוּא, אֶלָּא אַף אוֹתָנוּ גָּאַל עִמָּהֶם. שֶׁנֶּאֱמַר, וְאוֹתָנוּ הוֹצִיא מִשָּׁם, לְמַעַן הָבִיא אֹתָנוּ לָתֶת לָנוּ אֶת הָאָרֶץ אֲשֶׁר נִשְׁבַּע לַאֲבוֹתֵינוּ.[2]

The matzos are covered and the cup is lifted and held until it is to be drunk. According to some customs, however, the cup is put down after the following paragraph, in which case the matzos should once more be uncovered.

לְפִיכָךְ אֲנַחְנוּ חַיָּבִים לְהוֹדוֹת, לְהַלֵּל, לְשַׁבֵּחַ, לְפָאֵר, לְרוֹמֵם, לְהַדֵּר, לְבָרֵךְ, לְעַלֵּה, וּלְקַלֵּס, לְמִי שֶׁעָשָׂה לַאֲבוֹתֵינוּ וְלָנוּ אֶת כָּל הַנִּסִּים הָאֵלּוּ, הוֹצִיאָנוּ מֵעַבְדוּת לְחֵרוּת, מִיָּגוֹן לְשִׂמְחָה, וּמֵאֵבֶל לְיוֹם טוֹב, וּמֵאֲפֵלָה לְאוֹר גָּדוֹל, וּמִשִּׁעְבּוּד לִגְאֻלָּה, וְנֹאמַר לְפָנָיו שִׁירָה חֲדָשָׁה, הַלְלוּיָהּ.

הַלְלוּיָהּ הַלְלוּ עַבְדֵי יהוה, הַלְלוּ אֶת שֵׁם יהוה. יְהִי שֵׁם יהוה מְבֹרָךְ, מֵעַתָּה וְעַד עוֹלָם. מִמִּזְרַח שֶׁמֶשׁ עַד מְבוֹאוֹ, מְהֻלָּל שֵׁם יהוה. רָם עַל כָּל גּוֹיִם יהוה, עַל הַשָּׁמַיִם כְּבוֹדוֹ. מִי

הַלְלוּ עַבְדֵי ה׳ / *Praise, you servants of Hashem*

Fiery Angel of Moglenitza

One day the *Fiery Angel of Moglenitza* entered the *beis midrash* and stopped to listen to his disciple *R' Yissachar Ber of Volbroz* learning aloud with burning enthusiasm. The others noticed the Rebbe and fell silent. When R' Yissachar Ber sensed the quiet, he lifted his eyes and saw his Rebbe standing over him. He immediately closed the *sefer* and rose in awe.

"Is it proper to give preference to a man of flesh and blood, and honor him over the Torah?" asked the Fiery Angel.

R' Yissachar Dov asked permission to speak and said, "We find one verse which places praise of Hashem prior to praise of Hashem's servants (הַלְלוּ אֶת שֵׁם ה׳, הַלְלוּ עַבְדֵי ה׳; *Tehillim* 135:1), whereas another verse has the reverse order (הַלְלוּ עַבְדֵי ה׳, הַלְלוּ אֶת שֵׁם ה׳; *Tehillim* 113:1). This teaches us that the

for "me" when I went out of Egypt.'[1] It was not only our fathers whom the Holy One redeemed from slavery; we, too, were redeemed with them, as it is written: He brought "us" out from there so that He might take us to the land which He had promised to our fathers.[2]

The matzos are covered and the cup is lifted and held until it is to be drunk. According to some customs, however, the cup is put down after the following paragraph, in which case the matzos should once more be uncovered.

Therefore it is our duty to thank, praise, pay tribute, glorify, exalt, honor, bless, extol, and acclaim Him Who performed all these miracles for our fathers and for us. He brought us forth from slavery to freedom, from grief to joy, from mourning to festivity, from darkness to great light, and from servitude to redemption. Let us, therefore, recite a new song before Him! Halleluyah!

Halleluyah! Praise, you servants of HASHEM, praise the Name of HASHEM. Blessed be the Name of HASHEM from now and forever. From the rising of the sun to its setting, HASHEM's Name is praised. High above all nations is HASHEM, above the heavens is His

1. *Shemos* 13:8. 2. *Devarim* 6:23.

---

honor due to *tzaddikim*, Hashem's servants, is equal to the honor due Hashem" (*Ohel Yissachar* 23).

[This is an imaginative interpretation (דְּרָשָׁה) of the verses. Each verse is a *single*, and similar, command to the servants of Hashem to praise Hashem. The verb of command (הַלְלוּ) is merely repeated. For each הַלְלוּ in the verse the object is אֶת שֵׁם ה׳. R' Yissachar Ber — and he was not alone — treats the עַבְדֵי ה׳ as an object of הַלְלוּ and those addressed are the public in general. In this fashion, each verse consists of *two* commands: Praise Hashem, praise the servants of Hashem (*Tehillim* 113:1); Praise the servants of Hashem, praise Hashem (*Tehillim* 135:1). Although this interpretation of *Tehillim* is original, equating the honoring of one's teacher with honoring Hashem exists in *Chazal* and has halachic bearing; see *Rambam, Hilchos Talmud Torah*, 5:1.]

רָם עַל כָּל גּוֹיִם יהוה, עַל הַשָּׁמַיִם כְּבוֹדוֹ. מִי כַּיהוה אֱלֹהֵינוּ, הַמַּגְבִּיהִי לָשָׁבֶת. הַמַּשְׁפִּילִי לִרְאוֹת, בַּשָּׁמַיִם וּבָאָרֶץ. מְקִימִי מֵעָפָר דָּל, מֵאַשְׁפֹּת יָרִים אֶבְיוֹן. לְהוֹשִׁיבִי עִם נְדִיבִים, עִם נְדִיבֵי עַמּוֹ. מוֹשִׁיבִי עֲקֶרֶת הַבַּיִת, אֵם הַבָּנִים שְׂמֵחָה, הַלְלוּיָהּ.[1]

בְּצֵאת יִשְׂרָאֵל מִמִּצְרָיִם, בֵּית יַעֲקֹב מֵעַם לֹעֵז. הָיְתָה יְהוּדָה לְקָדְשׁוֹ, יִשְׂרָאֵל מַמְשְׁלוֹתָיו. הַיָּם רָאָה וַיָּנֹס, הַיַּרְדֵּן יִסֹּב לְאָחוֹר. הֶהָרִים רָקְדוּ כְאֵילִים, גְּבָעוֹת כִּבְנֵי צֹאן. מַה לְּךָ הַיָּם כִּי תָנוּס, הַיַּרְדֵּן תִּסֹּב לְאָחוֹר. הֶהָרִים תִּרְקְדוּ כְאֵילִים, גְּבָעוֹת כִּבְנֵי צֹאן. מִלִּפְנֵי אָדוֹן חוּלִי אָרֶץ, מִלִּפְנֵי אֱלוֹהַּ יַעֲקֹב. הַהֹפְכִי הַצּוּר אֲגַם מָיִם, חַלָּמִישׁ לְמַעְיְנוֹ מָיִם.[2]

According to all customs the cup is lifted and the matzos covered during the recitation of this blessing.

בָּרוּךְ אַתָּה יהוה אֱלֹהֵינוּ מֶלֶךְ הָעוֹלָם, אֲשֶׁר גְּאָלָנוּ וְגָאַל אֶת אֲבוֹתֵינוּ מִמִּצְרַיִם, וְהִגִּיעָנוּ הַלַּיְלָה הַזֶּה לֶאֱכָל בּוֹ מַצָּה וּמָרוֹר. כֵּן יהוה אֱלֹהֵינוּ וֵאלֹהֵי אֲבוֹתֵינוּ, יַגִּיעֵנוּ לְמוֹעֲדִים וְלִרְגָלִים אֲחֵרִים הַבָּאִים לִקְרָאתֵנוּ לְשָׁלוֹם, שְׂמֵחִים

הַמַּשְׁפִּילִי לִרְאוֹת / *Yet deigns to look*

R' Levi Yitzchak of Berdichev

When *R' Levi Yitzchak of Berdichev* was once on a trip, the wagon driver noticed a bale of fodder lying by the wayside. No one was in sight. He halted and jumped down, intending to take the bale, when he heard the Rebbe suddenly shout, "They're watching! They're watching!"

above all nations is HASHEM, above the heavens is His glory. Who is like HASHEM, our God, Who is enthroned on high, yet deigns to look, upon the heaven and earth? He raises the destitute from the dust, from the trash heaps He lifts the needy — to seat them with nobles, with nobles of His people. He transforms the barren wife into a glad mother of children. Halleluyah![1]

When Israel went forth from Egypt, Yaakov's household from a people of alien tongue, Yehudah became His sanctuary, Israel His dominion. The Sea saw and fled; the Jordan turned backward. The mountains skipped like rams, and the hills like young lambs. What ails you, O Sea, that you flee? O Jordan, that you turn backward? O mountains, that you skip like rams? O hills, like young lambs? Before HASHEM'S presence — tremble, O earth, before the presence of the God of Yaakov, Who turns the rock into a pond of water, the flint into a flowing fountain.[2]

According to all customs the cup is lifted and the matzos covered during the recitation of this blessing.

Blessed are You, HASHEM, our God, King of the universe, Who redeemed our ancestors from Egypt and enabled us to reach this night that we may eat matzah and maror. So, HASHEM, our God and God of our fathers, bring us also to future Festivals and holidays in peace, gladdened in the

1. *Tehillim* 113. 2. 114.

The driver dropped the fodder in fright, climbed onto the wagon and whipped up the horses. A long moment later, he peered about and saw no one. "Who was looking?" he asked in wonder.

"The Holy One, Blessed is He!" said the Rebbe (*Chasidim Mesaprim* III 814).

(On *Motzaei Shabbos* the phrase in parentheses substitutes for the preceding phrase.)

בְּבִנְיַן עִירֶךָ וְשָׂשִׂים בַּעֲבוֹדָתֶךָ, וְנֹאכַל שָׁם מִן הַזְּבָחִים וּמִן הַפְּסָחִים [מִן הַפְּסָחִים וּמִן הַזְּבָחִים] אֲשֶׁר יַגִּיעַ דָּמָם עַל קִיר מִזְבַּחֲךָ לְרָצוֹן. וְנוֹדֶה לְךָ שִׁיר חָדָשׁ עַל גְּאֻלָּתֵנוּ וְעַל פְּדוּת נַפְשֵׁנוּ. בָּרוּךְ אַתָּה יהוה, גָּאַל יִשְׂרָאֵל.

הֲרֵינִי מוּכָן וּמְזוּמָן לְקַיֵּם מִצְוַת כּוֹס שֵׁנִי מֵאַרְבַּע כּוֹסוֹת. לְשֵׁם יִחוּד קֻדְשָׁא בְּרִיךְ הוּא וּשְׁכִינְתֵּיהּ, עַל יְדֵי הַהוּא טָמִיר וְנֶעְלָם, בְּשֵׁם כָּל יִשְׂרָאֵל. וִיהִי נֹעַם אֲדֹנָי אֱלֹהֵינוּ עָלֵינוּ, וּמַעֲשֵׂה יָדֵינוּ כּוֹנְנָה עָלֵינוּ, וּמַעֲשֵׂה יָדֵינוּ כּוֹנְנֵהוּ:

בָּרוּךְ אַתָּה יהוה אֱלֹהֵינוּ מֶלֶךְ הָעוֹלָם, בּוֹרֵא פְּרִי הַגָּפֶן.

The second cup is drunk while leaning on the left side — preferably the entire cup, but at least most of it.

גָּאַל יִשְׂרָאֵל / *Who has redeemed Israel*

R' Avraham of Sadigura

Each year on the evening when the Search for Leaven (בְּדִיקַת חָמֵץ) is made, on the night before *Pesach, R' Avraham of Sadigura* told the following story:

In a village, not far from the city of Kolbasov, lived a Jew who rented the tavern from the local lord in whose estate the village lay. His affairs did not prosper and he was unable to pay the rent. The landlord warned him once, then again. And on the morning of the *Shabbos* before *Pesach* (*Shabbos HaGadol*), he sent his servants to vandalize the tavern keeper's home, as a warning. They spilled the pail of slops on the ground, overturned the pot of *cholent*, broke the table and smashed the dishes. They left confusion and destruction behind them, and a family shocked and weeping.

The taverner thought to soften his suffering and went to the city to listen to the sermon of the *Ohev Yisrael of Apta*, who served, at the time, as the *rav* of Kolbasov. When he came to the *beis knesses*, the *rav* was in the midst of his talk and he heard him say, "There are two blessings: one with a concluding phrase in the past tense — 'He Who *redeemed* Israel' (גָּאַל יִשְׂרָאֵל), which we say on the evening of the Seder, when we recite the *Haggadah*, and also just prior to the *Shemoneh Esrei* in every prayer-service; the other, which ends in the present tense — 'He Who *redeems* Israel' (גּוֹאֵל יִשְׂרָאֵל), is the seventh blessing of the *Shemoneh Esrei*, the blessing which begins 'Look upon our afflictions' (רְאֵה נָא בְעָנְיֵנוּ).

(On *Motzaei Shabbos* the phrase in parentheses substitutes for the preceding phrase.)

rebuilding of Your city, and joyful at Your service. There we shall eat of the offerings and Pesach sacrifices (of the Pesach sacrifices and offerings) whose blood will gain the sides of Your altar for gracious acceptance. We shall then sing a new song of praise to You for our redemption and for the liberation of our souls. Blessed are You, HASHEM, Who has redeemed Israel.

Behold, I am prepared and ready to fulfill the mitzvah of the second of the Four Cups. For the sake of the unification of the Holy One, Blessed is He, and His Presence, through Him Who is hidden and inscrutable – [I pray] in the name of all Israel. May the pleasantness of my Lord, our God, be upon us – may He establish our handiwork for us; our handiwork may He establish.

Blessed are You, HASHEM, our God, King of the universe, Who creates the fruit of the vine.

The second cup is drunk while leaning on the left side – preferably the entire cup, but at least most of it.

"The first speaks of the redemption that was, the deliverance from the exile of Egypt and the receiving of the Torah at Sinai. The second refers to the redemption which occurs at all times, so that, even if there is a Jew in some village who cannot manage to pay the rent on time and the landlord sends his Cossacks to overturn his house, even for such a Jew, the Holy One brings forth redemption and rescues him from his suffering."

The taverner heard this and was filled with joy. He returned home happily and sang, "The Rebbe said, 'He Who redeems Israel!' The Rebbe said, 'He Who redeems Israel!' " While he was in this mood, the landlord's servants arrived. Their master wished to see if the Jew had learned his lesson. The servants came back with an odd tale. The Jew was singing and dancing.

The landlord summoned the taverner and the Jew appeared before him with a shining countenance, certain that the words of the Rebbe would be made manifest. The landlord was convinced that the Jew had become mad from his sufferings. He felt compassion and said, "Moshke, why are you such an unfortunate? You are a pauper. You can't pay your debt and you don't even have money to buy spirits on which you might make a profit."

"What shall I do, then?" said the taverner.

"I'll tell you what to do. I'll give you a letter for the distillery, telling them to sell you spirits on credit. You'll sell at a profit, save a bit and pay your debt."

רחצה

The hands are washed for matzah and the following blessing is recited. It is preferable to bring water and a basin to the head of the household at the Seder table.

בָּרוּךְ אַתָּה יהוה אֱלֹהֵינוּ מֶלֶךְ הָעוֹלָם, אֲשֶׁר קִדְּשָׁנוּ בְּמִצְוֹתָיו, וְצִוָּנוּ עַל נְטִילַת יָדָיִם.

The taverner followed his suggestion and, in the short span of the few days between *Shabbos HaGadol* and the day before *Pesach*, he sold a huge amount of whiskey which netted a profit large enough to both pay the landlord and buy all his needs for the festival, with a liberal hand.

On the day before *Pesach* he tied money into a kerchief, came to the Rebbe and said, "Rebbe, I have brought the money of 'He Who *redeems* Israel' " (*Sipurei Chasidim, Moadim*, p. 267).

R' Yissachar Dov of Belz

R' Yissachar Dov of Belz would go out into the streets of town after completing his own Seder, to see how the common folk conducted theirs.

Once, he heard a simple Jew ending the blessing 'He Who redeemed Israel' (גָּאַל יִשְׂרָאֵל) with great fervor and immediately launching into *Shemoneh Esrei*.

The Rebbe's attendant burst out laughing, but the Rebbe said with great feeling, "He joined the blessing of redemption (גְאוּלָּה) to the *Shemoneh Esrei* prayer (תְּפִילָּה) with purposeful intention (כַּוָּנַת הַלֵּב) and his prayer will be received in Heaven! He is childless and now he will have children!" (*Admorei Belz* III 207).

[The last of the blessings of the *Shema*, immediately prior to the *Shemoneh Esrei* of the morning prayers, ends with גָּאַל יִשְׂרָאֵל. The *halachah* requires that *Shemoneh Esrei* follow it without interruption — not even a pause (*Shulchan Aruch, Orach Chaim* 111). The Rebbe saw a good omen in the man's mistake.]

רָחְצָה / *Rachtzah*

R' Chanoch Henoch of Alexander

R' Chanoch Henoch of Alexander:

When I first came to my master, *R' Menachem Mendel of Kotzk*, he said, "Come and I will teach you the meaning of *chasid*. The chasid constantly asks himself, 'Why?' just as the *gemara* often asks, 'What is the reason (מַאי טַעְמָא)?' "

I did not understand what the Rebbe wanted to say.

Some days later, I was about to wash my hands, in order to eat and, suddenly, I remembered the Rebbe's remarks. I began to think about the

RACHTZAH

The hands are washed for matzah and the following blessing is recited. It is preferable to bring water and a basin to the head of the household at the Seder table.

Blessed are You, HASHEM, our God, King of the universe, Who has sanctified us with His commandments, and has commanded us concerning the washing of the hands.

---

nature of the *mitzvah* which I was about to perform; about its purpose. I contemplated the thought that I was about to fulfill the *mitzvah* in the presence of the Divine. I stood, thus, for some two hours, washing-cup in hand, gripped by my thoughts. After I fully realized the great favor the Holy One had shown us when He sanctified us through His *mitzvos* and when He commanded us to wash hands, I made the blessing.

Would that I might have the fortune to make the blessing thus, today! (*Siach Sarfei Kodesh* I 556).

[*When he sanctified . . . to wash hands*. This is in effect the formula of the blessing itself: אֲשֶׁר קִדְּשָׁנוּ בְּמִצוֹתָיו וְצִוָּנוּ עַל נְטִילַת יָדָיִם. R' Chanoch Henoch felt the full import of the blessing that day. It transcended its formulaic bounds for him.]

נְטִילַת יָדָיִם / *The washing of hands*

R' Sar Shalom of Belz

R' Sar Shalom of Belz told the following story:

Not long ago, an evil man, a totally corrupt man, lived not far from our city. He was truly wicked and there was not a single sin which he had not committed, all with an air of defiance (לְהַכְעִיס). There was a lone *mitzvah*, a rabbinic *mitzvah* which he observed strictly, throughout his life; he would always wash his hands before meals.

Once, in the Intermediate Days (חוֹל הַמּוֹעֵד) of *Pesach*, he had to take a trip to a town some twenty miles distant. He saddled his horse and took several matzos with him. Whether he did so because he did not wish to eat *chametz*, I do not know. But he did take matzos for fare on the road. After having ridden several miles, he felt hungry, but did not wish to eat without first washing his hands. For he said, "I have committed all the sins in the world and not fulfilled *mitzvos*. But, since I have kept this single *mitzvah*, throughout my days, why should I give it up now?"

He rode on for some four miles and found that he no longer had any strength, due to his fasting. He sought here and there, but found no source of water. Then, he remembered that a path led off the road to a well. The well, however, was frequented by fierce bandits. He said to himself, "If I stay here, I will die a drawn-out, agonizing death from hunger. If I get there, the bandits will slay me. It's all one and the same. I prefer to die by their hands on a full stomach. But I will not eat without first washing my hands."

He rode to the well. Whether he said the blessing over the matzos

מוציא

The following two blessings are recited over matzah; the first is recited over matzah as food, and the second for the special *mitzvah* of eating matzah on the night of Pesach. [The latter blessing is to be made with the intention that it also apply to the 'sandwich' and the afikoman.]

הִנְנִי מוּכָן וּמְזוּמָן לְקַיֵּם מִצְוַת אֲכִילַת מַצָּה. לְשֵׁם יִחוּד קֻדְשָׁא בְּרִיךְ הוּא וּשְׁכִינְתֵּיהּ, עַל יְדֵי הַהוּא טָמִיר וְנֶעְלָם, בְּשֵׁם כָּל יִשְׂרָאֵל. וִיהִי נֹעַם אֲדֹנָי אֱלֹהֵינוּ עָלֵינוּ, וּמַעֲשֵׂה יָדֵינוּ כּוֹנְנָה עָלֵינוּ, וּמַעֲשֵׂה יָדֵינוּ כּוֹנְנֵהוּ:

The head of the household raises all the matzos on the Seder plate and recites the following blessing:

בָּרוּךְ אַתָּה יהוה אֱלֹהֵינוּ מֶלֶךְ הָעוֹלָם, הַמּוֹצִיא לֶחֶם מִן הָאָרֶץ.

The bottom matzah is put down and the following blessing is recited while the top (whole) matzah and the middle (broken) piece are still raised.

מצה

בָּרוּךְ אַתָּה יהוה אֱלֹהֵינוּ מֶלֶךְ הָעוֹלָם, אֲשֶׁר קִדְּשָׁנוּ בְּמִצְוֹתָיו, וְצִוָּנוּ עַל אֲכִילַת מַצָּה.

(הַמּוֹצִיא), I do not know. But I do know that he did not eat without washing. The bandits soon arrived, robbed him of his money and killed him.

In the heavens above, there was a great stir and commotion. A man had risked his life and knowingly put himself into mortal danger for the sake of a *mitzvah* of rabbinic force. This *mitzvah* had been so dear in his eyes, even though he had high-handedly transgressed and committed all possible sins.

Judgment was passed in his favor and he was granted a place in the light of life in Gan Eden.

Think and give your hearts over to imagine what will be the judgment of the man who observes the entire Torah — in all its principles and particulars (*Dover Shalom* 48).

Ba'al Shem Tov

Before he was revealed to the world at large, the *Ba'al Shem* would wander in solitude in the mountains about Okop. Once, robbers who were active in the area saw him approach a deep ravine. He was sunken in thought and unaware of the danger. They were certain that he would plunge into the abyss. But, to their amazement, the hill opposite moved and joined the hill on which the Ba'al Shem was walking; the canyon disappeared. The robbers realized that they were in the presence of a holy man. They approached and said, "Master, we know of a short route to *Eretz Yisrael*, through caves. If you so wish, come with us and we will show you the way."

MOTZI

The following two blessings are recited over matzah; the first is recited over matzah as food, and the second for the special *mitzvah* of eating matzah on the night of Pesach. [The latter blessing is to be made with the intention that it also apply to the 'sandwich' and the afikoman.]

The head of the household raises all the matzos on the Seder plate and recites the following blessing:

Behold, I am prepared and ready to fulfill the mitzvah of eating matzah. For the sake of the unification of the Holy One, Blessed is He, and His Presence, through Him Who is hidden and inscrutable – [I pray] in the name of all Israel. May the pleasantness of my Lord, our God, be upon us – may He establish our handiwork for us; our handiwork may He establish.

Blessed are You, HASHEM, our God, King of the universe, Who brings forth bread from the earth.

The bottom matzah is put down and the following blessing is recited while the top (whole) matzah and the middle (broken) piece are still raised.

MATZAH

Blessed are You, HASHEM, our God, King of the universe, Who has sanctified us with His commandments, and has commanded us concerning the eating of matzah.

They came to a deep, muddy marsh. A narrow plank was laid across it. The robbers passed over it. Yet, when the Ba'al Shem wished to cross, he sensed that he would be in terrible danger. He turned about to retrace his steps, but thought to himself, "I have certainly not come to this spot in vain!" And, lo and behold, there on the edge of the marsh sat a huge frog. He asked the frog, "Who are you?"

The frog told him that for the past five hundred years the soul of a wise man, a *talmid chacham*, had been interred within him. Even the sainted *Ari* who had made whole all the damaged souls had not been able to find the means to redeem this one and had put him far away in a place unfrequented by men, so that none should redeem him.

The Ba'al Shem asked what his sin had been. He answered that he had, one single time, treated the washing of hands before meals disparagingly and not washed properly. Satan had pointed an accusing finger, but had been told that a man cannot be indicted for a single transgression. However, since a sin tends to drag a further sin along in its wake, if he could cause the man to fall into an additional sin, he would be punished for this one, too. If the man would remember Hashem and sin no more, he would be cleansed of this sin, also. Satan tried him with another temptation and he did not resist. One sin brought on another and he violated almost the entire Torah. Because the first cause of all the sins was that of treating the washing of

Each participant is required to eat an amount of matzah equal in volume to an egg. Since it is usually impossible to provide a sufficient amount of matzah from the two matzos for all members of the household, the other matzos should be available at the head of the table from which to complete the required amounts. However, each participant should receive a piece from each of the top two matzos. The matzos are to be eaten while reclining on the left side and without delay; they need not be dipped in salt.

מרור

The head of the household takes a half-egg volume of maror, dips it into charoses, and gives each participant a like amount. The following blessing is recited with the intention that it also apply to the maror of the 'sandwich'. The maror is eaten without reclining, and without delay.

הִנְנִי מוּכָן וּמְזוּמָן לְקַיֵּם מִצְוַת אֲכִילַת מָרוֹר. לְשֵׁם יִחוּד קֻדְשָׁא בְּרִיךְ הוּא וּשְׁכִינְתֵּיהּ, עַל יְדֵי הַהוּא טָמִיר וְנֶעְלָם, בְּשֵׁם כָּל יִשְׂרָאֵל. וִיהִי נֹעַם אֲדֹנָי אֱלֹהֵינוּ עָלֵינוּ, וּמַעֲשֵׂה יָדֵינוּ כּוֹנְנָה עָלֵינוּ, וּמַעֲשֵׂה יָדֵינוּ כּוֹנְנֵהוּ:

בָּרוּךְ אַתָּה יהוה אֱלֹהֵינוּ מֶלֶךְ הָעוֹלָם, אֲשֶׁר קִדְּשָׁנוּ בְּמִצְוֹתָיו, וְצִוָּנוּ עַל אֲכִילַת מָרוֹר.

---

hands lightly, upon his death his soul had found its way into a frog which is constantly in water. He had been placed in an out-of-the-way spot, lest a Jew pass by and pronounce a blessing, or have a good thought, as this would redeem the souls which had been removed to that place.

The Ba'al Shem repaired the damage to the soul and raised it up; the frog fell dead (*Shivchei HaBesht* 49).

עַל אֲכִילַת מַצָּה /

Concerning the eating of matzah

Sainted Yehudi of Pshischa

The Sainted Yehudi (Jew) of Pshischa was powerful by nature. Once, on a visit to his master, the *Chozeh* of *Lublin*, there were those who wished to see how strong he really was. Many of the chasidim sat on one end of a table ten cubits long and a hands-width thick. The Yehudi leaned his weight on the other end and lifted them all up in the air. When his pipe was once clogged he blew through it to clean it, and the pipe shattered.

Yet, despite his bodily strength, and though he did not suffer from ill health, his teeth fell out in his youth. This was because of the fear of God which shook him when he said the *Shema*. One lone tooth remained and he called it 'the wicked one,' since it had not been stirred to fall out in fear of its Creator. He could not forgive that solitary tooth, until he remembered that it would help him in eating the matzah. That thought made him relent (*Niflaos HaYehudi* 5:8).

Each participant is required to eat an amount of matzah equal in volume to an egg. Since it is usually impossible to provide a sufficient amount of matzah from the twomatzos for all members of the household, the other matzos should be available at the head of the table from which to complete the required amounts. However, each participant should receive a piece from each of the top two matzos. The matzos are to be eaten while reclining on the left side and without delay; they need not be dipped in salt.

MAROR

The head of the household takes a half-egg volume of maror, dips it into charoses, and gives each participant a like amount. The following blessing is recited with the intention that it also apply to the maror of the 'sandwich'. The maror is eaten without reclining, and without delay.

Behold, I am prepared and ready to fulfill the mitzvah of eating maror. For the sake of the unification of the Holy One, Blessed is He, and His Presence, through Him Who is hidden and inscrutable — [I pray] in the name of all Israel. May the pleasantness of my Lord, our God, be upon us — may He establish our handiwork for us; our handiwork may He establish.

Blessed are You, HASHEM, our God, King of the universe, Who has sanctified us with His commandments, and has commanded us concerning the eating of maror.

מָרוֹר / *Maror*

R' Nachman of Breslav

R' Nachman of Breslav told the following story: A Jew and a German set out on a tour. Their money ran out while they were on the road and they no longer had provisions. This happened just on the eve of *Pesach* and the Jew said to the German, "I'll teach you some of the Jewish customs of *Pesach*. In the evening we'll go to a synagogue. Jews are a compassionate people. They will take pity on us and invite us to be guests at their *Seder*." He taught him about *kiddush*, about washing hands before the meal and other matters. But he forgot to tell him that *maror* is eaten before the meal.

In the evening they went to a synagogue and one householder invited the Jew and, another, assuming that his friend, too, was a Jew, invited the German.

The German came to the *Seder* after not having eaten the entire day. In the beginning of the evening they gave him a small portion of *karpas* dipped in salt water — hardly a satisfying morsel. And then they began reciting and reciting. He waited impatiently for them to end the recitation of the *Haggadah* and begin the meal. Finally, they washed hands and gave him a piece of matzah and he was happy. His friend, the Jew, had told him that this signaled the beginning of the meal. Now, they would serve fish and meat and other good things. And then, they passed him a portion of a vegetable. He bit into it. His mouth was filled with a bitter taste; his eyes watered. Certain that this

כורך

The bottom (thus far unbroken) matzah is now taken. From it, with the addition of other matzos, each participant receives a half-egg volume of matzah with an equal-volume portion of maror (dipped into charoses which is shaken off). The following paragraph is recited and the 'sandwich' is eaten while reclining.

זֵכֶר לְמִקְדָּשׁ כְּהִלֵּל. כֵּן עָשָׂה הִלֵּל בִּזְמַן שֶׁבֵּית הַמִּקְדָּשׁ הָיָה קַיָּם. הָיָה כּוֹרֵךְ (פֶּסַח) מַצָּה וּמָרוֹר וְאוֹכֵל בְּיַחַד. לְקַיֵּם מַה שֶּׁנֶּאֱמַר, עַל מַצּוֹת וּמְרֹרִים יֹאכְלֻהוּ.[1]

---

was the promised, looked-for meal, and that this was all that would be offered, he picked himself up and ran in anger from the table shouting, "Cursed Jews, after all the long Seder, you give such bitter food." He took himself to the synagogue to await his friend and reproach him for his "good advice."

Some time later his friend approached, happy and sated with food and drink. He asked the German how it had gone and the German gave vent to bitter disappointment. "Silly fool!" said the Jew. "What a pity! Had you waited but a bit longer, you would have enjoyed all the good things, just as I did."

The path of devotion to Hashem and drawing close to the true *tzaddik* is of a similar nature. After all the toil, when one is close to the goal, some bitterness enters the picture, to purify the body. Whoever bears it patiently and waits yet a bit, experiences all sorts of pleasures and feels a sense of vitality (*Avaneha Barzel*).

Yismach Yisrael of Alexander

It is important to accept suffering with love for Hashem (יִסּוּרִים שֶׁל אַהֲבָה). *Chazal* have alluded to this in saying: "If one swallows matzah (without first chewing and tasting it), he has fulfilled the *mitzvah*; if he swallows *maror*, he has not" (*Pesachim* 115b).

Maror was meant to be chewed well (*Chasidim Mesaprim* I 520).

מוֹצִיא, מַצָּה, מָרוֹר, כּוֹרֵךְ

Motzi, Matzah, Maror, Korech

Divrei Chaim of Sanz

The Divrei Chaim of Sanz was weak and sickly during the last year of his life and it was with exceptional sacrifice of self that he fulfilled the *mitzvos* of the Seder.

When he ate the matzah he said, "I wish to show and teach my children how one must really make a physical sacrifice for each and every *mitzvah*." Then, he took the *maror* and said, "I wish to show and teach my children that they are obliged to sacrifice themselves even for a *mitzvah* ordained by *Chazal* and not only those which appear in the Torah." Finally, he took up the *korech*

KORECH

The bottom (thus far unbroken) matzah is now taken. From it, with the addition of other matzos, each participant receives a half-egg volume of matzah with an equal-volume portion of maror (dipped into charoses which is shaken off). The following paragraph is recited and the 'sandwich' is eaten while reclining.

In remembrance of the Temple we do as Hillel did in Temple times: he would combine (the Pesach offering,) matzah and maror in a sandwich and eat them together, to fulfill what is written in the Torah: They shall eat it with matzos and bitter herbs.[1]

1. *Bamidbar* 9:11.

---

and ate it with the last of his strength, saying, "I wish to teach my children that one must make a sacrifice [not only for a *mitzvah*], but even for a custom (מִנְהָג)" (*Yisrael Saba*).

כְּזַיִת מִן הַמָּרוֹר / *An olive's volume of maror*

Divrei Chaim of Sanz

A chasid of Dinov suffered from mortal lung disease and traveled to the capital city of Vienna for medical advice. The doctors told him that his disease could not be cured, because the lung was not in its normal position. It was pushed to the side and was filled with phlegm which could not be drained and would cause decay. They suggested that he hurry home, lest he die among strangers.

The man started on his journey homeward with a broken heart. His way passed through Sanz and he thought to himself. "Since the *Divrei Chaim* [R' Chaim of Sanz] is famous as a great scholar and *halachic* authority, I will ask him what I should do about the eating of *maror* in the forthcoming Seder. I am unable to eat the required amount of *maror* , a *kezais* (כְּזַיִת). Am I however required to eat a lesser portion and should I pronounce a blessing over it?"

The Rebbe listened to his question. "It is said," he replied, "that *maror* is a 'healing food.' You should be able to eat the full prescribed amount and be healed."

After the man left the Rebbe's presence he remembered that the *Zohar* does not say that *maror* is a healing food, but rather, matzah. The *Divrei Chaim* had obviously made an error. And, with that thought, he pushed the incident out of his mind.

On the night of the Seder when the moment for eating *maror* arrived, the sick man took the tiniest portion of bitter herbs. He immediately began to cough strenuously, weakening himself greatly. "If my end is come," he cried out, "let me at least fulfill the *mitzvah* properly!" He took the full portion of *maror* and ate it. As soon as he swallowed the *kezais* (כְּזַיִת), the cough grew worse and his whole body shook dreadfully. His family became frightened and ran to fetch the doctor. But the doctor was himself conducting a Seder and did not come running. When he did arrive, he found the patient asleep.

שולחן עורך

The meal should be eaten in a combination of joy and solemnity, for the meal, too, is a part of the Seder service. While it is desirable that *zemiros* and discussion of the laws and events of Pesach be part of the meal, extraneous conversation should be avoided. It should be remembered that the *afikoman* must be eaten while there is still some appetite for it. In fact, if one is so sated that he must literally force himself to eat it, he is not credited with the performance of the *mitzvah* of *afikoman*. Therefore, it is unwise to eat more than a moderate amount during the meal.

צפון

From the *afikoman* matzah (and from additional matzos to make up the required amount), a half-egg-volume portion — according to some, a full egg's volume portion — is given to each participant. It should be eaten before midnight, while reclining, without delay, and uninterruptedly. Nothing may be eaten or drunk after the *afikoman* (with the exception of water and the like) except for the last two Seder cups of wine.

הִנְנִי מוּכָן וּמְזוּמָן לְקַיֵּם מִצְוַת אֲכִילַת אֲפִיקוֹמָן. לְשֵׁם יִחוּד קוּדְשָׁא בְּרִיךְ הוּא וּשְׁכִינְתֵּיהּ, עַל יְדֵי הַהוּא טָמִיר וְנֶעְלָם, בְּשֵׁם כָּל יִשְׂרָאֵל. וִיהִי נֹעַם אֲדֹנָי אֱלֹהֵינוּ עָלֵינוּ, וּמַעֲשֵׂה יָדֵינוּ כּוֹנְנָה עָלֵינוּ, וּמַעֲשֵׂה יָדֵינוּ כּוֹנְנֵהוּ:

He was told that the man had become exhausted from coughing, had fallen onto the bed and dropped off into slumber. The doctor said that rest was good for him and that he should not be awakened.

He slept until a late hour the following day and when the doctor came to examine him, he was amazed. The patient was completely cured. The force of the cough and the shuddering of his body had jarred the lung and it had returned to its normal position. The phlegm had been able to drain out.

The *maror* had indeed been, as the Rebbe of Sanz had said, a "healing food" (*Divrei Yechezkel Shraga* 143).

שֻׁלְחָן עוֹרֵךְ / *Shulchan Aruch, Set the Table*

Divrei Chaim of Sanz

The *Gaon of Rava,* author of *Derech HaMelech*, a commentary on the *Rambam,* decided to visit the *Divrei Chaim of Sanz*. When he arrived he found the Rebbe at a meal with his chasidim. It was the Rebbe's practice to conduct a formal public meal (*tish*) daily.

When the Rebbe saw him he said, "R' Berish'l of Lublin (for thus the *Gaon* was called in his youth) probably imagined that in Sanz he will find us attempting to understand a difficult passage in the *Mishneh LaMelech* (a work on the Rambam). And here he comes upon us busied with roast meat and gravy."

The Gaon answered, without hesitation, "And what would I have found had I had the fortune to come upon the *Kohen HaGadol*, the High Priest in the *Beis HaMikdash*? Would I not have found him busy with roast meat and gravy?"

SHULCHAN ORECH

The meal should be eaten in a combination of joy and solemnity, for the meal, too, is a part of the Seder service. While it is desirable that *zemiros* and discussion of the laws and events of Pesach be part of the meal, extraneous conversation should be avoided. It should be remembered that the *afikoman* must be eaten while there is still some appetite for it. In fact, if one is so sated that he must literally force himself to eat it, he is not credited with the performance of the *mitzvah* of *afikoman*. Therefore, it is unwise to eat more than a moderate amount during the meal.

TZAFUN

From the *afikoman* matzah (and from additional matzos to make up the required amount), a half-egg-volume portion — according to some, a full egg's volume portion — is given to each participant. It should be eaten before midnight, while reclining, without delay, and uninterruptedly. Nothing may be eaten or drunk after the *afikoman* (with the exception of water and the like) except for the last two Seder cups of wine.

Behold, I am prepared and ready to fulfill the mitzvah of eating the afikoman. For the sake of the unification of the Holy One, Blessed is He, and His Presence, through Him Who is hidden and inscrutable — [I pray] in the name of all Israel. May the pleasantness of my Lord, our God, be upon us — may He establish our handiwork for us; our handiwork may He establish.

The answer pleased the Rebbe. (From the Letter of the *Rabad of Strasbourg*, opening lines of *Pitchah Zuta*.)

צָפוּן / *Tzafun, The Hidden — Eating the Afikoman*

Tiferes Shmuel of Alexander

My father once gave me the portion of *afikoman* and said, "*Tzafun* — Hide it!" Perhaps he was alluding to the verse: "I have hidden (צָפַנְתִּי) Your word in my heart, that I might not sin" (*Tehillim* 119:11). When a man conceals his achievements and does not bring them forth into the open, they become implanted in his heart.

The Tiferes Shmuel once commented on a *tzaddik* of his day who had strange patterns of behavior. "True," he said, "it is good and becoming that one should act modestly, hide his light and be unknown. But *Chazal* have said: 'One does not keep food warm (on *Shabbos*) by concealing it in manure — זֶבֶל' (*mishnah, Shabbos* 4:1) — a man should not conceal himself through strange and odd practices" (*Tiferes Yisrael* 364;374).

בָּרֵךְ / *Barech, Recite Bircas HaMazon, Grace After Meals*

Chidushei HaRim

The Chidushei HaRim of Gur once asked an aged chasid, R' Abish by name, "What did you hear from the lips of our master, *the Rebbe of Kotzk*?"

"I heard him say," said the chasid, "that he wondered why people did not become God fearing through their reciting of the after-the-meal blessings (בִּרְכַּת הַמָּזוֹן). For it was through a post-meal blessing that our forefather

ברך

The third cup is poured and Bircas HaMazon (Grace After Meals) is recited. According to some customs, the Cup of Eliahu is poured at this point.

שִׁיר הַמַּעֲלוֹת, בְּשׁוּב יהוה אֶת שִׁיבַת צִיּוֹן, הָיִינוּ כְּחֹלְמִים. אָז יִמָּלֵא שְׂחוֹק פִּינוּ וּלְשׁוֹנֵנוּ רִנָּה, אָז יֹאמְרוּ בַגּוֹיִם, הִגְדִּיל יהוה לַעֲשׂוֹת עִם אֵלֶּה. הִגְדִּיל יהוה לַעֲשׂוֹת עִמָּנוּ, הָיִינוּ שְׂמֵחִים. שׁוּבָה יהוה אֶת שְׁבִיתֵנוּ, כַּאֲפִיקִים בַּנֶּגֶב. הַזֹּרְעִים בְּדִמְעָה בְּרִנָּה יִקְצֹרוּ. הָלוֹךְ יֵלֵךְ וּבָכֹה נֹשֵׂא מֶשֶׁךְ הַזָּרַע, בֹּא יָבֹא בְרִנָּה, נֹשֵׂא אֲלֻמֹּתָיו.[1]

If three or more males, aged thirteen or older, participated in the meal, the leader is required to formally invite the others to join him in the recitation of Grace after Meals. Following is the 'Zimun,' or formal invitation.

הִנְנִי מוּכָן וּמְזוּמָן לְקַיֵּם מִצְוַת עֲשֵׂה שֶׁל בִּרְכַּת הַמָּזוֹן, כַּכָּתוּב, וְאָכַלְתָּ וְשָׂבָעְתָּ וּבֵרַכְתָּ אֶת יהוה אֱלֹהֶיךָ עַל הָאָרֶץ הַטֹּבָה אֲשֶׁר נָתַן לָךְ:

The leader begins:

רַבּוֹתַי מִיר וֶועלֶען בֶּענְטְשֶׁען. or רַבּוֹתַי נְבָרֵךְ.

The group responds:

יְהִי שֵׁם יהוה מְבֹרָךְ מֵעַתָּה וְעַד עוֹלָם.[2]

The leader continues:

יְהִי שֵׁם יהוה מְבֹרָךְ מֵעַתָּה וְעַד עוֹלָם.[2]

If ten men join in the Zimun, the words (in parentheses) are included.

בִּרְשׁוּת מָרָנָן וְרַבָּנָן וְרַבּוֹתַי, נְבָרֵךְ (אֱלֹהֵינוּ) שֶׁאָכַלְנוּ מִשֶּׁלוֹ.

The group responds:

בָּרוּךְ (אֱלֹהֵינוּ) שֶׁאָכַלְנוּ מִשֶּׁלוֹ וּבְטוּבוֹ חָיִינוּ.

The leader continues:

בָּרוּךְ (אֱלֹהֵינוּ) שֶׁאָכַלְנוּ מִשֶּׁלוֹ וּבְטוּבוֹ חָיִינוּ.

The following line is recited if ten men join in the Zimun.

בָּרוּךְ הוּא וּבָרוּךְ שְׁמוֹ.

Avraham would bring his guests to take shelter under the wings of the Divine Presence. After they had eaten and drunk he would say, 'Bless the

BARECH

The third cup is poured and Bircas HaMazon (Grace After Meals) is recited. According to some customs, the Cup of Eliahu is poured at this point.

A song of Ascents. When HASHEM brings back the exiles to Zion, we will have been like dreamers. Then our mouth will be filled with laughter, and our tongue with glad song. Then will it be said among the nations: HASHEM has done great things for us, and we rejoiced. Restore our captives, HASHEM, like streams in the dry land. Those who sow in tears shall reap in joy. Though the farmer bears the measure of seed to the field in tears, he shall come home with joy, bearing his sheaves.[1]

If three or more males, aged thirteen or older, participated in the meal, the leader is required to formally invite the others to join him in the recitation of Grace after Meals. Following is the 'Zimun,' or formal invitation.

Behold, I am prepared and ready to fulfill the mitzvah of Grace after Meals, as it is written: 'And you shall eat and you shall be satisfied and you shall bless HASHEM, Your God, for the good land which He gave you.'

The leader begins:

Gentlemen, let us bless.

The group responds:

Blessed is the Name of HASHEM from this moment and forever![2]

The leader continues:

Blessed is the Name of HASHEM from this moment and forever![2]

If ten men join in the Zimun, the words (in parentheses) are included.

With the permission of the distinguished people present, let us bless [our God] for we have eaten from what is His.

The group responds:

Blessed is [our God] He of Whose we have eaten and through Whose goodness we live.

The leader continues:

Blessed is [our God] He of Whose we have eaten and through Whose goodness we live.

The following line is recited if ten men join in the Zimun.

Blessed is He and Blessed is His Name.

1. *Tehillim* 126. 2. 113:2.

בָּרוּךְ אַתָּה יהוה אֱלֹהֵינוּ מֶלֶךְ הָעוֹלָם, הַזָּן אֶת הָעוֹלָם כֻּלּוֹ, בְּטוּבוֹ, בְּחֵן בְּחֶסֶד וּבְרַחֲמִים, הוּא נֹתֵן לֶחֶם לְכָל בָּשָׂר, כִּי לְעוֹלָם חַסְדּוֹ.[1] וּבְטוּבוֹ הַגָּדוֹל, תָּמִיד לֹא חָסַר לָנוּ, וְאַל יֶחְסַר לָנוּ מָזוֹן לְעוֹלָם וָעֶד. בַּעֲבוּר שְׁמוֹ הַגָּדוֹל, כִּי הוּא אֵל זָן וּמְפַרְנֵס לַכֹּל, וּמֵטִיב לַכֹּל, וּמֵכִין

One from Whose goods you have eaten!' "

"These are words of Torah fit for a rebbe," said the Chidushei HaRim. "But I wonder that men do not become God fearing from the very eating itself. For the verse bears witness: 'The ox knows its owner and the donkey the manger of its master' (*Yeshayahu* 1:3)" (*Siach Sarfei Kodesh* V 9).

הוּא נֹתֵן לֶחֶם / *He gives nourishment*

R' Mordechai of Neschiz

R' Mordechai of Neschiz once asked his chasid, R' Velvel, "Where do you take the bread from?"

"From the shelf upon which it lies," he said.

"And who puts it there?" asked the Rebbe.

"My wife, after she has baked it."

"You have answered foolishly," said the Rebbe. "For had you mentioned Him Who truly gives bread — nourishment, you would have been blessed with wealth and a liberal livelihood" *(Zikaron Tov*, Conclusion, no. 8).

R' Zusha of Hanipoli

Each morning, after prayers, *R' Zusha of Hanipoli* would say, "Master of the world, Zusha is very hungry and wishes to eat. Please furnish him with his food." When his *shammash* (attendant) would hear this, he would enter and serve him refreshments, a portion of cake and drink.

One day, the *shammash* thought to himself, "Why doesn't the Rebbe ask *me* to bring him his food? Why does he turn to the Holy One with his request?" He decided that he would not serve the Rebbe unless he was asked to do so directly.

That morning, R' Zusha immersed himself in the *mikveh* before prayers as was his custom. It was a rainy day and the roads of Hanipoli were muddy. A path of narrow planks had been placed from one end of the street to the other to allow passageway. R' Zusha was pacing along the planks on his way to the *beis knesses* when, there in front of him, he saw a stranger, a visitor in town, walking towards him. The stranger saw an elderly, slight Jew hurrying in his direction. The desire to play a prank seized him and he pushed R'

Blessed are You, HASHEM, our God, King of the universe, Who nourishes the entire world, in His goodness — with grace, with kindness, and with mercy. He gives nourishment to all flesh, for His kindness is eternal.[1] And through His great goodness, we have never lacked, and may we never lack, nourishment, for all eternity. For the sake of His Great Name, because He is God Who nourishes and sustains all, and benefits all, and He prepares

1. *Tehillim* 136:25.

Zusha off the plank and into the mud. R' Zusha fell, dirtying his clothes, picked himself up without a word, and continued on his way. The stranger laughed heartily at the comical sight and could not stop laughing all the way to his lodgings. There, he told the innkeeper of the prank he had played.

When, in answer to his host's question, he had described the man whom he had pushed off the plank, the innkeeper smote his hands and said, "Oh my! What have you done? You shoved the Rebbe, R' Zusha, into the mud." The visitor shook and trembled. R' Zusha was known as a holy man of God. "Woe is me!" he cried out in fear, "What shall I do?"

"Listen to me," said his host. "R' Zusha spends a long time at his prayers and afterwards takes refreshments. Take some good-tasting pastry and quality liquor. Bring them to him as a present and ask his pardon. I'm positive that, righteous and modest as he is, he will forgive you wholeheartedly."

R' Zusha finished his prayers, took off his *tefillin* and said, "Master of the world, Zusha is very hungry and wishes to eat. Please furnish him with his food."

The *shammash* heard him and didn't make a move. "If the Rebbe turns to Hashem, let Hashem bring him refreshments," he thought.

The door suddenly opened and in walked a stranger bearing a tray of pastry and liquor. He entered the Rebbe's room and placed the tray before R' Zusha.

It was now evident to the *shammash* that it was not he who provided the Rebbe with food, but the Holy One (*Sipurei Tzaddikim* 74).

לְכָל בָּשָׂר / *To all flesh*

R' Yitzchak of Vurka

Wagon drivers fall into two categories. There is the wagon driver whom Hashem wishes to sustain and so provides him with a horse and wagon. Then there is the horse that Hashem wishes to sustain and so provides him with a driver.

Both drivers may gain an equal livelihood. But in one instance, the horse

מָזוֹן לְכָל בְּרִיּוֹתָיו אֲשֶׁר בָּרָא. כָּאָמוּר: פּוֹתֵחַ אֶת יָדֶךָ, וּמַשְׂבִּיעַ לְכָל חַי רָצוֹן.[1] בָּרוּךְ אַתָּה יהוה, הַזָּן אֶת הַכֹּל.

נוֹדֶה לְּךָ יהוה אֱלֹהֵינוּ, עַל שֶׁהִנְחַלְתָּ לַאֲבוֹתֵינוּ אֶרֶץ חֶמְדָּה טוֹבָה וּרְחָבָה. וְעַל שֶׁהוֹצֵאתָנוּ יהוה אֱלֹהֵינוּ מֵאֶרֶץ מִצְרַיִם, וּפְדִיתָנוּ מִבֵּית עֲבָדִים, וְעַל בְּרִיתְךָ שֶׁחָתַמְתָּ בִּבְשָׂרֵנוּ, וְעַל תּוֹרָתְךָ שֶׁלִּמַּדְתָּנוּ, וְעַל חֻקֶּיךָ שֶׁהוֹדַעְתָּנוּ, וְעַל חַיִּים חֵן וָחֶסֶד שֶׁחוֹנַנְתָּנוּ, וְעַל אֲכִילַת מָזוֹן שָׁאַתָּה זָן וּמְפַרְנֵס אוֹתָנוּ תָּמִיד, בְּכָל יוֹם וּבְכָל עֵת וּבְכָל שָׁעָה.

וְעַל הַכֹּל יהוה אֱלֹהֵינוּ אֲנַחְנוּ מוֹדִים לָךְ, וּמְבָרְכִים אוֹתָךְ, יִתְבָּרַךְ שִׁמְךָ בְּפִי

---

works for the driver; in the other, the driver toils his entire life for the horse.

That is what the *midrash* means: If man is found to be worthy, he is told, "You were created before the angels." If he is unworthy, he is told, "A fly preceded you, a mosquito preceded you, etc." (*Bereishis Rabbah* 8:1) — you were created so that the mosquitoes may feed on your blood (*Gedulas HaTzaddikim* II 3).

פּוֹתֵחַ אֶת יָדֶךָ, וּמַשְׂבִּיעַ לְכָל חַי רָצוֹן / *You open Your hand, and satisfy the desire of every living thing*

R' Pinchas of Koritz

A young man suffered from a serious illness which got progressively worse. He had been to many *tzaddikim*, but had not been cured. He came to *R' Pinchas of Koritz*, who assured him that he would get better. And so it turned out.

R' Pinchas said, "It is not that I stand on a higher plane than the others. They proceeded in a direct manner, while I made use of a roundabout path.

[* The *midrash* turns on the meaning of the puzzling verse: 'You fashioned me *first* and *last*' (אָחוֹר וָקֶדֶם צַרְתָּנִי — *Tehillim* 139:5). The particular view cited by the Rebbe is that of R' Shimon ben Lakish who takes *first* as referring to man's soul, which is, to him, the "spirit of *Elokim* which hovers above the waters" (*Bereishis* 1:2) and existed prior to the rest of Creation. *Last* refers to man's body which was created at the end of the sixth day of Creation (*Siach Sarfei Kodesh* V 24).]

food for all of His creatures which He has created. As it is said: 'You open Your hand, and satisfy the desire of every living thing.'[1] Blessed are You, HASHEM, Who nourishes all.

We thank You, HASHEM, our God, because You have given to our forefathers as a heritage a desirable, good and spacious land; because You removed us, HASHEM, our God, from the land of Egypt and You redeemed us from the house of bondage; for Your covenant which You sealed in our flesh; for Your Torah which You taught us and for Your statutes which You made known to us; for life, grace, and kindness which You granted us; and for the provision of food with which You nourish and sustain us constantly, in every day, in every season, and in every hour.

For all, HASHEM, our God, we thank You and bless You. May Your Name be blessed by the mouth of

1. *Tehillim* 145:16.

At first, like them, I tried to enter through the Gates of Healing and found them locked. I turned and made my way to the Gates of Sustenance (פַּרְנָסָה) and found them open. I prevailed upon Heaven to grant the sick man a livelihood. I then returned to the Gates of Healing and presented a statement of the *gemara*. *Chazal* say that the verse, 'You open Your hand and satisfy the desire of every living thing' (*Tehillim* 145:16) implies that 'when Heaven grants satisfaction (שׂוֹבֵעַ), it does so for the living.' This statement presented a just claim for the sick man which could not be disregarded. The Gates of Healing were opened and he was granted health and life'' (*Be'eros HaMayim* 81).

וְעַל הַכֹּל . . . אֲנַחְנוּ מוֹדִים לָךְ
For all . . . we thank You

R' Yaakov Shimshon of Shpitivka

R' Yaakov Shimshon of Shpitivka went up to *Eretz Yisrael* in 5559 (1799). When he saw the extreme poverty of the chasidim there, he set out to gather funds for them, in the far lands of the west. In his journeyings, he reached the home of a wise elder. When the man learned that R' Yaakov Shimshon hailed from Poland, he asked him if he knew *R' Baruch of Mezhibuz*. R'

כָּל חַי תָּמִיד לְעוֹלָם וָעֶד. כַּכָּתוּב, וְאָכַלְתָּ וְשָׂבָעְתָּ, וּבֵרַכְתָּ אֶת יהוה אֱלֹהֶיךָ, עַל הָאָרֶץ הַטֹּבָה אֲשֶׁר נָתַן לָךְ.[1] בָּרוּךְ אַתָּה יהוה, עַל הָאָרֶץ וְעַל הַמָּזוֹן.

רַחֵם יהוה אֱלֹהֵינוּ עַל יִשְׂרָאֵל עַמֶּךָ, וְעַל יְרוּשָׁלַיִם עִירֶךָ, וְעַל צִיּוֹן מִשְׁכַּן כְּבוֹדֶךָ, וְעַל מַלְכוּת בֵּית דָּוִד מְשִׁיחֶךָ, וְעַל הַבַּיִת הַגָּדוֹל וְהַקָּדוֹשׁ שֶׁנִּקְרָא שִׁמְךָ עָלָיו. אֱלֹהֵינוּ אָבִינוּ רְעֵנוּ זוּנֵנוּ פַּרְנְסֵנוּ וְכַלְכְּלֵנוּ וְהַרְוִיחֵנוּ, וְהַרְוַח לָנוּ יהוה אֱלֹהֵינוּ מְהֵרָה מִכָּל צָרוֹתֵינוּ. וְנָא אַל תַּצְרִיכֵנוּ יהוה אֱלֹהֵינוּ, לֹא לִידֵי מַתְּנַת בָּשָׂר וָדָם, וְלֹא לִידֵי

Yaakov Shimshon realized that the wise elder was a holy man who was aware of R' Baruch through Divine intuition (רוּחַ הַקֹּדֶשׁ). He answered that he did, indeed, know him and he was his submissive servant. His host asked that he repeat something of R' Baruch's Torah. Although he had never in all his days forgotten anything that his Rebbe had said, he now forgot all that he had ever heard. He felt terrible and the elderly *rav* wept that he had not had the good fortune to hear Torah of truth.

Finally, R' Yaakov Shimshon said, "I have remembered a small grain of my Rebbe's teachings.

"The Men of the Great Synod (אַנְשֵׁי כְּנֶסֶת הַגְּדוֹלָה) put 'We thank You Hashem' (נוֹדֶה לְּךָ) into the *Bircas HaMazon*. We say that we thank Him for giving us the Holy Land, for taking us out of Egypt, for the covenant of circumcision, for the Torah etc., and we end with* 'and above everything, Hashem our God we thank You etc.' (וְעַל הַכֹּל). We say, in effect, 'above everything else we must thank You for being Hashem, our God — that we are fortunate enough to approach Your faith.' "

When the *rav* heard this he exclaimed in wonder, "Is this a 'small grain'? It is a profound thought." And he proceeded to expand on the topic through the hidden paths of the Torah for three days, until R' Yaakov Shimshon's mind could no longer embrace his words (*Mekor Baruch* 12).

[**And above everything* (וְעַל הַכֹּל). R' Baruch treated עַל not in the sense of *for*, or *on account of*, but in the sense of *above*. He saw ה׳ אֱלֹקֵינוּ not as a form of address — we thank You, *Hashem, our God* — parallel to *You* (לָךְ), but as part of a phrase modifying *thank* (מוֹדִים) — we thank You *for being Hashem*.]

all the living, continuously for all eternity. As it is written: 'And you shall eat and you shall be satisfied and you shall bless HASHEM, your God, for the good land which He gave you.'[1] Blessed are You, HASHEM, for the land and for the nourishment.

Have mercy HASHEM, our God, on Israel Your people; on Jerusalem, Your city, on Zion, the resting place of Your Glory; on the monarchy of the house of David, Your anointed; and on the great and holy House upon which Your Name is called. Our God, our Father — tend us, nourish us, sustain us, support us, relieve us; HASHEM, our God, grant us speedy relief from all our troubles. Please, make us not needful — HASHEM, our God — of the gift of human hands nor of their

1. *Devarim* 8:10.

כַּכָּתוּב . . . וּבֵרַכְתָּ

As it is written . . . and you shall bless

Maggid of Mezritch The *Maggid of Mezritch* cautioned his disciples to take greater pains with the thoughtful purpose (כַּוָּנָה) with which they pronounced the after-the-meal blessing, *Bircas HaMazon,* than that with which they approached prayer (תְּפִלָּה). For prayer was ordained by the Rabbis, whereas the after-the-meal blessing is expressly dictated by the Torah *(Toledos Aharon, Shoftim)*.

לֹא לִידֵי מַתְּנַת בָּשָׂר וָדָם

Not . . . of the gift of human hands

R' Yaakov Aryeh of Radzimin In the days of his want, *R' Yaakov Aryeh of Radzimin* went about in tatters. He grew in Torah and devotion to Hashem without any awareness of his material state. A chasid, R' Yissachar Dov Horvitz, provided him with handsome, befitting clothing.

"What are these for?" asked R' Yaakov Aryeh.

"It is not becoming for you to go about like a pauper," was the answer.

"What!" said the rebbe. "Should I be ashamed of the poverty which is Hashem's gift and adorn myself with the gift which comes from a man of flesh and blood?"

And he did not accept them (*Chasidim MeSaprim* I 296).

הַלְוָאָתָם, כִּי אִם לְיָדְךָ הַמְּלֵאָה הַפְּתוּחָה הַקְּדוֹשָׁה וְהָרְחָבָה, שֶׁלֹּא נֵבוֹשׁ וְלֹא נִכָּלֵם לְעוֹלָם וָעֶד.

On Shabbos add the following paragraph.

רְצֵה וְהַחֲלִיצֵנוּ יהוה אֱלֹהֵינוּ בְּמִצְוֹתֶיךָ, וּבְמִצְוַת יוֹם הַשְּׁבִיעִי הַשַּׁבָּת הַגָּדוֹל וְהַקָּדוֹשׁ הַזֶּה, כִּי יוֹם זֶה גָּדוֹל וְקָדוֹשׁ הוּא לְפָנֶיךָ, לִשְׁבָּת בּוֹ וְלָנוּחַ בּוֹ בְּאַהֲבָה כְּמִצְוַת רְצוֹנֶךָ, וּבִרְצוֹנְךָ הָנִיחַ לָנוּ יהוה אֱלֹהֵינוּ, שֶׁלֹּא תְהֵא צָרָה וְיָגוֹן וַאֲנָחָה בְּיוֹם מְנוּחָתֵנוּ, וְהַרְאֵנוּ יהוה אֱלֹהֵינוּ בְּנֶחָמַת צִיּוֹן עִירֶךָ, וּבְבִנְיַן יְרוּשָׁלַיִם עִיר קָדְשֶׁךָ, כִּי אַתָּה הוּא בַּעַל הַיְשׁוּעוֹת וּבַעַל הַנֶּחָמוֹת.

אֱלֹהֵינוּ וֵאלֹהֵי אֲבוֹתֵינוּ, יַעֲלֶה, וְיָבֹא, וְיַגִּיעַ, וְיֵרָאֶה, וְיֵרָצֶה, וְיִשָּׁמַע, וְיִפָּקֵד, וְיִזָּכֵר

וְלֹא לִידֵי הַלְוָאָתָם / *Nor of their loans*

R' Menachem Mendel of Riminov

A chasid came before *R' Menachem Mendel of Riminov* and asked that the Rebbe pray that he find favor in the eyes of a particular lord, so that the lord would agree to give him a loan.

"I cannot pray that you receive a loan from a non-Jew," said the Rebbe, "because that is one of the curses contained in the Passage of Rebuke (תּוֹכֵחָה) — 'he (the non-Jew) will lend to you' (*Devarim* 28:44). I can only pray that you won't need a loan" (*Ateres Menachem* 32).

וַאֲנָחָה / *Or lament (sigh, groan)*

R' Yissachar Ber of Radoshitz

In my youth I took upon myself a self-imposed exile. In my wanderings, I came to a hamlet and asked the local Jewish baker to put me up for the night. He made up a bed over the oven. At midnight, when the house was deep in darkness, I heard the baker sigh. The sigh was such as could break a man's entire body.

I felt miserable and depressed. If a simple village baker could sigh thus and pray at midnight over the destruction of the *Beis HaMikdash* and the self-concealment (הֶסְתֵּר פָּנִים) of the Divine Presence (שְׁכִינָה), how could I hold up my head? What could I say? What could I utter? Of what worth was my self-exile?

And, then, I heard his wife ask him, "What are you sighing about?"

loans, but only of Your Hand that is full, open, holy, and generous, that we not feel inner shame nor be humiliated for ever and ever.

On Shabbos add the following paragraph.

May it please You, HASHEM, our God — give us rest through Your commandments and through the commandment of the seventh day, this great and holy Shabbos. For this day is great and holy before You to rest on it and be content on it in love, as ordained by Your will. May it be Your will, HASHEM, our God, that there be no distress, grief, or lament on this day of our contentment. And show us, HASHEM, our God, the consolation of Zion, Your city, and the rebuilding of Jerusalem, City of Your holiness, for You are the Master of salvations and Master of consolations.

Our God and God of our forefathers, may there rise, come, reach, be noted, be favored, be heard, be considered, and be remembered —

"How long are you going to cook potatoes? Again and again and again! The time has come for you to make cheese blintzes," he answered (*Niflaos HaSaba Kadisha II* 43).

R' Pinchas of Koritz

R' Pinchas of Koritz was a seeker of truth. For seven years, he toiled to know what truth is; for seven years more, he labored to define falsehood; and for seven additional years he sought to learn how to acquire truth and avoid falsehood.

R' Shem of Kalshitz would immerse himself in the *mikveh* in the dark of each night, before he sat down to learn. He once found his *shammash* (attendant) asleep and, refraining from arousing him, went to the *mikveh* alone.

Caught up in his thoughts, he fell into a pit and broke a rib. When he was found there in the morning, he was carried home where he was abed, in pain, for many days. But, during that entire span of time, he did not emit a single groan. He was asked how he could contain himself.

He answered, "I thought of what R' Pinchas of Koritz has said, 'If a man groans more than his pain requires, that, too, reflects a tinge of falsehood' " (*Beis Rabbi* and Introduction to *Ohel Shem*).

אֱלֹהֵינוּ וֵאלֹהֵי אֲבוֹתֵינוּ / *Our God and God of our forefathers*

R' Shmuel Eliyahu of Z'volim

A son of a rebbe came before *R' Shmuel Eliyahu of Z'volim*. The Rebbe asked him,

זִכְרוֹנֵנוּ וּפִקְדּוֹנֵנוּ, וְזִכְרוֹן אֲבוֹתֵינוּ, וְזִכְרוֹן מָשִׁיחַ בֶּן דָּוִד עַבְדֶּךָ, וְזִכְרוֹן יְרוּשָׁלַיִם עִיר קָדְשֶׁךָ, וְזִכְרוֹן כָּל עַמְּךָ בֵּית יִשְׂרָאֵל לְפָנֶיךָ, לִפְלֵיטָה לְטוֹבָה לְחֵן וּלְחֶסֶד וּלְרַחֲמִים, לְחַיִּים (טוֹבִים) וּלְשָׁלוֹם בְּיוֹם חַג הַמַּצּוֹת הַזֶּה. זָכְרֵנוּ יהוה אֱלֹהֵינוּ בּוֹ לְטוֹבָה, וּפָקְדֵנוּ בוֹ לִבְרָכָה, וְהוֹשִׁיעֵנוּ בוֹ לְחַיִּים טוֹבִים. וּבִדְבַר יְשׁוּעָה וְרַחֲמִים, חוּס וְחָנֵּנוּ וְרַחֵם עָלֵינוּ וְהוֹשִׁיעֵנוּ, כִּי אֵלֶיךָ עֵינֵינוּ, כִּי אֵל חַנּוּן וְרַחוּם אָתָּה.[1]

"Who are you?" "I am the son of Rebbe so-and-so," he said.

"But who are *you*?" said the Rebbe. "We say, '*Our* God and God of our forefathers.' One's personal attributes are to be considered before family lineage."

R' Yisrael of Ruzhin

A noble had a faithful dog who accompanied him on all his hunting trips and kept steadfast watch over his home. Years passed; the dog grew old and could no longer perform his duty. The noble was reluctant to have him killed and thought of a solution to his problem. He had the dog wrapped in the hides of a leopard, a lion, a bear, and a wolf and had him sent into the forest.

Just then, the lion was holding forth to the other beasts and saw that, one by one, his audience was dwindling away before him. "What's happening today?" he asked the fox.

"A new king of the beasts has come to the forest," said the fox, "a combination lion, leopard, bear, and wolf."

Fear came over the lion and he said to the fox, "Go see what this king is like and return to tell me."

The fox went, bowed down before the new king and asked humbly, "Who are you, sir?"

"My great-great-grandfather was a lion," he answered proudly.

The fox bowed again and asked, "Who are you, sir?"

"My great-grandfather was a leopard."

"But who are you, sir?"

"My grandfather was a bear."

"And who are you, sir?"

"My father was a wolf."

"And who are you, sir?"

"I? I am a dog."

the remembrance and consideration of ourselves; the remembrance of our forefathers; the remembrance of Messiah, son of David, Your servant; the remembrance of Jerusalem, the City of Your Holiness; the remembrance of Your entire people, the Family of Israel — before You for deliverance, for goodness, for grace, for kindness, and for compassion, for (good) life, and for peace on this day of the Festival of Matzos. Remember us on it, HASHEM, our God, for goodness; consider us on it for blessing; and help us on it for good life. In the matter of salvation and compassion, pity, be gracious and compassionate with us and help us, for our eyes are turned to You, because You are God, the gracious, and compassionate.[1]

1. *Nechemiah* 9:31.

The fox bowed mockingly and ran off to tell the lion.

Famed ancestors are like a string of zeros. If any other number stands at the head of the row, the zeros multiply it and make it all the greater, each one by ten-fold more than the previous zero. But if a descendant is himself a zero, the string of zeros which stand beside him are of no use whatsoever (*Ner Yisrael*).

R' Yechiel Meir of Ostrovtza

R' Yechiel Meir of Ostrovtza was the son of a simple, but God-fearing, baker. Through his native genius, his diligence, his holiness and prayers, he rose to be one of the greatest rebbes of his generation.

He was once in the company of another rebbe who boasted of his distinguished family tree and of the host of teachings which he had absorbed in the household of his father.

"And my father," said the Rebbe of Ostrovtza, "was a bagel baker. I learned one thing from him. A fresh bagel is better than an old one" (*Sichos HaTzaddikim*).

Fiery Angel of Kotzk

When the *Fiery Angel of Kotzk* returned from his first trip to Lublin (to the *Chozeh of Lublin*) his father, who was an opponent (*misnaged*) of chasidus, asked him, "Is it proper to leave the customs of one's fathers and follow new paths?"

To which his son answered, "First the verse states: 'This is *my* God and I will declare His praise' and only then do we find: 'the God of *my father* and I will exalt Him' (*Shemos* 15:2)" (*Sipurei Chasidim*, *Beshalach* 165).

וּבְנֵה יְרוּשָׁלַיִם עִיר הַקֹּדֶשׁ בִּמְהֵרָה בְיָמֵינוּ. בָּרוּךְ אַתָּה יהוה, בּוֹנֵה (בְרַחֲמָיו) יְרוּשָׁלָיִם. אָמֵן.

בָּרוּךְ אַתָּה יהוה אֱלֹהֵינוּ מֶלֶךְ הָעוֹלָם, הָאֵל אָבִינוּ מַלְכֵּנוּ אַדִּירֵנוּ בּוֹרְאֵנוּ גּוֹאֲלֵנוּ יוֹצְרֵנוּ קְדוֹשֵׁנוּ קְדוֹשׁ יַעֲקֹב, רוֹעֵנוּ רוֹעֵה יִשְׂרָאֵל, הַמֶּלֶךְ הַטּוֹב וְהַמֵּטִיב לַכֹּל, שֶׁבְּכָל יוֹם וָיוֹם הוּא הֵטִיב, הוּא מֵטִיב, הוּא יֵיטִיב לָנוּ. הוּא גְמָלָנוּ הוּא גוֹמְלֵנוּ הוּא יִגְמְלֵנוּ לָעַד, לְחֵן וּלְחֶסֶד וּלְרַחֲמִים וּלְרֶוַח הַצָּלָה וְהַצְלָחָה, בְּרָכָה וִישׁוּעָה נֶחָמָה פַּרְנָסָה וְכַלְכָּלָה וְרַחֲמִים וְחַיִּים וְשָׁלוֹם וְכָל טוֹב, וּמִכָּל טוּב לְעוֹלָם אַל יְחַסְּרֵנוּ.

הָרַחֲמָן הוּא יִמְלוֹךְ עָלֵינוּ לְעוֹלָם וָעֶד. הָרַחֲמָן הוּא יִתְבָּרַךְ בַּשָּׁמַיִם וּבָאָרֶץ. הָרַחֲמָן

אָבִינוּ / *our Father*

R' Shlomo of Zvihl My father, R' Mordechai, supported his children after their marriage. One day, I decided that there is a Father above and I didn't need the support of my flesh-and-blood father. A day passed, then two days and the larder began to empty. Two more days passed and we had reached the point where we hungered for bread itself. I thought to myself, "Perhaps Heaven has ordained that my sustenance must come by way of my father." I sent my wife to my father and he gave her a full ruble.

At the time, two chasidim were visiting my father. They decided to pay me a visit, also, as I had celebrated my marriage only a short while earlier. One of them had taken a ruble out of his pocket to give to me as a wedding gift. Just as my wife returned with the ruble which she had received from my father, the chasid put his ruble, absentmindedly, back into his pocket.

I had been given a clear sign from Heaven: See, the ruble had already been prepared for you and it returned to where it had come from, to teach you that everything is ordained by Heaven (*Tzaddik Yesod Olam*).

Rebuild Jerusalem, the Holy City, soon in our days. Blessed are You, HASHEM, Who rebuilds Jerusalem (in His mercy). Amen.

Blessed are You, HASHEM, our God, King of the universe, the Almighty, our Father, our King, our Sovereign, our Creator, our Redeemer, our Maker, our Holy One, Holy One of Yaakov, our Shepherd, the Shepherd of Israel, the King Who is good and Who does good for all. For every single day He did good, He does good, and He will do good to us. He was bountiful with us, He is bountiful with us, and He will forever be bountiful with us — with grace and with kindness and with mercy, with relief, salvation, success, blessing, help, consolation, sustenance, support, mercy, life, peace, and all good; and of all good things may He never deprive us.

The compassionate One! May He reign over us forever. The compassionate One! May He be blessed in heaven and on earth. The compassionate

---

אָבִינוּ מַלְכֵּנוּ / *our Father, our King*

Beis Aharon of Karlin

The basic task of the evil desire (יֵצֶר הָרָע) is to make man forget that he is a King's son (*Darchei Aharon* 24).

הָרַחֲמָן / *The compassionate One*

R' Tzvi Elimelech of Dinov

The Maggid of Mezritch lived in extreme poverty before he was known to the world. Once, his wife wept before him, lamenting the hunger of their children and their lack of clothing in the bitter cold. The Maggid listened and sighed. And in that instant he heard a voice from heaven telling him that, with that sigh, he had lost his portion of the World-to-Come. He stood up trembling. For, in a single moment, he had been thrust out of both worlds. He did not enjoy this world of the here and now, for he and his family were pressed by hunger and want. And now, he had lost access to the World-to-Come. But, in a brief moment, he came to himself and said, "On the contrary! Now that I have lost both worlds I can truly serve Hashem. It will now be devotion for its own sake, solely to please my Creator." And he continued to learn with joy.

הוּא יִשְׁתַּבַּח לְדוֹר דּוֹרִים, וְיִתְפָּאַר בָּנוּ לָעַד וּלְנֵצַח נְצָחִים, וְיִתְהַדַּר בָּנוּ לָעַד וּלְעוֹלְמֵי עוֹלָמִים. הָרַחֲמָן הוּא יְפַרְנְסֵנוּ בְּכָבוֹד. הָרַחֲמָן הוּא

Thereupon, he was informed by Heaven that, because of his attitude, his portion in the World-to-Come was being returned to him, but with a condition attached: From that day on, he was not to sigh in compassion over his children's state, for he was not more compassionate than the Holy One (*Agra D' Firka* 22).

הָרַחֲמָן הוּא יְפַרְנְסֵנוּ / *The compassionate One! May He sustain us*

Chidushei HaRim

The world is topsy-turvy. A man's sustenance (*parnasah*) is in the hands of the Creator. Yet everyone pursues it and makes grand plans to obtain it. And on the other hand, it is in *man's* power to devote himself to God. Do not *Chazal* say that everything is in the hands of heaven except the fear of heaven? And on this issue, man relies on his Creator. Man expects *Him* to plant the love and fear of Hashem in his heart (*Siach Sarfei Kodesh* I 481).

R' Mordechai of Tchernobil

A number of chasidim who had spent *Shabbos* in the presence of *R' Mordechai of Tchernobil* were on their way home. They reviewed the Torah which they had heard from the Rebbe; the words gave them joy and were sweeter than honey. And they agreed among themselves that they had never experienced such a *Shabbos* in their lives.

Among them sat a frightfully ignorant innkeeper who also had a comment and said, "I never had a visit to the Rebbe like this one."

The others were astonished and asked, "What did you find special about the *Shabbos*?"

The innkeeper replied, "When I went to say my farewell to the Rebbe and receive his blessing, he asked me about my daily program. I told him that I rise early and go to the village to buy produce from the peasants. When I've finished my dealings, I return home, say the morning blessings (בִּרְכּוֹת הַשַּׁחַר), and pray. The Rebbe said, 'It is not good that you put off your *tefillah* (prayers) until after you've taken care of your business affairs.' I told the Rebbe that the peasant farmers get up early to go out to their fields and if I would pray first, I would not find anyone left from whom to buy my produce."

" 'Let me tell you a story,' said the Rebbe:

A young man, when he was first married, stayed with, and was supported by, his father-in-law. His family grew and the time came for him to engage in trade. He left his family and went off to build up capital. Hiring himself out as a school teacher in the village, he saved penny after penny and, in three

One! May He be praised throughout all generations, may He be glorified through us forever to the ultimate ends, and be honored through us forever and for all eternity. The compassionate One! May He sustain us in honor. The compassionate One! May He

---

years, he amassed funds which were sufficient to enter the world of business. It was time to return home.

On a Friday afternoon, he arrived in a village not far from his town. But, he was too distant to reach home before *Shabbos* and he had to take quarters in a local inn.

What was he to do with his money? It was a handsome sum, twelve bags of gold coins and, among the gold, a single copper coin. He couldn't carry it about on his person; that was not allowed on *Shabbos;* money was *muktzeh*. If he left it in his bags, it might be stolen. Should he leave it with the innkeeper? Perhaps the man was dishonest and wouldn't give it back.

Shabbos grew closer and closer. There wasn't much time left. And the young man was God fearing and had no wish to desecrate the *Shabbos*. He finally gave the money to the innkeeper for safekeeping. But, throughout the *Shabbos*, his heart beat wildly and fear was a constant companion.

Shabbos departed, the innkeeper made *havdalah*, went to his chest and handed the twelve bags of gold coins to his guest. A heavy weight fell away from the young man's chest. He counted the bags. There were really twelve, not one missing! He then opened them up and poked about in their contents.

"What are you looking for?" asked the innkeeper.

"I had a small copper coin among the gold ones in one of the bags. I want to see if that's come back, too," said the young man.

" 'What a foolish young man he was,' said the Rebbe. 'Although all his bags of gold had been returned, he thought that the innkeeper might have stolen his piddling copper coin. And you, you act in a like manner. Each night you place your soul, your most valuable possession, in the Holy One's hand, and lie down to sleep like a corpse. You arise on the morrow and see that the Holy One has kept faith and returned your bag of gold, your soul. How then, can you doubt that He will assure you your livelihood, even if you turn to your affairs only after *tefillah*?' Thus the Rebbe spoke to me and invigorated me with his words."

"Indeed," said the other chasidim, "your profit from the *Shabbos* is greater than ours" (*Admorei Tchernobil* 205).

יְפַרְנְסֵנוּ בְּכָבוֹד / *Sustain us in honor*

R' Nachum of Tchernobil

R' Nachum of Tchernobil gave whatever he had to charity and lived in poverty. In contrast, his son *R' Mordechai of Tchernobil* lived in grand, royal style. When R'

יִשְׁבּוֹר עֻלֵּנוּ מֵעַל צַוָּארֵנוּ, וְהוּא יוֹלִיכֵנוּ קוֹמְמִיּוּת לְאַרְצֵנוּ. הָרַחֲמָן הוּא יִשְׁלַח לָנוּ בְּרָכָה מְרֻבָּה בַּבַּיִת הַזֶּה, וְעַל שֻׁלְחָן זֶה שֶׁאָכַלְנוּ עָלָיו. הָרַחֲמָן הוּא יִשְׁלַח לָנוּ אֶת אֵלִיָּהוּ הַנָּבִיא זָכוּר לַטּוֹב, וִיבַשֶּׂר לָנוּ בְּשׂוֹרוֹת טוֹבוֹת יְשׁוּעוֹת וְנֶחָמוֹת.

הָרַחֲמָן הוּא יְבָרֵךְ

Guests recite the following.
Children at their parents' table add words in parentheses.

אֶת (אָבִי מוֹרִי)בַּעַל הַבַּיִת הַזֶּה,
וְאֶת (אִמִּי מוֹרָתִי)בַּעֲלַת הַבַּיִת הַזֶּה,

Nachum heard of his son's way of life he questioned him about it.

"*Chazal* tell us," said R' Mordechai. "that *Rabbeinu HaKodesh* (R' Yehudah HaNasi) was fabulously wealthy. Yet, when he was on death's threshold, he lifted his ten fingers and said that even his little finger had not enjoyed the pleasures of this world. If *Chazal* tell us this, they certainly indicate that his is a possible road to follow in the service of the Creator."

When R' Nachum fell ill, his chasidim wished to have him brought to Kiev, to be seen by a prominent physician. But the trip would be a long and hard one, and R' Nachum was weak and suffering from pain. They sought a carriage that would ease the journey. R' Mordechai, his son, possessed just such a grand, upholstered carriage, but he had kept it out of sight of his father, who lived the simple life. The need of the hour dictated that it be used, however. The carriage was brought around, and R' Nachum was told that it had been hired from one of the gentry. R' Nachum entered it, sat down and commented, "This doesn't belong to one of the gentry. You are hiding the truth from me." They were forced to admit that it belonged to his son. "I immediately felt that it was the carriage of a *tzaddik*. Now, I see that a man can lead a holy life amid wealth and plenty" (*Admorei Tchernobil* pp. 76,93).

וְהוּא יוֹלִיכֵנוּ קוֹמְמִיּוּת לְאַרְצֵנוּ
And guide us erect to our Land

Yismach Moshe

The *Yismach Moshe* lived in old, shabby, rented quarters. When his chasidim wished to buy a large, spacious home for him, he did not agree. For *Mashiach* would soon come, he said, and he had an estate prepared for him in the Holy Land, along with everyone else of Israel. Each evening, as he retired, he would lay out his festival clothes and cane near the bed, so that he need not waste a minute

break the yoke of oppression from our necks and guide us erect to our Land. The compassionate One! May He send us abundant blessing to this house and upon this table at which we have eaten. The compassionate One! May He send us Eliyahu, the Prophet — he is remembered for good — to proclaim to us good tidings, salvations, and consolations. The compassionate One! May He bless

Guests recite the following.
Children at their parents' table add words in parentheses.

(my father, my teacher) the master of this house, and (my mother, my teacher) lady of this house,

---

before greeting the *Mashiach* when he came. And he left orders with his *shammash* (attendant) to awake him, immediately, should the *Mashiach* come, so that he would not be late by even a single moment.

Before he passed away, while he lay in his bed in pain, he said, "Master of the world, You know that I am the least and worst among men. But You also know that I never lie, and now, before my death, I would certainly not lie.

"I say before You, that had I known that I would reach old age before *Mashiach* had come, I would not have been able to bear it; I would have died long ago. But heaven fooled me from day to day.

"I ask you: Isn't it overdoing it to make fun of an old man like me? I beg of You that You allow *Mashiach* to come immediately. It is clear and known to You that I do not make the request for my own good. As for me, I will waive my share and will be the offering of atonement for Israel, so that His great name may be magnified and sanctified (יִתְגַּדֵּל וְיִתְקַדֵּשׁ שְׁמֵהּ רַבָּא)'" (*MiGedolei HaChasidus* VIII 81-84).

הָרַחֲמָן הוּא יִשְׁלַח לָנוּ אֶת אֵלִיָּהוּ הַנָּבִיא

The compassionate One! May He send us Eliyahu, the Prophet

R' Levi Yitzchak of Berdichev

The prophet informs us: "Behold I will send Eliyahu the Prophet to you, before the coming of the great and awesome day of Hashem" (*Malachi* 3:23). How was it, then, that when R' Yehoshua ben Levi asked the *Mashiach*, "When are you coming, sir?" he answered (in the words of *Tehillim* 95:7), "Today, if you hearken to His voice" (*Sanhedrin* 98a). And, indeed, *why* must Eliyahu come a day before the *Mashiach*?

Mankind is sunken into the comings and goings of the world and preoccupied by its vanities. Eliyahu must come to sever them from their affairs and ready them to receive the *Mashiach*. However, "if you hearken to His voice" and shake yourselves free of the trivialities of the present, of your

Those eating at their own table recite the following, adding the appropriate parenthesized phrases:

אוֹתִי (וְאֶת אִשְׁתִּי/בַּעְלִי. וְאֶת זַרְעִי) וְאֶת כָּל אֲשֶׁר לִי.

All guests recite the following:

אוֹתָם וְאֶת בֵּיתָם וְאֶת זַרְעָם וְאֶת כָּל אֲשֶׁר לָהֶם.

All continue here:

אוֹתָנוּ וְאֶת כָּל אֲשֶׁר לָנוּ, כְּמוֹ שֶׁנִּתְבָּרְכוּ אֲבוֹתֵינוּ אַבְרָהָם יִצְחָק וְיַעֲקֹב בַּכֹּל מִכֹּל כֹּל, כֵּן יְבָרֵךְ אוֹתָנוּ כֻּלָּנוּ יַחַד בִּבְרָכָה שְׁלֵמָה, וְנֹאמַר, אָמֵן.

בַּמָּרוֹם יְלַמְּדוּ עֲלֵיהֶם וְעָלֵינוּ זְכוּת, שֶׁתְּהֵא לְמִשְׁמֶרֶת שָׁלוֹם. וְנִשָּׂא בְרָכָה מֵאֵת יהוה, וּצְדָקָה מֵאֱלֹהֵי יִשְׁעֵנוּ, וְנִמְצָא חֵן וְשֵׂכֶל טוֹב בְּעֵינֵי אֱלֹהִים וְאָדָם.[1]

On Shabbos add the following sentence:

הָרַחֲמָן הוּא יַנְחִילֵנוּ יוֹם שֶׁכֻּלּוֹ שַׁבָּת וּמְנוּחָה לְחַיֵּי הָעוֹלָמִים.

---

own accord, then the *Mashiach* can come "today" — immediately. There will be no need for the prior preparation by Eliyahu (*Sifsei Tzaddikim, Beha'aloscha*).

יוֹם שֶׁכֻּלּוֹ שַׁבָּת / *The day which will be completely a Shabbos*

Chidushei HaRim *Shabbos* is a miniature World-to-Come (*Berachos* 57b). Just as a man cannot enter the World-to-Come until he departs from this world, so, too, he cannot feel the holiness of *Shabbos* unless he separates himself from the weekdays (*Siach Sarfei Kodesh* III 142).

R' David of Lelov *R' David of Lelov* would often say that there is no such person as a bad Jew. If he does exist it is because there is a non-Jew part within him. Since the *halachah* states that a non-Jew who observes *Shabbos* deserves the death penalty, a Jew cannot enter into the *Shabbos* with the non-Jew part of himself. He must banish it before *Shabbos* arrives (ibid. I 77).

Those eating at their own table recite the following, adding the appropriate parenthesized phrases:

me (my wife/husband and family) and all that is mine,

All guests recite the following:

them, their house, their family, and all that is theirs,

All continue here:

ours and all that is ours — just as our forefathers Avraham, Yitzchak, and Yaakov were blessed in everything, from everything, with everything. So may He bless us all together with a perfect blessing. And let us say: Amen!

On high, may merit be pleaded upon them and upon us, for a safeguard of peace. May we receive a blessing from HASHEM and just kindness from the God of our salvation, and find favor and good understanding in the eyes of God and man.[1]

On Shabbos add the following sentence:

The compassionate One! May He cause us to inherit the day which will be completely a Shabbos and rest day for eternal life.

1. *Mishlei* 3:4.

וּמְנוּחָה לְחַיֵּי הָעוֹלָמִים / *And rest day for eternal life*

R' Sar Shalom of Belz

Many, many people come to me, each with his bundle of troubles. Each cries out for deliverance. And each secretly complains, in his heart of hearts, against the Holy One, Who has wronged him. There is nothing new in this, for it is stated: "Man's foolishness twists his path — and his heart is angry with Hashem" (*Mishlei* 19:3). But in the time to come (לְעָתִיד לָבֹא), when the world will function as it should, and the earth will be filled with an awareness of God (דֵּעָה), everyone will see that "whatever heaven does is for the good." They will be convinced that He has directed each generation with kindness, "a God of truth without injustice, just and upright" (*Devarim* 32:4). Then Hashem will have a rest, so to speak, from the complaints of the Children of Israel. That will be *"a day which will be completely a *Shabbos — and rest day for eternal life*" (*Dover Shalom* 68).

* [*A day which will be etc.*: וּמְנוּחָה לְחַיֵּי הָעוֹלָמִים is to be understood in context, as "a rest for eternal life." R' Sar Shalom takes (חַיֵּי הָעוֹלָמִים as a variant of חֵי הָעוֹלָמִים, Life of the universe (Hashem) and thus gave the phrase a new interpretation.]

The words in parentheses are added on the two Seder nights in some communities.

הָרַחֲמָן הוּא יַנְחִילֵנוּ יוֹם שֶׁכֻּלּוֹ טוֹב. (יוֹם שֶׁכֻּלּוֹ אָרוּךְ. יוֹם שֶׁצַּדִּיקִים יוֹשְׁבִים וְעַטְרוֹתֵיהֶם בְּרָאשֵׁיהֶם וְנֶהֱנִים מִזִּיו הַשְּׁכִינָה וִיהִי חֶלְקֵנוּ עִמָּהֶם.)

הָרַחֲמָן הוּא יְזַכֵּנוּ לִימוֹת הַמָּשִׁיחַ וּלְחַיֵּי הָעוֹלָם הַבָּא. מִגְדּוֹל יְשׁוּעוֹת מַלְכּוֹ וְעֹשֶׂה חֶסֶד לִמְשִׁיחוֹ לְדָוִד וּלְזַרְעוֹ עַד עוֹלָם.[1] עֹשֶׂה שָׁלוֹם בִּמְרוֹמָיו, הוּא יַעֲשֶׂה שָׁלוֹם עָלֵינוּ וְעַל כָּל יִשְׂרָאֵל. וְאִמְרוּ, אָמֵן.

יְראוּ אֶת יהוה קְדֹשָׁיו, כִּי אֵין מַחְסוֹר לִירֵאָיו. כְּפִירִים רָשׁוּ וְרָעֵבוּ, וְדֹרְשֵׁי יהוה

יְזַכֵּנוּ לִימוֹת הַמָּשִׁיחַ

May He make us worthy of the days of Mashiach

R' Tzvi Elimelech of Bluzhov

R' Tzvi Elimelech of Bluzhov sat in his *succah* surrounded by his chasidim. "*Chazal* tell us," he said, "that the *Mashiach* will not come on a *Shabbos* or Festival (*Eruvin* 43a). How can we understand this? Here, all of Israel awaits him, all are consumed with troubles, pains and terrible tribulations — and the *Mashiach* is to pick and choose times; he will come on this day; he will not come on that day. Wonder of wonders!"

The Rebbe sat, head bowed, caught up in his thoughts. After what seemed an interminable time, he lifted his head and said, "The truth of the matter is that the *Mashiach* is shrewd. Imagine if he were to come now when we sit in company of our sainted guests, Avraham, Yitzchak, Yaakov, Moshe, Aharon, Yosef and David. When do we ever feel ourselves enveloped in such sanctity? We can veritably taste the pleasures of *Gan Eden* itself. If they were to come and tell us that *Mashiach* is here, waiting outside, we wouldn't even go out to greet him. We would choose to remain in our *Gan Eden,* in the company of our sainted guests. The *Mashiach* knows this, and therefore does not come on such days."

His disciple, the *Shomer Emunim,* explained his comments:

The Rebbe wished to give us the sense of purpose of the *mishnah* in *Avos*

The words in parentheses are added on the two Seder nights in some communities.

The compassionate One! May He cause us to inherit that day which is altogether good (that everlasting day, the day when the just will sit with crowns on their heads, enjoying the reflection of God's majesty – and may our portion be with them!).

The compassionate One! May He make us worthy of the days of Mashiach and the life of the World-to-Come. He Who is a tower of salvations to His king and does kindness for His anointed, to David and to his descendants forever.[1] He Who makes peace in His heights, may He make peace upon us and upon all Israel. Now respond: Amen!

Fear HASHEM, you – His holy ones – for there is no deprivation for His reverent ones. Young lions may want and hunger, but those who seek HASHEM

1. *II Shmuel* 22:51.

---

in concrete terms. The *mishnah* writes: "One hour of repentance and good deeds in this world outweighs the entire existence in the World-to-Come" (*Avos* 4:17). He wished to teach us that our soul's good and its soundness were not dependent, at all, on the coming of *Mashiach*. We are to "work" on the eve of *Shabbos* to ensure ourselves of "food" on the *Shabbos*; we are to devote ourselves to and serve *Hashem*, if we wish to have a proper reception in the World-to-Come (*Uvda D'Aharon* 85).

וּלְחַיֵּי הָעוֹלָם הַבָּא / *And the life of the World-to-Come*

Maggid of Kozhnitz

A merchant, a chasid of the sainted *Maggid of Kozhnitz*, was on the road one snowy, stormy night. He was to make his way through Kozhnitz. When he arrived in town, the entire city was deep in sleep. Only the Rebbe's house showed a light; the *Maggid* was up learning. The merchant knocked on the Rebbe's door and entered. The Rebbe did not at first recognize his chasid who was covered with snow from head to toe. When the snow melted and the chasid saw that he had been recognized, he wept before the Rebbe and cried out, "Rebbe, I have nothing of this world of the here and now (עוֹלָם הַזֶּה); I wander here and there, driven by, and completely submerged in, my affairs. I hope that at least I will be found worthy enough to gain the World-to-Come (עוֹלָם הַבָּא)."

לֹא יַחְסְרוּ כָל טוֹב.[1] הוֹדוּ לַיהוה כִּי טוֹב, כִּי לְעוֹלָם חַסְדּוֹ.[2] פּוֹתֵחַ אֶת יָדֶךָ, וּמַשְׂבִּיעַ לְכָל חַי רָצוֹן.[3] בָּרוּךְ הַגֶּבֶר אֲשֶׁר יִבְטַח בַּיהוה, וְהָיָה יהוה מִבְטַחוֹ.[4] נַעַר הָיִיתִי גַּם זָקַנְתִּי, וְלֹא רָאִיתִי צַדִּיק נֶעֱזָב, וְזַרְעוֹ מְבַקֶּשׁ לָחֶם.[5] יהוה עֹז לְעַמּוֹ יִתֵּן, יהוה יְבָרֵךְ אֶת עַמּוֹ בַשָּׁלוֹם.[6]

Upon completion of Bircas HaMazon the blessing over wine is recited and the third cup is drunk while reclining on the left side. It is preferable to drink the entire cup, but at the very least, most of the cup should be drained.

הֲרֵינִי מוּכָן וּמְזוּמָן לְקַיֵּם מִצְוַת כּוֹס שְׁלִישִׁי שֶׁל אַרְבַּע כּוֹסוֹת. לְשֵׁם יִחוּד קֻדְשָׁא בְּרִיךְ הוּא וּשְׁכִינְתֵּיהּ, עַל יְדֵי הַהוּא טָמִיר וְנֶעְלָם, בְּשֵׁם כָּל יִשְׂרָאֵל. וִיהִי נֹעַם אֲדֹנָי אֱלֹהֵינוּ עָלֵינוּ, וּמַעֲשֵׂה יָדֵינוּ כּוֹנְנָה עָלֵינוּ, וּמַעֲשֵׂה יָדֵינוּ כּוֹנְנֵהוּ:

בָּרוּךְ אַתָּה יהוה אֱלֹהֵינוּ מֶלֶךְ הָעוֹלָם, בּוֹרֵא פְּרִי הַגָּפֶן.

"Monumental fool," said the Rebbe, "if you don't possess this world, which you strive so hard to gain through exhausting toil, how will you ever possess the World-to-Come, for which you do not labor at all?" (*Gedulas HaTzaddikim* 52).

וְדֹרְשֵׁי ה' לֹא יַחְסְרוּ כָל טוֹב

But those who seek Hashem will not lack any good

R' Yitzchak of Nishchiz

There was, in Apta, a great and righteous *rav* who once proclaimed in a speech that he could guarantee that anyone who would occupy himself with learning Torah would be provided with bread and *borscht* without any work or effort. A man who dug and sold clay for a living believed what he had heard, went home, sat himself in a corner by the stove, began saying *Tehillim* and refused to go to work. His wife was unable to persuade him to stop saying *Tehillim* and he did not reveal his reason to her. She thought that he had gone mad.

In order to make ends meet, she sent a man off on her husband's wagon to dig clay in his place, with the understanding that the profits would be divided between the worker and herself.

While digging, the man found a treasure chest of money which he loaded onto the wagon and covered with a matting. Before he could climb aboard, the horse ran off and returned, wagon and all, to his owner's home. Husband and wife rolled back the matting and discovered the treasure. After dividing it with the worker, they were able to live in wealth for the rest of their days (*Emunas HaTzaddikim* 155).

will not lack any good.[1] Give thanks to God for He is good; His kindness endures forever.[2] You open Your hand and satisfy the desire of every living thing.[3] Blessed is the man who trusts in HASHEM, then HASHEM will be his security.[4] I was a youth and also have aged, and I have not seen a righteous man forsaken, with his children begging for bread.[5] HASHEM will give might to His people; HASHEM will bless His people with peace.[6]

Upon completion of Bircas HaMazon the blessing over wine is recited and the third cup is drunk while reclining on the left side. It is preferable to drink the entire cup, but at the very least, most of the cup should be drained.

Behold, I am prepared and ready to fulfill the mitzvah of the third of the Four Cups. For the sake of the unification of the Holy One, Blessed is He, and His presence, through Him Who is hidden and inscrutable — [I pray] in the name of all Israel. May the pleasantness of my Lord, our God, be upon us — may He establish our handiwork for us; our handiwork may He establish.

Blessed are You, HASHEM, our God, King of the universe, Who creates the fruit of the vine.

1. *Tehillim* 34:10-11. 2. 136:1. 3. 145:16.
4. *Yirmeyahu* 17:7. 5. *Tehillim* 37:25. 6. 29:11.

R' Simchah Bunim of Pshischa

"Those who seek Hashem will not lack" because "everything is good" (כָּל טוֹב). They know that whatever *Hashem* does to them is only for the good (*Siach Sarfei Kodesh* II 396).

וְלֹא רָאִיתִי צַדִּיק נֶעֱזָב וְזַרְעוֹ מְבַקֶּשׁ לָחֶם

And I have not seen a righteous man forsaken, with his children begging for bread

R' Yissachar Ber of Volbroz

After *R' Yissachar Ber of Volbroz* passed away, his chasidim wished to drape the mantle of leadership over the shoulders of his son *R' Yaakov Moshe*. But he vigorously refused to accept it, and went off to the industrial city of Lodz to find a livelihood.

While he was there, a man, who was unknown to him, entered his room and said to him, "The *tzaddik*, while alive, is worried about, and takes care of, his children. But when he leaves the world and can no longer help them, he stands before the Heavenly Throne and argues, 'Does the verse not assure us that: "I have not seen a righteous man forsaken, with his children begging bread" (*Tehillim* 37:25)? What will happen to my son?' It stands to reason that his words make an impression, and they turn to him and say, 'How do

The fourth cup is poured. According to most customs, the cup of Eliahu is poured at this point, after which the door is opened in accordance with the verse, 'It is a guarded night.' Then the following paragraph is recited.

שְׁפֹךְ חֲמָתְךָ אֶל הַגּוֹיִם אֲשֶׁר לֹא יְדָעוּךָ וְעַל מַמְלָכוֹת אֲשֶׁר בְּשִׁמְךָ לֹא קָרָאוּ. כִּי אָכַל אֶת יַעֲקֹב וְאֶת נָוֵהוּ הֵשַׁמּוּ.[1] שְׁפָךְ עֲלֵיהֶם זַעְמֶךָ

---

you wish your children to find sustenance?' To this he answers, 'I wish that their blessing not return unanswered and that their advice to those who turn to them always be effective.' "

The man turned to R' Yaakov Moshe and added, "Those are your provisions for the journey. From this day on, go forth and bless Israel."

R' Yaakov Moshe accepted the mantle of leadership and in later days told those who were close to him, "A rebbe is a man whom Eliahu the Prophet, himself, has placed on the chair of authority" (*Ohel Yissachar* 67).

כּוֹס שֶׁל אֵלִיָּהוּ / *The cup of Eliahu*

R' Yisrael of Ruzhin

One of the chasidim of *R' Yisrael of Ruzhin* was fabulously wealthy and, each year, he was accustomed to add to and embellish the cup of Eliahu by setting it with more exceptional and precious stones. However, his fortunes slipped and he became poverty stricken, so much so, that as Pesach rapidly approached, he was left without a penny. No one as yet knew of his condition and he did not wish to accept charity, "Perhaps," he said to his wife, "we should sell Eliahu's cup."

"Better that we suffer starvation rather than sell the cup which we fashioned to honor Eliahu, may he be mentioned for the good," replied his wife.

It was the eve of Pesach and the house was empty of food. The man went to the *beis midrash* long hours before the festival evening was to begin and in his absence, an honorable-looking individual arrived at his home. He was a stranger to the place, and he would like to be a guest at their *Seder,* he told the woman. When she said that the house was bare, he told her not to worry and gave her money with which to buy all that was needed with a liberal hand. After the *ma'ariv* prayers, he said, he would come to the house.

After *ma'ariv* the husband remained in the *beis knesses* until all of the congregation had left; he did not wish anyone to sense that his house was bare and unlit. When he did leave and finally approached the house, he was surprised to see light streaming from the windows. He opened the door to a table set to perfection. His wife told him of all that had occurred.

Before the man made *kiddush*, the guest entered and blessed them that they be granted wealth and all that was good; thereupon he immediately disappeared. They understood that this was not an ordinary matter and,

The fourth cup is poured. According to most customs, the cup of Eliahu is poured at this point, after which the door is opened in accordance with the verse, 'It is a guarded night.' Then the following paragraph is recited.

Pour Your wrath upon the nations that do not recognize You and upon the kingdoms that do not invoke Your Name. For they have devoured Yaakov and destroyed His habitation.[1] Pour Your

1. *Tehillim* 79:6-7.

---

after the festival, they traveled to the Rebbe of Ruzhin. The Rebbe told him that they had been visited by Eliahu the Prophet. Because they had taken such pains with his cup, they had been judged worthy to see him. And he had appeared twice to the woman, because it had been she who did not agree to sell the cup (*Ginzei Yisrael, L'Nechad HaRav HaKadosh MeRuzhin*).

שְׁפֹךְ חֲמָתְךָ עַל הַגּוֹיִם
Pour Your wrath upon the nations

R' Aharon of Karlin

One year, while reciting the confessional prayer (*vidui*) of Yom Kippur, *R' Aharon the Great of Karlin* omitted two words. Instead of saying, "and the sins which I have committed before You erase in Your great mercy, **but not** through sufferings and evil diseases," he said, ". . . erase in Your great mercy through sufferings and evil diseases." His body immediately broke out in sores and boils and he suffered dreadful pains until Pesach. On the evening of the *Seder* when he reached the passage of "Pour Your wrath upon the nations," he stamped furiously on the floor. Immediately all the sores on his body burst open. The pus which flowed forth seeped through all his clothes and soaked his *kittel*.

The *kittel* was preserved in Stolin for many years (*Sipurei Chasidim, Moadim* 93).

פּוֹתְחִין הַדֶּלֶת / *The door is opened*

R' Tzvi Elimelech of Dinov

R' Pesach, the father of *R' Tzvi Elimelech of Dinov*, once served in a hamlet as the teacher of children for a miserly, tight-fisted man. R' Pesach pitied the poor who were given nothing and sent away in shame from the miser's door. He suggested to his employer that he give charity and take it off his, R' Pesach's, salary. The miser agreed and at the end of the period for which R' Pesach had been hired, when the festival of Pesach was approaching, the employer made a reckoning. Not only did the money given for charity equal the wages, but surpassed them by five gold coins. The miser was unwilling to overlook the five coins which were owed him and since he had no money, R' Pesach left his *Shabbos* clothes with the miser as payment.

R' Pesach had been away from home for the long term of teaching and

וַחֲרוֹן אַפְּךָ יַשִּׂיגֵם.[1] תִּרְדֹּף בְּאַף וְתַשְׁמִידֵם מִתַּחַת שְׁמֵי יהוה.[2]

---

now, he was left without a penny to show for his efforts. He was embarrassed to return home empty handed, so he made his way to the *beis midrash*. There he met his son, Tzvi Elimelech, who ran home to tell his mother the good news: Father had arrived. R' Pesach's wife prepared a grand homecoming meal and sent her son to call her husband. Against his will, R' Pesach, countenance drooping and soul downcast, dragged his reluctant feet behind the skipping steps of his son.

On the way, a carriage dashed by and its passenger threw a purse towards them. R' Pesach picked it up and ran after the carriage shouting. But the galloping horses went even faster, and the man within paid no attention to R' Pesach's cries.

R' Pesach understood that this was not a chance affair. He opened the purse and found a sum exactly matching his wages, plus five gold coins — the sum that had been given away for charity.

On the evening of the *Seder*, which was celebrated on a grand scale, the youngster, Tzvi Elimelech, was sent to open the door when "Pour Your wrath" (שְׁפֹךְ חֲמָתְךָ) was said. "Look, Father!" he cried out. "It's the man who threw the purse from the carriage" (*Meha R' Tzvi Elimelech M'Dinov* 18).

R' Mordechai of Tchernobil

R' Mordechai of Tchernobil supported the secret *tzaddikim* (צַדִּיקִם נִסְתָּרִים) of his generation and would have his chasidim contribute to this cause. The wealthy chasid, R' Chaim Mendel, was outstanding in giving great sums with a willing heart.

Once, however, he said to the Rebbe, "I have given great sums to help the secret *tzaddikim* but I have not had the fortune to know them. I am ready to give whatever sum is asked if only I might be allowed to see one of them."

Before the Rebbe had a chance to reply, R' Chaim Mendel continued, "I have a further request, Rebbe. My only son, Shalom Shachna, is a scholar (*talmid chacham*) and God fearing. Could the Rebbe bless him that he find his true match quickly?"

When the Rebbe questioned him, R' Chaim Mendel said that his son had rejected all the proposals that had been suggested to him. And what pained the father most of all was his son's hint that he would not be averse to marrying the daughter of Baruch Leib, the forest watchman — a pauper, common and unlearned. "Although," said R' Chaim Mendel, "my son is humble and of high moral standing, even humility has its limits. *Chazal* say that a man should even sell all that he has to marry the daughter of a sage. And I am, indeed, ready and willing to spend a fortune to marry my son to the wellborn daughter of a great man."

The Rebbe thought a while and answered, "My son, you have presented

anger upon them and let Your fiery wrath overtake them.[1] Pursue them with wrath and annihilate them from beneath the heavens of HASHEM.[2]

1. *Tehillim* 69:25. 2. *Eichah* 3:66.

two difficult requests. It is not in my power to grant either. The secret *tzaddikim* must be unknown; that is their essence and that is their destiny. As for the matter of a proper match for your son, it is the Holy One who sits in Heaven and joins the partners. The task is as difficult as the parting of the Red Sea. And who am I to intervene in the affair?"

After a few moments of additional thought the Rebbe said, "Listen, Chaim Mendel. I am not permitted to disclose who the secret *tzaddikim* are, but perhaps, you will be fortunate and Eliahu will reveal himself to you. It is no small matter to see Eliahu; not everyone is found worthy to do so. Come to me on the night of the *Seder* and perhaps Eliahu will reveal himself to you when the door is opened after the *Bircas HaMazon*. Perhaps, perhaps, he will appear in the guise of one of the secret *tzaddikim* — and your request will have been honored."

R' Chaim Mendel's heart quickened. He, a simple chasid, would see Eliahu? In preparation for the great event, he prayed with twice the thoughtful purpose (כַּוָּנָה) with which he usually prayed and he learned with twice the diligence (הַתְמָדָה). Before Pesach he doubled his contributions of festival needs to the poor. He was hurt that Baruch Leib, the forest watchman, had sent back the package of provisions which he had given. "A beggar putting on airs," he thought to himself. But he repressed his feelings. He had no time to harbor resentment, not when he was preparing to see the prophet Eliahu!

The evening of the *Seder* arrived. The Maggid of Tchernobil sat reclining at the table, robed in a white *kittel* edged with silver, his eight saintly sons about him. His face was radiant, his eyes shone brilliantly and pearls poured forth from his lips — explanations, interpretations, statements — all bathed in purity.

The meal had been served; they had already said the after-the-meal blessing (בִּרְכַּת הַמָּזוֹן); they were pouring the wine into Eliahu's cup and the *shammash* (attendant) was about to open the door. All eyes turned as the door swung on its hinges. Who knows who saw the prophet? But R' Chaim Mendel *did* see him!

He saw a figure of a man with shining face and smiling lips, in the opening. He was dressed like a peasant in sheepskin coat with a leather belt. He seemed to float towards the table. Suddenly, a thump was heard. Everyone stared in alarm. R' Chaim Mendel had fainted and lay stretched out on the floor. R' Chaim Mendel had seen and recognized the man in whose guise Eliahu had chosen to appear; the guise of Baruch Leib, the forest watchman.

They revived him with difficulty. When he had come to, the Rebbe

הלל

The door is closed and the recitation of the *Haggadah* is continued.

לֹא לָנוּ יהוה לֹא לָנוּ, כִּי לְשִׁמְךָ תֵּן כָּבוֹד, עַל חַסְדְּךָ עַל אֲמִתֶּךָ. לָמָּה יֹאמְרוּ הַגּוֹיִם, אַיֵּה נָא אֱלֹהֵיהֶם. וֵאלֹהֵינוּ בַשָּׁמָיִם, כֹּל אֲשֶׁר חָפֵץ עָשָׂה. עֲצַבֵּיהֶם כֶּסֶף וְזָהָב, מַעֲשֵׂה יְדֵי אָדָם. פֶּה

---

indicated that he was to keep his silence. The figure of Eliahu had disappeared and the Rebbe, his face aglow, said, "See, R' Chaim Mendel, heaven agreed to grant you both requests. Now you will no longer be ashamed to join families with your neighbor Baruch Leib."

"Yes, indeed," thought R' Chaim Mendel, "my two requests were granted and I gained a favor which I had never had the impertinence to even dream about; I saw Eliahu" (*Beis Karlin-Stolin* 69).

Fiery Angel of Kotzk

On the evening of the *Seder*, before the recitation of 'Pour Your wrath' (שְׁפֹךְ חֲמָתְךָ), the *Fiery Angel of Kotzk* directed one of the participants to open the door. The chasid ran with speed and joy. But when he returned to his seat, his face betrayed his disappointment; he had failed to see Eliahu.

"Fool!" said the Rebbe. "Eliahu doesn't come through the door. He comes through the mind" (*Bircas Chaim* II).

לָמָּה יֹאמְרוּ הַגּוֹיִם / *Why should the nations say*

Zecher Chaim of Vishva-Vizhnitz

Our death stood before our eyes in Auschwitz. We were starved, humiliated and suffering forced labor, amidst blows and curses, till the last of our strength drained away. All of this did not touch my inner soul. But when a German screamed, "Work, work, cursed Jews, forgotten by God," my heart was torn within me, and I remembered the verse (*Tehillim* 42:4): "My tears were my bread, by day and by night, when it was said to me throughout the day, 'Where is your God?' " (*Zecher Chaim, Yalkut HaTeshuvah*, p. 288).

וֵאלֹקֵינוּ בַשָּׁמָיִם / *Our God is in the heavens*

R' Shmuel Aba of Zichlin

In Lodz there lived a rich Jew, Mordechai by name, who had thrown off the yoke of Torah and *mitzvos*. A member of his family fell ill and, since the doctors could find no cure, he decided to travel to *R' Shmuel Aba of Zichlin* who had become famous as a wonder-worker.

In Zichlin, he waited in line among all the others who had come there and

HALLEL

The door is closed and the recitation of the *Haggadah* is continued.

Not for our sake, HASHEM, not for our sake, but for Your Name's sake give glory, for Your kindness and for Your truth! Why should the nations say, 'Where is their God now?' Our God is in the heavens; whatever He pleases, He does! Their idols are silver and gold, the handiwork of man. They have a mouth,

---

happened to be next to the great Torah scholar R' Shimshon of Lipno. Suddenly, the door to the Rebbe's chamber opened; the Rebbe came out and surveyed the line of the waiting. He approached the wealthy man and examined his expensive fur coat and, in particular, the collar, which was exceptionally handsome.

"Where did you get such a fine coat?" asked the Rebbe.

The man was in shock. Fear had seized him and he was unable to answer.

"How much did you pay for this marvelous collar?" asked the Rebbe.

"Several hundred rubles," answered the man.

The Rebbe now turned to R' Shimshon who was also wearing a coat trimmed with a fur collar. "And what did your coat cost?" he asked.

R' Shimshon mentioned a low sum.

"Why is there such a difference in price?" asked the rebbe.

Mordechai explained that his collar was fashioned from the fur of a rare animal.

"And if all the fur was removed from the two coats, would there still be such a vast difference in their values?" asked the Rebbe.

"No," said the rich man. "Then they would lose whatever worth they have."

"Is that how things are?" said the Rebbe heatedly. "Men strive so hard to attain the fur, the hair of the animal, and without it the value of the coat disappears, yet, you strive so hard to shave off the hair of your beard?" And with that, he returned to his chamber, leaving the rich man stunned.

It was Mordechai's turn to see the Rebbe. He went in and handed the Rebbe his note of request. Even before he read the note, the Rebbe asked him, "Tell me, Mordechai, what's doing in heaven?"

"Rebbe, am I, then, in heaven?" said the man in amazement.

"But you were there!" insisted the Rebbe.

"I don't know what the Rebbe means," he said.

"What are you wondering about? Certainly you were there — in heaven. For had you not been there, how would you know that there is no *gehinnom* in heaven? And I see that you are certain that there is no *gehinnom*, because you are not afraid to sin. You must have been there.

לָהֶם וְלֹא יְדַבֵּרוּ, עֵינַיִם לָהֶם וְלֹא יִרְאוּ. אָזְנַיִם לָהֶם וְלֹא יִשְׁמָעוּ, אַף לָהֶם וְלֹא יְרִיחוּן. יְדֵיהֶם וְלֹא יְמִישׁוּן, רַגְלֵיהֶם וְלֹא יְהַלֵּכוּ, לֹא יֶהְגּוּ בִּגְרוֹנָם. כְּמוֹהֶם יִהְיוּ עֹשֵׂיהֶם, כֹּל אֲשֶׁר בֹּטֵחַ

"Now, I've never been to heaven. But I believe in what *Chazal* tell us — and the paths of heaven were clear to them. They tell us that a *gehinnom* exists and those who violate the commandments of the Torah are punished there. And that is why I am afraid to sin."

The burning words of the Rebbe shook the wealthy man and changed the whole course of his life, and he became a complete *ba'al teshuvah* (ibid. 24).

R' Levi Yitzchak of Berdichev

The father-in-law of *R' Levi Yitzchak of Berdichev* was opposed to chasidus. His son-in-law once traveled to *R' Shmelke of Nikolsburg* and stayed there for several months. Upon his return, his father-in-law said, "I won't reprimand you for joining the sect of chasidim, nor for your leaving home. What happened, happened. But let me just ask you this: Before you went you were already exceptionally learned and devoted to Hashem. What did you learn in your long absence?"

"I learned to know that there is God in heaven," said R' Levi Yitzchak.

His father-in-law smiled, summoned the gentile maid and asked her, "Tell me! Do you know that there is a God in heaven?"

"Certainly!" she said.

"The difference between us," said R' Levi Yitzchak, "is that she *says* she knows, but I *know*!" (*Siach Sarfei Kodesh* V 46).

רַגְלֵיהֶם וְלֹא יְהַלֵּכוּ / *Their feet — they cannot walk*

Divrei Chaim of Sanz

A man came before the *Divrei Chaim of Sanz* and complained of his bitter poverty. The Rebbe advised him to pull up his roots, move to a particular village and open a tavern there. The man took a trip to see the village and found a cluster of huts, isolated and unknown. He returned to the Rebbe with a complaint. "Can a living be had," he asked, "from a few gentiles who are busy in their fields? The village is off the beaten track."

But the Rebbe insisted, "Go there, and you will prosper."

The man borrowed money, bought a cask of whiskey, put his family aboard the wagon and moved to the village. When he arrived, he found a large gathering. The peasants told him, with emotion, that the cross in the church had moved. The report spread rapidly and the village became an

but cannot speak; they have eyes, but cannot see. They have ears, but cannot hear; they have a nose, but cannot smell. Their hands — they cannot feel; their feet — they cannot walk; they cannot utter a sound from their throat. Those who make them should become like them, whoever trusts

---

attraction to throngs of peasants who came on pilgrimage to the church and would drop in for a drink in the local tavern.

The poor Jew prospered and became a man of substance. He married off his children in honorable fashion and managed to save a goodly sum. And since things had gone so well, he traveled to his Rebbe and said, "Rebbe, I'm sick of staying in the village, a Jew in the company of boorish non-Jews. I've saved enough to allow me to move to the city, to pray in a *minyan* and to frequent the court of the Rebbe!"

The Rebbe agreed and the man hired a wagon to move his possessions from the village.

When he arrived in the village, he again encountered a huge gathering of stunned and agitated peasants. He was told that the local priest had suddenly taken ill and had requested that they call the priest from the neighboring village. He had confessed that many years ago, he had been peeved to serve as a priest in such a remote spot. He had moved the cross and spread the report that it had moved of itself, in order to turn the village and its church into a drawing center and thereby have his own star shine more brightly. Now that he was lying in a bed of pain he had revealed what he had done. The peasants who had been duped wished to exact punishment, but the priest forestalled them by dying.

The Jew packed his goods and left. The village once more became an isolated hamlet far off the beaten track (*Divrei Yechezkel Shraga*, pp. 141, 162).

עֵינַיִם לָהֶם וְלֹא יִרְאוּ . . . כְּמוֹהֶם יִהְיוּ עֹשֵׂיהֶם

They have eyes, but cannot see —
Those who make them should become like them

Divrei Chaim of Sanz

At the age of twenty, Yosef Shtecksthil was a delightful young man, diligent in learning, and exceptional in his knowledge of Torah; besides that, healthy and sturdy as an oak. In those days the Austrian regime was exceptionally strict about enforcing its draft laws and there was no prospect that Yosef would be freed from army service. Yosef's father took his tale of trouble and poured it forth to the *Divrei Chaim of Sanz*.

The Rebbe communed with himself and then said, "One folds."

Yosef's father didn't understand the answer, and repeated his story. The Rebbe, for his part, repeated, "One folds."

בָּהֶם. יִשְׂרָאֵל בְּטַח בַּיהוה, עֶזְרָם וּמָגִנָּם הוּא. בֵּית אַהֲרֹן בִּטְחוּ בַיהוה, עֶזְרָם וּמָגִנָּם הוּא. יִרְאֵי יהוה בִּטְחוּ בַיהוה, עֶזְרָם וּמָגִנָּם הוּא.

יהוה זְכָרָנוּ יְבָרֵךְ, יְבָרֵךְ אֶת בֵּית יִשְׂרָאֵל, אֶת בֵּית אַהֲרֹן. יְבָרֵךְ יִרְאֵי יהוה, הַקְּטַנִּים עִם הַגְּדֹלִים. יֹסֵף יהוה עֲלֵיכֶם, עֲלֵיכֶם וְעַל בְּנֵיכֶם. בְּרוּכִים אַתֶּם לַיהוה, עֹשֵׂה שָׁמַיִם וָאָרֶץ. הַשָּׁמַיִם שָׁמַיִם לַיהוה, וְהָאָרֶץ נָתַן לִבְנֵי אָדָם. לֹא הַמֵּתִים יְהַלְלוּ יָהּ, וְלֹא כָּל יֹרְדֵי דוּמָה. וַאֲנַחְנוּ נְבָרֵךְ יָהּ, מֵעַתָּה וְעַד עוֹלָם, הַלְלוּיָהּ.

Yosef's father left, disappointed and depressed. At home he waited daily for the arrival of the induction orders. But days passed, then weeks and months. The authorities seemed to have forgotten about the existence of his son Yosef.

The young man married and had children. When they reached adulthood, he decided to go up to the Holy Land; it had been his long standing dream. He went to the Registration Office to apply for a passport. But, to his surprise, he was told that his name did not appear in the citizen rolls. R' Yosef rushed about from one clerk to another, from one official to another. Finally, they conducted a basic investigation into the matter and discovered that his name did appear in an old register where births were recorded. It had been written on the bottom line of the page; the edge of the sheet had been folded over and the fold had concealed the name. It had never been transferred anew to the draft register. Only then did they understand the Divrei Chaim's comment — "One folds" (*Dos Yiddishe Licht*).

יְבָרֵךְ יִרְאֵי ה׳, הַקְּטַנִּים עִם הַגְּדוֹלִים
He will bless those who fear Hashem, the small as well as the great

R' Shlomo Leib of Lenchno

Those who fear *Hashem* will be considered blessed if the great and the small will live *together*, without the great being haughty towards the small (*Eser Ataros* 56).

in them! O Israel, trust in HASHEM; — their help and their shield is He! House of Aaron, trust in HASHEM; their help and their shield is He! You who fear HASHEM, trust in HASHEM; their help and their shield is He!

HASHEM Who has remembered us will bless — He will bless the House of Israel; He will bless the House of Aharon; He will bless those who fear HASHEM, the small as well as the great. May HASHEM increase upon you, upon you and upon your children! You are blessed of HASHEM, maker of heaven and earth. As for the heavens — the heavens are HASHEM's, but the earth He has given to mankind. Neither the dead can praise God, nor any who descend into silence; but we will bless God from this time and forever. Halleluyah!

הַשָּׁמַיִם שָׁמַיִם לַה׳ וְהָאָרֶץ נָתַן לִבְנֵי אָדָם

The heavens are Hashem's, but the earth He has given to mankind

R' Chanoch Henoch of Alexander

The heavens are *Hashem's* — they are already heavenly; the earth He has given to mankind — to make it heavenly (*Siach Sarfei Kodesh* I 545).

וְהָאָרֶץ נָתַן לִבְנֵי אָדָם – לְאַחַר בְּרָכָה

But the earth He has given to mankind — after they recite the blessing (Berachos 35a)

R' Yissachar Ber of Volbroz

When *R' Yissachar Ber of Volbroz* dwelt in the shadow of his rebbe, the *Fiery Angel of Moglenitza*, he would fast from *Shabbos* to *Shabbos*. Once, when the Fiery Angel was returning from the *mikveh*, on a Wednesday, he made his way to R' Yissachar Ber's lodgings. The disciple received his master with awe and wished to serve him a cup of coffee.

"How can you serve someone with food that does not belong to you?" asked his master. "*Chazal* say that 'the earth and it's fullness is *Hashem*'s' (*Tehillim* 24:1) — before man pronounces a blessing over the produce of the earth it is to be viewed as the property of God. But after man pronounces the blessing, it becomes his, for the verse says: 'the earth He has given to mankind' (ibid. 115:16). If *you* first make a blessing and taste of the food it will be yours. Only then can you serve of it to me."

אָהַבְתִּי כִּי יִשְׁמַע יהוה, אֶת קוֹלִי תַּחֲנוּנָי. כִּי הִטָּה אָזְנוֹ לִי, וּבְיָמַי אֶקְרָא. אֲפָפוּנִי חֶבְלֵי מָוֶת, וּמְצָרֵי שְׁאוֹל מְצָאוּנִי, צָרָה וְיָגוֹן אֶמְצָא. וּבְשֵׁם יהוה אֶקְרָא, אָנָּה יהוה מַלְּטָה נַפְשִׁי. חַנּוּן יהוה וְצַדִּיק, וֵאלֹהֵינוּ מְרַחֵם. שֹׁמֵר פְּתָאִים יהוה, דַּלּוֹתִי וְלִי יְהוֹשִׁיעַ. שׁוּבִי נַפְשִׁי לִמְנוּחָיְכִי, כִּי יהוה גָּמַל עָלָיְכִי. כִּי חִלַּצְתָּ נַפְשִׁי מִמָּוֶת, אֶת עֵינִי מִן דִּמְעָה, אֶת רַגְלִי מִדֶּחִי. אֶתְהַלֵּךְ לִפְנֵי יהוה, בְּאַרְצוֹת הַחַיִּים. הֶאֱמַנְתִּי כִּי אֲדַבֵּר, אֲנִי עָנִיתִי מְאֹד. אֲנִי אָמַרְתִּי בְחָפְזִי, כָּל הָאָדָם כֹּזֵב.

מָה אָשִׁיב לַיהוה, כָּל תַּגְמוּלוֹהִי עָלָי. כּוֹס יְשׁוּעוֹת אֶשָּׂא, וּבְשֵׁם יהוה אֶקְרָא.

R' Yissachar Ber said nothing in return, but made the blessing immediately and tasted the drink.

When the Rebbe left he said with astonishment to his *shammash* (attendant), "That is a true disciple. Today is Wednesday. He had but two more days to go to complete a fast from *Shabbos* to *Shabbos* which the devotional literature praises highly. Yet, he broke his fast without a word in order to serve me, because he considers me to be his Rebbe!" (*Ohel Yissachar* 23).

לֹא הַמֵּתִים יְהַלְלוּ יָ־הּ / *Neither the dead can praise God*

Sainted Yehudi

The *Sainted Yehudi* once felt, during a meal, that he was enjoying the food. He prayed to be afflicted with epilepsy and fell down in a convulsion. The family summoned his disciple, *R' Simchah Bunim of Pshische,* and he directed that they sing "neither the dead can praise God." They sang and the Sainted Yehudi arose, sat down to the table and finished the meal.

R' Simchah Bunim said that it was time for the *ma'ariv* prayer, to which the Rebbe replied, "When I rolled about on the ground, I had a victory over my great adversary, my body. And I decided to pray *ma'ariv*, then and there, because there was nothing to stop me in my service to Hashem. I felt very pleased with the yoke of heaven and wished to cling to the Creator and not rise again. But when I heard them singing 'neither the dead can praise God,' I decided to rise and continue to live" (*Or HaNer* p. 12).

I love Him, for HASHEM hears my voice, my supplications. As He has inclined His ear to me, so in my days shall I call. The pains of death encircled me; the confines of the grave have found me; trouble and sorrow I would find. Then I would invoke the Name of HASHEM: 'Please HASHEM, save my soul.' Gracious is HASHEM and righteous, our God is merciful. HASHEM protects the simple; I was brought low, but He saved me. Return, my soul, to your rest; for HASHEM has been kind to you. For You have delivered my soul from death, my eyes from tears, my feet from stumbling. I shall walk before HASHEM in the lands of the living. I have kept faith although I say: 'I suffer exceedingly.' I said in my haste: 'All mankind is deceitful.'

How can I repay HASHEM for all His kindness to me? I will raise the cup of salvations and the Name of

---

צָרָה וְיָגוֹן אֶמְצָא. וּבְשֵׁם ה׳ אֶקְרָא, אָנָּה ה׳ מַלְּטָה נַפְשִׁי / *Trouble and sorrow I would find. Then I would invoke the Name of Hashem: 'Please Hashem, save my soul'*

R' Dovid of Lelov

There are those who imagine that when they are in trouble — "trouble and sorrow I would find" — then it is the time to "invoke the name of Hashem." But when the Holy One aids them and they lack nothing, they have nothing for which to pray. David *HaMelech* begs: "Please *Hashem,* save my soul" — save me from the improper idea that only troubles can effect prayer (*Tiferes Beis David* 104).

R' Yitzchak of Bohush

The *mishnah* declares that man should bless the Holy One in the same spirit both for the good which he receives and the bad (*Berachos* 9:5). The *gemara* (*Berachos* 60b) suggests that this is derived from two passages in *Tehillim* which use the identical phrase to express praise of God: "I will raise the cup of salvations *and the name of Hashem I will invoke*" (116:13), which refers to the good which man experiences; "trouble and sorrow I would find. *Then I would invoke the name of Hashem*" (ibid. 3,4), which speaks of the bad.

However, the praise in the instance of the good appears in the same verse as the reference to the good, whereas reference to trouble, the bad, is found in one verse and the praise in the following verse. There is a break in the flow.

נְדָרַי לַיהוה אֲשַׁלֵּם, נֶגְדָה נָּא לְכָל עַמּוֹ. יָקָר בְּעֵינֵי יהוה, הַמָּוְתָה לַחֲסִידָיו. אָנָּה יהוה כִּי אֲנִי עַבְדֶּךָ, אֲנִי עַבְדְּךָ, בֶּן אֲמָתֶךָ, פִּתַּחְתָּ לְמוֹסֵרָי. לְךָ אֶזְבַּח זֶבַח תּוֹדָה, וּבְשֵׁם יהוה אֶקְרָא. נְדָרַי לַיהוה אֲשַׁלֵּם, נֶגְדָה נָּא לְכָל עַמּוֹ. בְּחַצְרוֹת בֵּית יהוה, בְּתוֹכֵכִי יְרוּשָׁלָיִם הַלְלוּיָהּ.

הַלְלוּ אֶת יהוה, כָּל גּוֹיִם, שַׁבְּחוּהוּ כָּל הָאֻמִּים. כִּי גָבַר עָלֵינוּ חַסְדּוֹ, וֶאֱמֶת יהוה לְעוֹלָם, הַלְלוּיָהּ.

הוֹדוּ לַיהוה כִּי טוֹב, כִּי לְעוֹלָם חַסְדּוֹ.
יֹאמַר נָא יִשְׂרָאֵל, כִּי לְעוֹלָם חַסְדּוֹ.
יֹאמְרוּ נָא בֵית אַהֲרֹן, כִּי לְעוֹלָם חַסְדּוֹ.
יֹאמְרוּ נָא יִרְאֵי יהוה, כִּי לְעוֹלָם חַסְדּוֹ.

This both reflects a truism and suggests a directive. One can express praise for the good immediately, in an instant response, but not so with the bad. Then, one must pause and give thought to what good is concealed within it and recognize, thereby, that whatever heaven does is only for the good. Then, and only then, is it possible to express praise (*Ner Yisrael* I 148).

הַלְלוּ אֶת ה׳, כָּל גּוֹיִם . . . כִּי גָבַר עָלֵינוּ חַסְדּוֹ

Praise Hashem, all nations . . . for His kindness has overwhelmed us

Chozeh of Lublin

The difficulty of the verse is well known: Why should the nations praise Hashem because His kindness overwhelmed *us*?

A non-Jew was an out-and-out anti-Semite in general, and in particular, he had an even more-burning hatred towards a chasid who was exceptional in his service to Hashem. The chasid could be found in the *beis knesses* each day, from before dawn to late at night. The Jew-hater dug a deep pit on the road where the chasid regularly walked early in the morning on his way to the *beis knesses*. He was certain that the Jew would not sense the pit in the pre-dawn dark.

The Holy One, however, arranged that the chasid receive a distinguished guest that night and the two were up to a late hour "speaking in learning."

HASHEM I will invoke. My vows to HASHEM I will pay, in the presence, now, of His entire people. Difficult in the eyes of HASHEM is the death of His devout ones. Please, HASHEM — for I am Your servant, I am Your servant, son of Your handmaid — You have released my bonds. To You I will sacrifice thanksgiving offerings, and the name of HASHEM I will invoke. My vows to HASHEM I will pay, in the presence, now, of His entire people. In the courtyards of the House of HASHEM, in your midst, O Jerusalem, Halleluyah!

Praise HASHEM, all nations; praise Him, all the states! For His kindness has overwhelmed us, and the truth of HASHEM is eternal, Halleluyah!

Give thanks to HASHEM for He is good;
His kindness endures forever!
Let Israel say: His kindness endures forever!
Let the House of Aharon say:
His kindness endures forever!
Let those who fear HASHEM say:
His kindness endures forever!

Thus, the chasid awoke later than usual — after the light of day. On his way to the *beis knesses*, he saw the pit and avoided it. The non-Jew noticed him and asked him why he had gotten up later that day. The chasid told him about his guest. And then, the gentile praised the Holy One Who had saved the chasid, without his knowledge, from death.

That is the meaning of the verse. Only the gentiles know what evils they contrive for us and how the Holy One foils their plans. We, on our part, exemplify that which *Chazal* say: "He who experiences a miracle is unaware of it" (*Nifleos HaRabi* 366).

יֹאמְרוּ נָא יִרְאֵי ה׳ / *Let those who fear Hashem say . . .*

Maggid of Tchernobil

They were trying times for Israel. The draft laws weighed heavily on the Jews of Russia. The soldiers of the czar would swoop down and snatch youngsters from their mother's lap. The *tzaddikim* of the time assembled in alarm and traveled to the eldest among them, to *R' Mordechai, the Maggid of Tchernobil*.

Some forty had gathered together and were in Tchernobil for *Shabbos*. And just as the Rebbe came to the table and was about to recite the *kiddush*,

מִן הַמֵּצַר קָרָאתִי יָּהּ, עָנָנִי בַמֶּרְחָב יָהּ. יהוה לִי לֹא אִירָא, מַה יַּעֲשֶׂה לִי אָדָם. יהוה לִי בְּעֹזְרָי, וַאֲנִי אֶרְאֶה בְשֹׂנְאָי. טוֹב לַחֲסוֹת בַּיהוה, מִבְּטֹחַ בָּאָדָם. טוֹב לַחֲסוֹת בַּיהוה, מִבְּטֹחַ בִּנְדִיבִים. כָּל גּוֹיִם סְבָבוּנִי, בְּשֵׁם יהוה כִּי אֲמִילַם. סַבּוּנִי גַם סְבָבוּנִי, בְּשֵׁם יהוה כִּי אֲמִילַם.

---

a woman burst into the room and cried out in a broken voice, "Help me, Rebbe! They have taken away my only son, the apple of my eye!" All present wept, but the Rebbe, who was caught up in his devotions, moved not a whit.

The others gave a sign to *R' Moshe of Slavito*, the son of *R' Pinchas of Koritz*, to act as their spokesman. He called out in a tearful tone, "Sainted Maggid, where is Hashem's kindness (חַסְדֵי ה׳)?"

The Rebbe answered not a word. He made *kiddush*, broke bread and ate the required measure (כְּזַיִת). And, as all kept their silence, he began. "In *Hallel* we find," he said, " 'Let Israel say, His kindness endures forever. Let the House of Aharon say . . . Let those who fear Hashem say.' We have three categories here: There are clear acts of kindness for which all of Israel can give praise to Hashem and say, 'His kindness endures forever.' There are hidden acts of kindness which the masses of Israel see as harsh decrees. We pray that at least the 'House of Aharon,' those of the generation who are devoted to Hashem, might fathom their true meaning and see the kindness of Hashem within them. But there are edicts which are so terrible that even the servants of Hashem, the *tzaddikim*, are confused by them and see them as a sign of dread self-concealment of Hashem from the world (הֶסְתֵּר פָּנִים). Then, we pray that at least 'those who fear Hashem,' the greatest of the *tzaddikim* of the age, should understand and see Hashem's kindness within them.

"What can I do if heaven has revealed to me that even this decree is filled with heavenly kindness from the kiln of the All-present? How can I pray that it be abolished?" (*Admorei Tchernobil* 246).

R' Mordechai Menachem Mendel of Vurka

When the authorities decreed that Jews must shave off their beards, R' Moshe Kohen fled from Warsaw to the court of his rebbe, *R' Mordechai Menachem Mendel of Vurka*. *R' Yisrael of Ruzhin* had just departed this world at the time and the Rebbe remarked to his disciple, "My father and the Rebbe of Ruzhin are rejoicing now."

"Can anyone be happy in this time of trouble?" said R' Moshe, in pain.

"They see, in heaven, that all the decrees are for the good and they feel no suffering because of them," said the Rebbe.

From the straits did I call upon God; God answered me with expansiveness. HASHEM is with me, I have no fear; how can man affect me? HASHEM is with me through my helpers; therefore I can face my foes. It is better to take refuge in HASHEM than to rely on man. It is better to take refuge in HASHEM than to rely on nobles. All the nations surround me; in the Name of HASHEM I cut them down! They encircle me, they also surround me; in the Name of HASHEM I cut them down!

"But wasn't your father aware, while he was alive, that all the decrees are for the good? And yet, we saw that he was always pained by the sufferings of Israel," said the chasid.

To which the Rebbe replied, "Hearing is not seeing" (*Eser Zechuyos* 19).

R' Yitzchak of Skver

When my sainted grandfather, *R' Nachum of Tchernobil*, visited *R' Baruch of Mezhibuz*, R' Baruch asked him, "What do you think of me?"

"I think that you are truly God fearing," said R' Nachum.

Some time later, R' Baruch met *R' Levi Yitzchak of Berdichev*, and R' Baruch asked him, "What do you think of me?"

"I think that you are truly God fearing," answered R' Levi Yitzchak.

R' Baruch was happy. "Now I know that I am God fearing," he said, "because two honest and proper witnesses have said so."

"Is fear of Heaven a small thing?" asks the *gemara*. And it answers, "Yes, to Moshe it is a small matter" (*Berachos* 33b). Wonder of wonders! There are chasidim who have reached the level of our teacher Moshe, and fear of Heaven is a small matter in their eyes. R' Baruch of Mezhibuz was proud that he was said to possess it. Yet these chasidim do not find it proper to praise their rebbes for this quality. They think that it's not enough to consider him a rebbe for only such an inconsequential trait (*Ma'asios U'Ma'amarim Yekarim*).

טוֹב לַחֲסוֹת בַּה׳ מִבְּטֹחַ בִּנְדִיבִים

It is better to take refuge in Hashem than to rely on nobles

Fiery Angel of Kotzk

A very poor man came before the *Fiery Angel of Kotzk* and told him that he had a grown daughter to marry off, but he could not raise the dowry. The Rebbe gave him a letter for the princely, rich R' Moshe Rotenberg of Chantshin, asking him to help the bearer of the letter to the best of his ability.

The poor man wore out his legs on the journey, until he finally reached Chantshin and the wealthy home of R' Moshe; he was well received.

סַבּוּנִי כִדְבֹרִים דֹּעֲכוּ כְּאֵשׁ קוֹצִים, בְּשֵׁם יהוה כִּי אֲמִילַם. דָּחֹה דְחִיתַנִי לִנְפֹּל, וַיהוה עֲזָרָנִי. עָזִּי וְזִמְרָת יָהּ, וַיְהִי לִי לִישׁוּעָה. קוֹל רִנָּה וִישׁוּעָה, בְּאָהֳלֵי צַדִּיקִים, יְמִין יהוה עֹשָׂה חָיִל. יְמִין יהוה רוֹמֵמָה, יְמִין יהוה עֹשָׂה חָיִל. לֹא אָמוּת כִּי אֶחְיֶה, וַאֲסַפֵּר מַעֲשֵׂי יָהּ. יַסֹּר יִסְּרַנִּי יָּהּ, וְלַמָּוֶת לֹא נְתָנָנִי. פִּתְחוּ לִי שַׁעֲרֵי צֶדֶק, אָבֹא בָם אוֹדֶה יָהּ. זֶה הַשַּׁעַר לַיהוה, צַדִּיקִים יָבֹאוּ בוֹ. אוֹדְךָ כִּי עֲנִיתָנִי, וַתְּהִי לִי לִישׁוּעָה. אוֹדְךָ כִּי עֲנִיתָנִי, וַתְּהִי לִי לִישׁוּעָה. אֶבֶן מָאֲסוּ הַבּוֹנִים, הָיְתָה לְרֹאשׁ פִּנָּה. אֶבֶן מָאֲסוּ הַבּוֹנִים, הָיְתָה לְרֹאשׁ פִּנָּה. מֵאֵת יהוה הָיְתָה זֹּאת, הִיא נִפְלָאת בְּעֵינֵינוּ. מֵאֵת יהוה הָיְתָה זֹּאת, הִיא נִפְלָאת בְּעֵינֵינוּ. זֶה הַיּוֹם עָשָׂה יהוה, נָגִילָה וְנִשְׂמְחָה בוֹ. זֶה הַיּוֹם עָשָׂה יהוה, נָגִילָה וְנִשְׂמְחָה בוֹ.

R' Moshe inquired as to his wishes and was given the Rebbe's letter. The poor man knew that the rich R' Moshe gave charity widely and generously. Now, with the letter, he would probably give far and above what was usual for him. To the poor man's surprise, he was given a single, lone ruble! He was highly insulted and complained that his expenses for the trip amounted to more than that, let alone the toil and troubles of the road. And there was the return trip. But nothing he said could move the man; he left dejected.

He began to make his way back with downcast shoulders. And lo! A grand carriage pulled up beside him and R' Moshe's face peered out. The servants descended and unloaded costly dress and many gifts; the philanthropist, in person, handed him a bag of money, sufficient to cover the costs of the wedding.

The poor man could not contain himself. "Since you intended giving so much, why did you cause me all that anguish?" he asked.

"I'll tell you," said R' Moshe. "When you came to me with the Rebbe's letter, I saw that you had forgotten that there is a God in Israel. I wanted you to be aware that it is useless to seek salvation from man; you must trust in Hashem. Now, help has come from Him, and you must give praise only to Him" (*Siach Sarfei Kodesh* IV 32).

They encircle me like bees, but they are extinguished as a fire does thorns; in the Name of HASHEM I cut them down! You pushed me hard that I might fall, but HASHEM assisted me. God is my might and my praise, and He was a salvation for me. The sound of rejoicing and salvation is in the tents of the righteous: 'HASHEM's right hand does valiantly. HASHEM's right hand is raised triumphantly; HASHEM's right hand does valiantly!' I shall not die! But I shall live and relate the deeds of God. God has chastened me exceedingly, but He did not let me die. Open for me the gates of righteousness, I will enter them and thank God. This is the gate of HASHEM; the righteous shall enter through it. I thank You for You have answered me and become my salvation. I thank You for You have answered me and become my salvation. The stone the builders despised has become the cornerstone. The stone the builders despised has become the cornerstone. This emanated from HASHEM; it is wondrous in our eyes. This emanated from HASHEM; it is wondrous in our eyes. This is the day HASHEM has made; let us rejoice and be glad on it. This is the day HASHEM has made; let us rejoice and be glad on it.

לֹא אָמוּת כִּי אֶחְיֶה / *I shall not die, but I shall live*

R' Shlomo Leib of Lenchno

The verse can be understood as follows: "I shall not die *while I live" — while I am still alive. I will not be like the wicked who are called dead even when still alive (*Eser Ataros* 59).

[*while I live* (כִּי אֶחְיֶה). כִּי can be used as *when*; see *Rosh Hashanah* 3a and *Rashi's* commentary there. R' Shlomo Leib interpreted the כִּי here as *when* or *while.*]

פִּתְחוּ לִי שַׁעֲרֵי צֶדֶק / *Open for me the gates of righteousness*

Chidushei HaRim

"Fortunate is the man who hearkens *to me to keep guard at my doors, day by day; to guard the doorposts of my openings" (*Mishlei* 8:34). Each man must wait expectantly at the door for the moment it opens, so that he might immediately enter, before it closes once more.

---

*to me: *wisdom* which *Chazal* interpret as Torah.]

אָנָּא יהוה הוֹשִׁיעָה נָּא.
אָנָּא יהוה הוֹשִׁיעָה נָּא.
אָנָּא יהוה הַצְלִיחָה נָא.
אָנָּא יהוה הַצְלִיחָה נָא.

בָּרוּךְ הַבָּא בְּשֵׁם יהוה, בֵּרַכְנוּכֶם מִבֵּית יהוה.
בָּרוּךְ הַבָּא בְּשֵׁם יהוה, בֵּרַכְנוּכֶם מִבֵּית
יהוה. אֵל יהוה וַיָּאֶר לָנוּ, אִסְרוּ חַג בַּעֲבֹתִים, עַד
קַרְנוֹת הַמִּזְבֵּחַ. אֵל יהוה וַיָּאֶר לָנוּ, אִסְרוּ חַג
בַּעֲבֹתִים, עַד קַרְנוֹת הַמִּזְבֵּחַ. אֵלִי אַתָּה וְאוֹדֶךָּ,
אֱלֹהַי אֲרוֹמְמֶךָּ. אֵלִי אַתָּה וְאוֹדֶךָּ, אֱלֹהַי אֲרוֹמְמֶךָּ.
הוֹדוּ לַיהוה כִּי טוֹב, כִּי לְעוֹלָם חַסְדּוֹ. הוֹדוּ לַיהוה
כִּי טוֹב, כִּי לְעוֹלָם חַסְדּוֹ.

הוֹדוּ לַיהוה כִּי טוֹב כִּי לְעוֹלָם חַסְדּוֹ.
הוֹדוּ לֵאלֹהֵי הָאֱלֹהִים כִּי לְעוֹלָם חַסְדּוֹ.
הוֹדוּ לַאֲדֹנֵי הָאֲדֹנִים כִּי לְעוֹלָם חַסְדּוֹ.
לְעֹשֵׂה נִפְלָאוֹת גְּדֹלוֹת לְבַדּוֹ כִּי לְעוֹלָם חַסְדּוֹ.

When the gates of the heart open, one should increase his efforts in serving Hashem. For when those gates lock, it becomes very difficult to enter. That is why we plead: "Open for me the gates of righteousness," and follow it up, immediately, with "I will enter them and thank God" (*Siach Sarfei Kodesh* I 468).

לְעֹשֵׂה נִפְלָאוֹת גְּדֹלוֹת לְבַדּוֹ
To Him Who alone performs great wonders

Ba'al Shem Tov

On his way to *Eretz Yisrael* the *Ba'al Shem Tov* was detained in Constantinople. It was the eve of Pesach and the Ba'al Shem and his daughter were in the strange, foreign city. He went to the *beis midrash* to study; she took her father's shirt to the river for washing. And while scrubbing the shirt, she wept that although all the other Jews would sit down to a *Seder* in their homes that evening, she and her

Please, HASHEM, save now!
Please, HASHEM, save now!
Please, HASHEM, bring success now!
Please, HASHEM, bring success now!

Blessed is he who comes in the Name of HASHEM; we bless you from the House of HASHEM. Blessed is he who comes in the Name of HASHEM; we bless you from the House of HASHEM. HASHEM is God, He illuminated for us; bind the festival offering with cords until the corners of the Altar. HASHEM is God, He illuminated for us; bind the festival offering with cords until the corners of the Altar. You are my God, and I will thank You; my God, I will exalt You. You are my God, and I will thank You; my God, I will exalt You. Give thanks to HASHEM, for He is good; His kindness endures forever. Give thanks to HASHEM, for He is good; His kindness endures forever.

Give thanks to HASHEM for He is good,
for His kindness endures forever.
Give thanks to the God of the heavenly powers,
for His kindness endures forever.
Give thanks to the Lord of the lords,
for His kindness endures forever.
To Him Who alone performs great wonders,
for His kindness endures forever.

---

father had no place to celebrate the festival. A rich Jew passed by and saw the weeping girl; he asked why she wept and she, in turn, told him about her father's greatness and described their solitude in the great city.

"Don't cry," said the wealthy man. "You and your father are invited to be my guests." The girl led him to the Ba'al Shem and the rich man invited him to his home, gave him a room and honored him greatly.

When it was time for the *minchah* prayer, the host entered the guest room to call the Ba'al Shem. In amazement he saw the great man asleep with tears running from his eyes. Heart pounding, he stood and contemplated the sight. The Ba'al Shem woke suddenly and said with great fervor, "To Him Who alone performs great wonders," and he went off to the *beis knesses*.

When they returned home, the Ba'al Shem conducted the *Seder* with

לְעֹשֵׂה הַשָּׁמַיִם בִּתְבוּנָה כִּי לְעוֹלָם חַסְדּוֹ.
לְרֹקַע הָאָרֶץ עַל הַמָּיִם כִּי לְעוֹלָם חַסְדּוֹ.
לְעֹשֵׂה אוֹרִים גְּדֹלִים כִּי לְעוֹלָם חַסְדּוֹ.
אֶת הַשֶּׁמֶשׁ לְמֶמְשֶׁלֶת בַּיּוֹם כִּי לְעוֹלָם חַסְדּוֹ.
אֶת הַיָּרֵחַ וְכוֹכָבִים לְמֶמְשְׁלוֹת בַּלָּיְלָה
כִּי לְעוֹלָם חַסְדּוֹ.
לְמַכֵּה מִצְרַיִם בִּבְכוֹרֵיהֶם כִּי לְעוֹלָם חַסְדּוֹ.
וַיּוֹצֵא יִשְׂרָאֵל מִתּוֹכָם כִּי לְעוֹלָם חַסְדּוֹ.

---

emotion and sanctity, and when they reached the verse "To Him Who alone performs great wonders," he repeated it, time and again, his face radiant like a torch of fire. When they had finished reciting the *Haggadah,* the Ba'al Shem rose and said, " 'In every generation, they rise against us to annihilate us. But the Holy One, Blessed is He, rescues us from their hand!' Listen and I will tell you of the miracle that Hashem has worked on this night.

"As you know, the sultan, the Turkish ruler, has a Jewish advisor, named Moshe. Moshe has many enemies at court, and one of them accompanied the sultan to the Jewish quarter, that he might use the occasion of the festival to incite the sultan against the Jews. When they saw the sparkling lights and heard the happy voices, the sultan asked what it was all about, and this enemy of the Jews vilified them and their festivals. He said that their customs differed from those of the rest of the populace and they held themselves apart from all others. This led to a denouncement of the sultan's advisor, Moshe, as a traitor who was prepared to make a pact with the sultan's enemies and hand the kingdom over into their hands. And his fellow Jews would be the first to side with those enemies. It would be in the best interests of His Highness, the sultan, he said, to banish the Jews from the realm and hang Moshe, the advisor, that all might hear and fear! The sultan was persuaded; he removed his signet ring and gave it to the enemy of the Jews that he might sign and seal the decree of banishment and the writ of execution of the advisor.

"When I saw this, I wept and pleaded before the Heavenly Throne; my prayers did not return unanswered. The sultan returned to his palace and told his mother, the dowager queen, about what had happened. She burst into tears and said, 'What have you done? Do you wish to bring destruction upon us? Remember the fate of all those who oppressed the Jews — Pharaoh and Haman and Titus! What evil have the Jews ever done to you? What crime have you found among them? They are loyal to the empire; they enrich the country with their trade and fill your coffers with their taxes. And

To Him Who made the heavens with understanding,
for His kindness endures forever.
To Him Who spread out the earth upon the waters,
for His kindness endures forever.
To Him Who made great lights,
for His kindness endures forever.
The sun for the reign of the day,
for His kindness endures forever.
The moon and the stars for the reign of the night,
for His kindness endures forever.
To Him Who smote Egypt through their firstborn,
for His kindness endures forever.
And brought Israel forth from their midst,
for His kindness endures forever.

Moshe was your father's advisor before you. He has served the court loyally and his advice has always proven sound! What have you done, my son?'

"The sultan's face fell and he said, 'Truly, I have acted foolishly. But what can I do now? I gave the Jew-hater my signet ring.'

" 'Summon Moshe,' said his mother. 'His advice will help us this time, also.'

"The sultan summoned Moshe, who, after due consideration, said, 'There is a simple solution. When my enemy comes to present the sealed edict tomorrow, let the palace guards seize him; let him be accused of stealing the ring and be executed immediately, without delay.'

"The sultan and his mother accepted the clever solution. When I saw this, I praised Hashem 'Who alone performs great wonders.' "

The next day, when the Jews assembled for prayer, they learned that the Jew-hater had arrived at the palace before daybreak, the guards found the sultan's ring on his person and he was executed. The sensational news did not surprise Moshe the advisor, nor the wealthy man who had heard about it the previous night, at the close of the *Seder* before the event had even taken place. He told all those present who it was that had been responsible, through his tears, for the miracle. Everyone turned to give praise to the Ba'al Shem. But he said, "Do not praise me. 'Give thanks to Hashem, for He is good — to Him Who alone performs great wonders!' " *(Sipurei Chasidim)*.

לְעֹשֵׂה הַשָּׁמַיִם בִּתְבוּנָה / *To Him Who made the heavens with understanding*

R' Simchah Bunim of Pshischa

Certainly the Holy One made the heavens with understanding. Did anyone ever

בְּיָד חֲזָקָה וּבִזְרוֹעַ נְטוּיָה כִּי לְעוֹלָם חַסְדּוֹ.
לְגֹזֵר יַם סוּף לִגְזָרִים כִּי לְעוֹלָם חַסְדּוֹ.
וְהֶעֱבִיר יִשְׂרָאֵל בְּתוֹכוֹ כִּי לְעוֹלָם חַסְדּוֹ.
וְנִעֵר פַּרְעֹה וְחֵילוֹ בְיַם סוּף כִּי לְעוֹלָם חַסְדּוֹ.
לְמוֹלִיךְ עַמּוֹ בַּמִּדְבָּר כִּי לְעוֹלָם חַסְדּוֹ.
לְמַכֵּה מְלָכִים גְּדֹלִים כִּי לְעוֹלָם חַסְדּוֹ.
וַיַּהֲרֹג מְלָכִים אַדִּירִים כִּי לְעוֹלָם חַסְדּוֹ.
לְסִיחוֹן מֶלֶךְ הָאֱמֹרִי כִּי לְעוֹלָם חַסְדּוֹ.
וּלְעוֹג מֶלֶךְ הַבָּשָׁן כִּי לְעוֹלָם חַסְדּוֹ.
וְנָתַן אַרְצָם לְנַחֲלָה כִּי לְעוֹלָם חַסְדּוֹ.
נַחֲלָה לְיִשְׂרָאֵל עַבְדּוֹ כִּי לְעוֹלָם חַסְדּוֹ.
שֶׁבְּשִׁפְלֵנוּ זָכַר לָנוּ כִּי לְעוֹלָם חַסְדּוֹ.
וַיִּפְרְקֵנוּ מִצָּרֵינוּ כִּי לְעוֹלָם חַסְדּוֹ.
נֹתֵן לֶחֶם לְכָל בָּשָׂר כִּי לְעוֹלָם חַסְדּוֹ.
הוֹדוּ לְאֵל הַשָּׁמָיִם כִּי לְעוֹלָם חַסְדּוֹ.

---

imagine that they were sewn with needles?

The verse is not discussing the *means* by which the heavens were fashioned but their **purpose*. Hashem fashioned the heavens for the sake of contemplation, so that by contemplating them, we might understand His greatness, as it is written: "Lift your eyes on high, and see who created these" (*Yeshayahu* 40:26) (*Siach Sarfei Kodesh* I 221).

נֹתֵן לֶחֶם לְכָל בָּשָׂר
He gives nourishment to all flesh

R' Tzvi Elimelech of Dinov

R' Tzvi Elimelech of Dinov dedicated a particular hour each day to meeting with tradesmen and merchants in his community, one at a time. Each would

---

* *purpose*. The ב can be used to express *purpose*; see *Rashi* to *Bereishis* 1:1.

With strong hand and outstretched arm,
for His kindness endures forever.
To Him Who divided the Sea of Reeds into parts,
for His kindness endures forever.
And caused Israel to pass through it,
for His kindness endures forever.
And threw Pharaoh and his army into the Sea of
Reeds, for His kindness endures forever.
To Him Who led His people through the wilderness,
for His kindness endures forever.
To Him Who smote great kings,
for His kindness endures forever.
And slew mighty kings,
for His kindness endures forever.
Sichon, king of the Emorites,
for His kindness endures forever.
And Og, king of Bashan,
for His kindness endures forever.
And presented their land as a heritage,
for His kindness endures forever.
A heritage for Israel, His servant,
for His kindness endures forever.
In our lowliness He remembered us,
for His kindness endures forever.
And released us from our tormentors,
for His kindness endures forever.
He gives nourishment to all flesh,
for His kindness endures forever.
Give thanks to God of the heavens,
for His kindness endures forever.

---

present a detailed account of his income and expenses for the entire year. He was able to show each one, clear as day, that his expenses outweighed his income. This proved to them that their sustenance was not a natural phenomenon; they thus came face to face with the Divine Presence (*Eser Tzachtzachos* 28).

נִשְׁמַת כָּל חַי תְּבָרֵךְ אֶת שִׁמְךָ יהוה אֱלֹהֵינוּ וְרוּחַ כָּל בָּשָׂר תְּפָאֵר וּתְרוֹמֵם זִכְרְךָ מַלְכֵּנוּ תָּמִיד. מִן הָעוֹלָם וְעַד הָעוֹלָם אַתָּה אֵל וּמִבַּלְעָדֶיךָ אֵין לָנוּ מֶלֶךְ גּוֹאֵל וּמוֹשִׁיעַ פּוֹדֶה וּמַצִּיל וּמְפַרְנֵס וְעוֹנֶה וּמְרַחֵם בְּכָל עֵת צָרָה וְצוּקָה. אֵין לָנוּ מֶלֶךְ עוֹזֵר וְסוֹמֵךְ אֶלָּא אָתָּה. אֱלֹהֵי הָרִאשׁוֹנִים וְהָאַחֲרוֹנִים אֱלוֹהַּ כָּל בְּרִיּוֹת אֲדוֹן כָּל תּוֹלָדוֹת הַמְהֻלָּל בְּרֹב הַתִּשְׁבָּחוֹת הַמְנַהֵג עוֹלָמוֹ בְּחֶסֶד

נִשְׁמַת כָּל חַי תְּבָרֵךְ אֶת שִׁמְךָ / *The soul of every living being shall bless Your name*

Chozeh of Lublin

If a man, for a moment, forgets to cling to his Creator, he deserves instant death. Yet, if he clings to his Creator, night and day, then he is no different from the littlest worm which constantly does the will of its Maker. That is the purpose for which man was created. What, then, does he have to be proud of — of the fact that he is not derelict in his duty? (*Tefillah LeMoshe, Nitzavim*).

כָּל חַי / *Every living being*

R' Mordechai Yosef of Izbitza

A very young Gershon Henoch (later the Rebbe of Radzin) ran to the river and bumped into the erudite Rabbi of Lomaz, R' David, who was numbered among the elder chasidim of Gershon Henoch's grandfather, *R' Mordechai Yosef of Izbitza*. The elderly R' David scolded him saying, "Have respect, young man."

"Why?" asked the boy.

"Because I'm the grandson of the *Chozeh of Lublin*," said the Rabbi.

"And I'm the grandson of the Rebbe," said the youngster.

"But I'm the grandson of the Chozeh," repeated R' David.

This was a novel idea for the little boy. Was someone greater than his grandfather? He went to his grandfather in a rush and complained that the Rabbi of Lomaz had said that the Chozeh was greater than the Rebbe.

The Rebbe listened to his grandson and said, "Go back and tell R' David that there is no comparison at all between me and the Chozeh of Lublin! I don't come up to his toenails. But there is a great distinction between us. I am still among the living; I still have a desire to rise and there is still a possibility of my rising and I have hopes to reach far loftier heights" (*Admorei Izbitza-Radzin*).

The soul of every living being shall bless Your Name, HASHEM our God; the spirit of all flesh shall always glorify and exalt Your remembrance, our King. From This World to the World-to-Come, You are God, and other than You we have no king, redeemer or savior. Liberator, Rescuer, Sustainer, Answerer and Merciful One in every time of distress and anguish, we have no king, helper or supporter but You! — God of the first and of the last, God of all creatures, Master of all generations, Who is extolled through a multitude of praises, Who guides His

---

פּוֹדֶה וּמַצִּיל / *Liberator, Rescuer*

Fiery Angel of Moglenitza

When *R' Yitzchak of Vurka* was ill, messengers came to the *Fiery Angel of Moglenitza* begging that he pray for him. The Fiery Angel directed his chasidim to say *tehillim*. *R' Yissachar Ber of Volbroz*, the Angel's disciple, was very distressed by the plight of the Rebbe of Vurka. He prayed mightily and said, "Master of the world, mankind needs that *tzaddik*; and I, for what purpose do I exist? Let my plea have weight before You and let me take his place, whatever his fate may be!"

The following day a messenger reached Moglenitza informing them that the Rebbe of Vurka's state was improving. But in equal measure, weakness overcame R' Yissachar Ber. He understood that his prayer had been answered and that his life was endangered. He hurried to his Rebbe and told him about his weakness and its cause.

"In our prayers we say, 'Blessed are You Who liberate and rescue,' " said the Fiery Angel. "There is no repetition here. It indicates that the Holy One liberates one man through the intercession of his fellow. Afterwards, he saves the second man by whose prayer the sick one was rescued."

And, indeed, R' Yissachar Dov regained his strength and enjoyed a long life (*Ohel Yissachar* 33).

כָּל בְּרִיּוֹת / *Of all creatures*

R' Chaim of Sanz

The Rabbi of Litovisk was firm, unbending and fearless in the face of those who threw off the yoke of *mitzvos*. This caused many of the townsmen to oppose him and embitter his life. The Rabbi came before *R' Chaim of Sanz* and told him that he had decided to leave his position and find some other means of sustenance; he was even willing to be a woodcutter.

"What brings you to such a state?" asked the Rebbe.

"*Chazal* say," replied the rabbi, "that if a man does not find favor in the

וּבְרִיּוֹתָיו בְּרַחֲמִים וַיהוה עֵר, הִנֵּה לֹא יָנוּם וְלֹא יִישָׁן הַמְעוֹרֵר יְשֵׁנִים וְהַמֵּקִיץ נִרְדָּמִים (מְחַיֵּה מֵתִים, וְרוֹפֵא חוֹלִים, פּוֹקֵחַ עִוְרִים), וְהַמֵּשִׂיחַ אִלְּמִים וְהַמַּתִּיר אֲסוּרִים וְהַסּוֹמֵךְ נוֹפְלִים וְהַזּוֹקֵף

---

eyes of men (בְּרִיּוֹת), he will not find favor before the All-present (הַמָּקוֹם) [*Avos* 3:13]. And since I do not find favor in the eyes of men, why should I serve as rabbi against the will of Hashem?''

The Rebbe became exceptionally angry and said, ''Do you think that those who harass you deserve the name of *men*? They are inferior to randomly strewn rocks. The *mishnah* does not have such men in mind; it has men like me in mind. And I am as fond of you as I am of myself! Thus, you find favor before the All-present, too; you are highly viewed in heaven. Do not fear nor feel dread, and Hashem will aid you to achieve peace and tranquility, calm and security'' (*Mekor Chaim*).

הַמְעוֹרֵר יְשֵׁנִים וְהַמֵּקִיץ נִרְדָּמִים / *Who arouses the sleepers and awakens the slumberers*

R' Shmelke of Nikolsburg

There are two categories of ''sleepers'': There are those who are in a deep sleep with regard to their devotion to Hashem (יְשֵׁנִים). They must be aroused from the coma-like slumber which the flow of time of this world has imposed upon them. And it is the Holy One Who arouses them (הַמְעוֹרֵר יְשֵׁנִים). But there are those who, at times, do remember and serve Hashem, and at times, forget him; they doze off. And the Holy One also awakens these slumberers (וְהַמֵּקִיץ נִרְדָּמִים) (*Eretz HaChaim* 423).

R' Yehoshua of Belz

When *R' Yehoshua of Belz* reached this passage, on the evening of the *Seder*, he would note, ''When my sainted father said these words, all the sick who needed to be healed were saved. We, unfortunately cannot effect a cure solely with *our* speech. We turn to Him 'Who arouses the sleepers and awakens the slumberers' to awaken those who sleep the eternal sleep. And we beg of them that they summon up their influence and lay *their* prayers before *Hashem* to support the fallen and heal the sick'' (*Admorei Belz* I 322).

וְרוֹפֵא חוֹלִים / *(And) heals the sick*

R' Mordechai of Nishchiz

A chasid who was mortally ill came before *R' Mordechai of Nishchiz*. He had visited many doctors and taken various medicines, but nothing had helped. He had turned, in his desperation, to the Rebbe.

world with kindness and His creatures with mercy. HASHEM is awake, behold He neither slumbers nor sleeps. He Who arouses the sleepers and awakens the slumberers (Who resuscitates the dead, heals the sick, and gives sight to the blind), Who makes the mute speak and releases the bound; Who supports the fallen and straightens the bent (and

---

"Go to the specialist in Anipoli. He will cure you," said the Rebbe.

Without delay, the chasid went off to Anipoli. The journey was long and difficult in those days before the railroads. On his arrival he immediately inquired about the specialist.

"But there is no specialist here," said the puzzled townsmen.

"Perhaps a doctor?" asked the man.

"There's no doctor here either," they said.

"A druggist?"

"There's no druggist, either."

"No specialist, no doctor, no druggist?" said the man in amazement. "What do you people do if someone takes ill?"

"What can we do?" they said. "We put our trust in Hashem and pray that He will save us."

The man now understood to which specialist the Rebbe had sent him. And the Specialist who aided the townsmen of Anipoli would also aid him (*Sipurei Chasidim, Beshalach* 168).

R' Shlomo of Bobov

A young man, who was afflicted with a severe case of tuberculosis, lived with a poor man in Sanz. Before Pesach the landlord, the poor man, wished to whitewash his house, as he did each year. However, the doctor warned him that the smell of the whitewash would hasten the young man's death, though he did not have much time to live as it was, since his lungs were badly eaten away.

The landlord ran to the *Divrei Chaim of Sanz* and told him, in anguished tones, that he could not forgo whitewashing his house for Pesach; he felt he had no choice and must turn the sick young man out.

The Rebbe was shaken by the tale and asked the man to wait a short while, until the illness would pass, and then he would be able to whitewash the house.

The doctor heard about what the Rebbe had said and laughed it to scorn. But when a few days had passed, he was forced to admit that the patient had improved. And, shortly thereafter, the sick man was found to be completely cured.

The Rebbe of Bobov asked the doctor, "Well, what do you have to say now?"

כְּפוּפִים (וְהַמְפַעֲנֵחַ נֶעֱלָמִים). וּלְךָ לְבַדְּךָ אֲנַחְנוּ מוֹדִים. אִלּוּ פִינוּ מָלֵא שִׁירָה כַּיָּם וּלְשׁוֹנֵנוּ רִנָּה כַּהֲמוֹן גַּלָּיו וְשִׂפְתוֹתֵינוּ שֶׁבַח כְּמֶרְחֲבֵי רָקִיעַ וְעֵינֵינוּ מְאִירוֹת כַּשֶּׁמֶשׁ וְכַיָּרֵחַ וְיָדֵינוּ פְרוּשׂוֹת כְּנִשְׁרֵי שָׁמָיִם וְרַגְלֵינוּ קַלּוֹת כָּאַיָּלוֹת אֵין אֲנַחְנוּ

"It would seem that I was mistaken when I said the lungs were eaten away and disintegrated," said the doctor.

"Why don't you admit, rather, that you were wrong in mocking the words of my grandfather, the Rebbe of Sanz?" asked the Rebbe of Bobov.

"If your grandfather can create new lungs, why doesn't he make the blind see and give speech to the dumb?" replied the doctor.

"If my grandfather were to give sight to the blind, you would have no choice but to repent," said the Rebbe of Bobov. "However, Hashem wants man to have free choice and choose the good of his own will. That is why the *tzaddik* only performs miracles of this sort which allow the doctor to say, 'I was mistaken in my diagnosis' " (*Mekor Chaim* 197).

פִּינוּ מָלֵא שִׁירָה / *Our mouth as full of song*

R' Tzvi Elimelech of Dinov

R' Tzvi Elimelech of Dinov would say the *Nishmas* prayer in a captivating melody, while standing at a window of his *beis midrash*, which looked out on the valley below. The melody was so sweet and vibrant that the gentile shepherds would gather with their flocks to listen.

R' Tzvi Elimelech passed away, and on the first *Shabbos* after his departure an air of sorrow rested on the *beis midrash*, an air which became seven-fold more oppressive as they approached the *Nishmas* prayer. And then, to the amazement of all, the sweet melody floated into the *beis midrash*.

The shepherds who had been accustomed to stand and listen had, on their own, burst forth into song (*Rabbi Tzvi Elimelech of Dinov*, p. 166).

וְעֵינֵינוּ מְאִירוֹת / *And our eyes as brilliant*

Maggid of Mezritch

The *Maggid of Mezritch* would pray alone in his chamber. When he reached *Ein Kelokeinu* (אֵין כֵּאלֹקֵינוּ) he would gather a bare quorum (*minyan*). When the *Chozeh of Lublin* reached Mezritch in his youth, he too once entered the private *minyan*. The Maggid said, "Bring someone else in his place; he is not capable (בַּטְלָן)." Though they sought a substitute, they could not find one and the Chozeh remained.

When the Maggid began to say *Ein Kelokeinu*, the Chozeh fainted and was

uncovers the hidden). And to You alone we give thanks. Were our mouth as full of song as the sea, and our tongue as full of joyous song as its multitude of waves, and our lips as full of praise as the breadth of the heavens, and our eyes as brilliant as the sun and the moon, and our hands as outspread as eagles of the sky and our feet as swift

---

revived only with great difficulty. "I said he was incapable," said the Maggid. "He just took one glimpse at the Heavenly Retinue (פַּמַלְיָא שֶׁל מָעְלָה) and fainted. It would have been better to have someone who doesn't see such sights and would not fear" (*Eser Oros* 25).

R' Yechiel Yehoshua of Biale

On a wintry *Shabbos* morning, before sunrise, when the light was still very dim, *R' Yechiel Yehoshua of Biale* asked of his grandson that he bring a *siddur* (prayerbook) so that he might say the 'for Torah-study blessings' (בִּרְכוֹת הַתּוֹרָה) and the *Shema*. His grandson did not succeed in finding the proper place in the *siddur* and was forced to approach the candle burning in the corner of the room; there he found it easily. He asked his grandfather if he wished to sit near the light, but the Rebbe said that it was not necessary. He took the *siddur,* said the blessings, turned the pages to the Thirteen Principles of Faith (י״ג עִקָּרִים), and then to the *Shema*.

His grandson was amazed. For, in his last years, the Rebbe's right eye was useless and he saw through his left eye only with difficulty. How could he read in darkness where his grandson could not see with his healthy vision?

The Rebbe took his grandson's hand lovingly and said, "Just understand! If one keeps guard over one's eyes throughout all the years, that which is holy shines forth" (*Kedushas Einayim* 343).

וְעֵינֵינוּ מְאִירוֹת כַּשֶּׁמֶשׁ וְכַיָּרֵחַ / *And our eyes as brilliant as the sun and the moon*

R' BenZion of Bobov

"Our eyes" (עֵינֵינוּ) refers to the righteous, the *tzaddikim*, who are called "the eyes of the assembly" (עֵינֵי הָעֵדָה). Even if they are as brilliant as the sun (שֶׁמֶשׁ) at its height, they see themselves as the moon (יָרֵחַ) only, which has no radiance of its own but reflects that of the sun. They see their power as having its source in Israel who cling to them (*Heichal Bobov* 156).

וְרַגְלֵינוּ קַלּוֹת / *And our feet (as) swift*

R' Chaim of Kosov

R' Chaim of Kosov would dance with great and saintly enthusiasm each *Shabbos* night, his face

מַסְפִּיקִים לְהוֹדוֹת לְךָ יהוה אֱלֹהֵינוּ וֵאלֹהֵי אֲבוֹתֵינוּ וּלְבָרֵךְ אֶת שְׁמֶךָ מַלְכֵּנוּ עַל אַחַת מֵאֶלֶף אֶלֶף אַלְפֵי אֲלָפִים וְרִבֵּי רְבָבוֹת פְּעָמִים הַטּוֹבוֹת נִסִּים וְנִפְלָאוֹת שֶׁעָשִׂיתָ עִם אֲבוֹתֵינוּ וְעִמָּנוּ. מִלְּפָנִים מִמִּצְרַיִם גְּאַלְתָּנוּ יהוה אֱלֹהֵינוּ וּמִבֵּית עֲבָדִים פְּדִיתָנוּ בְּרָעָב זַנְתָּנוּ וּבְשָׂבָע כִּלְכַּלְתָּנוּ מֵחֶרֶב הִצַּלְתָּנוּ וּמִדֶּבֶר מִלַּטְתָּנוּ וּמֵחֳלָיִם רָעִים וְרַבִּים וְנֶאֱמָנִים דִּלִּיתָנוּ. עַד הֵנָּה עֲזָרוּנוּ רַחֲמֶיךָ וְלֹא עֲזָבוּנוּ חֲסָדֶיךָ יהוה אֱלֹהֵינוּ. וְאַל תִּטְּשֵׁנוּ

---

radiant like a torch. Once a heavy bench fell on his feet and he stopped dancing for some time. But after a few weeks had passed, he began to dance once more with his customary fervor. When his chasidim tried to prevent him, because of his injured feet, he said, "You thought I had stopped dancing because my feet hurt me, but in truth my feet hurt because I had stopped dancing" (*Sipurei Chasidim, Moadim* 162).

Maggid of Kozhnitz The *Maggid of Kozhnitz* became so weak and gaunt that the doctors were amazed that he continued to live. He was not even able to bear clothes on his body and special clothing of paper was sewn for him. They wrapped him in rabbit furs and spread bear hides on the floor. Because he was so weak, he could not stand on his feet and his chasidim carried him in a chair from his home to the *beis midrash*. But when he reached the door of the *beis midrash*, he would leap from the chair and run in like a vigorous young man and in his great fervor he would roar like a lion, "Who am I that I should be worthy to pray to the high, exalted King?" Then he would quote from *Bereishis* 28:17, "How fearful is this place. It is none other than the House of God, and this is the gateway of heaven!" (*Toledos HaMaggid* 15).

בְּרָעָב זַנְתָּנוּ / *In famine You nourished us*

R' Chanoch Henoch of Alexander *R' Chanoch Henoch of Alexander* complained to his rebbe, *R' Simchah Bunim of Pshischa* that he didn't sense that he ate good food and he had no appetite. The Rebbe replied, "The verse says: 'Behold, the eye of Hashem looks towards those who fear Him . . . to keep them alive in famine' (*Tehillim* 33:18-19), which may be interpreted as 'keeps them alive while

as hinds — we still could not thank You sufficiently, HASHEM our God and God of our forefathers, and bless Your Name, our King, for even one of the thousand thousand, thousands of thousands and myriad myriads of favors, miracles and wonders that You performed for our ancestors and for us. At first You redeemed us from Egypt, HASHEM our God, and liberated us from the house of bondage. In famine You nourished us and in plenty You sustained us. From sword You saved us; from plague You let us escape; and from severe, numerous and enduring diseases You spared us. Until now Your mercy has helped us, and Your kindness has not forsaken us HASHEM our God. Do not abandon us, HASHEM our

---

they hunger and lack appetite.' And therefore we say, 'in famine You nourished us' " (*Siach Sarfei Kodesh* I 595).

בְּרָעָב זַנְתָּנוּ וּבְשָׂבָע כִּלְכַּלְתָּנוּ / *In famine You nourished us and in plenty You sustained us*

R' David'l of Tolna

A group of wealthy grain merchants came before *R' David'l of Tolna* to ask advice and seek his blessing. The previous year had been a year of drought and the prices of grain had risen very steeply. They had thought that the current year would follow the same pattern and they had not sold their produce, waiting for the prices to rise even higher. But the rains did fall and the prices had plummeted drastically. Now, they stood to lose vast sums.

The Rebbe replied, "He Who fed and sustained the poor in the year of *famine* will feed and sustain the wealthy in the year of *plenty*" (*Sipurei Tzaddikim, Lecha*).

עַד הֵנָּה עֲזָרוּנוּ . . . וְאַל תִּטְּשֵׁנוּ
Until now (Your mercy) has helped us . . . Do not abandon us

R' Yitzchak of Skver

This is not a prayer and a plea, but a declaration of faith.

Had You aided us until now, because we were found worthy by virtue of our good deeds and righteousness, we would, of necessity, be concerned about the future. Would we continue to be so favored?

But we have been helped because of Your mercy and Your kindness. These will never be exhausted and spent. We are certain that You will never abandon us (*Besoros Tovos*).

יהוה אֱלֹהֵינוּ לָנֶצַח. עַל כֵּן אֵבָרִים שֶׁפִּלַּגְתָּ בָּנוּ וְרוּחַ וּנְשָׁמָה שֶׁנָּפַחְתָּ בְּאַפֵּינוּ וְלָשׁוֹן אֲשֶׁר שַׂמְתָּ בְּפִינוּ הֵן הֵם יוֹדוּ וִיבָרְכוּ וִישַׁבְּחוּ וִיפָאֲרוּ וִישׁוֹרְרוּ וִירוֹמְמוּ וְיַעֲרִיצוּ וְיַקְדִּישׁוּ וְיַמְלִיכוּ אֶת שִׁמְךָ מַלְכֵּנוּ תָּמִיד. כִּי כָל פֶּה לְךָ יוֹדֶה וְכָל לָשׁוֹן לְךָ תִשָּׁבַע, וְכָל עַיִן לְךָ תְצַפֶּה, וְכָל בֶּרֶךְ לְךָ תִכְרַע וְכָל קוֹמָה לְפָנֶיךָ תִשְׁתַּחֲוֶה וְכָל הַלְּבָבוֹת יִירָאוּךָ

עַל כֵּן אֵבָרִים שֶׁפִּלַּגְתָּ בָּנוּ . . . הֵן הֵם יוֹדוּ

Therefore, the organs that You set within us . . . all of them shall thank

Maggid of Mezritch

Previously, we said that even if our mouth were "as full of song as the sea . . . we still could not thank You sufficiently." How is it that we do a turnabout and say that our organs give thanks and praise?

Let us suggest a parable:

A king summoned his servant and ordered him to prepare a meal at home, fit for a king and his entourage. The servant was seized by trembling at the thought of the great responsibility placed upon him. What food, what drinks should he provide? With what dishes should he set the table? How to clean the house?

In the midst of his fearful contemplations, the king said, "I'll have all that is necessary prepared in the palace, my servants will carry it to your home, and we'll eat there." The weight disappeared from the future host's shoulders.

When we assume that the mouth and tongue are *our* mouth and *our* tongue, we feel that we are inadequate for the task of praise. But when we realize that our organs have been set within us by Hashem, and He has placed the tongue within our mouths — the organs are all Hashem's, then we can say, "All of them shall thank," for You have fashioned it all and given it to us from Your Hand (*Eser Oros* 37).

הֵן הֵם יוֹדוּ / ***All of them shall thank***

Fiery Angel of Kotzk

When the *Fiery Angel of Kotzk* became known to the world, a man who lived in Tomashov was amazed to hear that he had become a rebbe. "He?" he said. "We were together in *cheder* as youngsters."

The chasidim wished to learn about the Rebbe's childhood and asked the man what the Fiery Angel had been like as a boy.

God, forever. Therefore, the organs that You set within us, and the spirit and soul that You breathed into our nostrils, and the tongue that You placed in our mouth — all of them shall thank and bless, praise and glorify, sing about, exalt and revere, sanctify and declare the sovereignty of Your Name, our King, continuously. For every mouth shall offer thanks to You; every tongue shall vow allegiance to You; every eye shall look toward You; every knee shall bend to You; every erect spine shall prostrate itself before You; all the hearts shall fear You, and all

---

"I have nothing to tell you," he said. "He was a boy like all boys. But," he said after a pause, "I now recall that the teacher once took us for a hike in the hills on *Lag B'Omer*. We returned at a late hour and, when we reached town, we realized that Menachem Mendel was not with us. We went back and searched for him; he was stretched out full length on the ground, arms widespread, repeating again and again, 'My heart and flesh sing to the living God' " (*Tehillim* 84:3) (*Siach Sarfei Kodesh* V 48).

וְכָל קוֹמָה לְפָנֶיךָ תִשְׁתַּחֲוֶה

Every erect spine shall prostrate itself before You

R' Baruch of Mezhibuz

The highest level of prostration is achieved when man appears to stand with *a fully erect posture, in the eyes of the beholder, and his inner self feels a sense of complete obeisance (*Betzina D' Nehora*).

[**a fully erect posture*. R' Baruch invested the כָּל (of כָּל קוֹמָה) with the meaning of *entirely*, rather than *every*; like בְּכָל לְבָבְךָ with your *entire* heart, (*Devarim* 6:5).]

R' Menachem Mendel of Vurka

R' Menachem Mendel of Vurka, the Silent Rebbe, would add: It is right and proper that a chasid know how to feel the spirit of dance while sitting, of bowing while erect and of crying aloud in prayer while silent (*Gedulas HaTzaddikim* II 69).

יִירָאוּךָ / *(All) shall fear You*

Ba'al HaTanya

R' Aharon the Great of Karlin's fear of Hashem was like the fear of a man condemned to death who is bound to the pole and sees the soldier stand before him, aim his rifle and fire the bullet. That was the fear he felt when involved in petty everyday matters. It is

וְכָל קֶרֶב וּכְלָיוֹת יְזַמְּרוּ לִשְׁמֶךָ. כַּדָּבָר שֶׁכָּתוּב כָּל עַצְמֹתַי תֹּאמַרְנָה יהוה מִי כָמוֹךָ מַצִּיל עָנִי מֵחָזָק מִמֶּנּוּ וְעָנִי וְאֶבְיוֹן מִגֹּזְלוֹ. שַׁוְעַת עֲנִיִּים אַתָּה תִשְׁמַע, צַעֲקַת הַדַּל תַּקְשִׁיב וְתוֹשִׁיעַ. מִי יִדְמֶה

---

impossible to describe his fear when he was on an exalted plane (*Beis Rabi* I, ch. 25).

R' Levi Yitzchak of Berdichev

The *Noam Elimelech* bore witness that the heart of *R' Levi Yitzchak of Berdichev* pounded furiously in his sleep from fear of Hashem, like the heart of a man who walks in the thickness of a forest and suddenly finds himself surrounded by murderous bandits.

Imagine what that fear of Hashem was when he woke from his sleep. (*Toledos Kedushas Levi* 50, quoted in the name of the *Divrei Chaim*)

Chidushei HaRim

The *Chidushei HaRim of Gur* was once traveling by wagon up a steep mountain. When the wagon made the sheer decline, the horses went into a gallop and the travelers were in danger of plunging into the abyss. The fear of death, plain and simple, seized the others, but when they glanced at the Rebbe, they saw he was as unmoved as if they had been driving on a plain. They asked him how he could be so tranquil in the face of such clear danger.

"Whoever constantly experiences the fear of death because of the dread of his Creator does not note any difference between travel on level ground and down a steep decline," he said (*Siach Sarfei Kodesh* I 453).

R' Yisrael of Ruzhin

R' Yisrael of Ruzhin prayed in a special chamber close by his *beis midrash*. When he would finish his prayer he would give a sign indicating that he had done so.

One Yom Kippur during *Ne'ilah*, the Rebbe gave no sign that he had completed his prayers, although the hour was late. They waited for two hours in fasting and fear. Finally, his firstborn son, *R' Shalom Yosef*, took courage and entered his father's chamber. He approached the *shtender* where the Rebbe's *machzor* lay and turned the page. Moments later the Rebbe indicated that he had ended his prayers.

When R' Shalom Yosef was asked what had occurred, he said, "I realized that my father stood before Hashem in such fear that he did not dare lift his hand to turn the page of the *machzor*. And since he did not wish to pray

innermost feelings and thoughts shall sing praises to Your name, as it is written: "All my bones shall say: 'HASHEM, who is like You?' You save the poor man from one stronger than he, the poor and destitute from one who would rob him." The outcry of the poor You hear, the screams of the destitute You listen to, and You save. Who is like unto You?

---

from memory, he could not continue, but stood in silent trembling. I turned the page and he was able to complete the prayers'' (*Avkas Rochlim*).

כָּל עַצְמֹתַי תֹּאמַרְנָה / *All my bones shall say*

Kol Aryeh of Bregsas

The *Kol Aryeh of Bregsas* saw a man praying without swaying back and forth. ''My master, the *Chasam Sofer* did, indeed, pray without any movement,'' he said to him. ''But when I looked at his face, it was radiant. Flaming like a torch. Suddenly, he blanched, as though about to faint. I wished to shout, for I feared that his soul had flown from his body. Whoever prays with such a sense of closeness to God can allow himself to stand motionless. But we lesser mortals must pray with motion, so that 'all my bones shall say' '' (*Toledos Kol Arye* 29).

צַעֲקַת / *The outcry*

Shomer Emunim

The *Shomer Emunim* implanted into his chasidim the idea that prayer was especially powerful when expressed forcefully and fervently, with full voice. Such had been the manner of prayer, in days gone by, of *R' Uri the Fiery Angel of Strelisk*. When R' Uri was about to pass away, he had intimated to his chasidim that they should find shelter in the shade of *R' Yisrael of Ruzhin*.

The *Shomer Emunim* told the following:

In Ruzhin they prayed in a low voice; their lips would move but their voice was not heard. The chasidim of Strelisk arrived in Ruzhin and prayed loudly in their usual manner. The Rebbe was amazed at the outcry and was told that this was how they prayed in Strelisk.

After the prayers the Rebbe called them over and asked, ''Why in such a loud voice? Isn't it possible to pray quietly?''

They answered that they did not wish to pray in the same voice in which they spoke about everyday matters.

The Rebbe smiled and said, ''Fine! But why have you decided to use the pleasant manner of speech for your everyday use and the unpleasant manner for prayer? It would be fitting to pray quietly and shout at other times.''

They remained silent.

לָךְ וּמִי יִשְׁוֶה לָּךְ וּמִי יַעֲרָךְ לָךְ הָאֵל הַגָּדוֹל הַגִּבּוֹר וְהַנּוֹרָא אֵל עֶלְיוֹן, קֹנֵה שָׁמַיִם וָאָרֶץ. נְהַלֶּלְךָ וּנְשַׁבֵּחֲךָ וּנְפָאֶרְךָ וּנְבָרֵךְ אֶת שֵׁם קָדְשֶׁךָ כָּאָמוּר לְדָוִד בָּרְכִי נַפְשִׁי אֶת יהוה וְכָל קְרָבַי אֶת שֵׁם קָדְשׁוֹ:

הָאֵל בְּתַעֲצֻמוֹת עֻזֶּךָ הַגָּדוֹל בִּכְבוֹד שְׁמֶךָ הַגִּבּוֹר לָנֶצַח וְהַנּוֹרָא בְּנוֹרְאוֹתֶיךָ הַמֶּלֶךְ הַיּוֹשֵׁב עַל כִּסֵּא רָם וְנִשָּׂא:

שׁוֹכֵן עַד מָרוֹם וְקָדוֹשׁ שְׁמוֹ. וְכָתוּב רַנְּנוּ צַדִּיקִים בַּיהוה לַיְשָׁרִים נָאוָה תְהִלָּה:

בְּפִי יְשָׁרִים תִּתְרוֹמָם.
וּבְשִׂפְתֵי צַדִּיקִים תִּתְבָּרַךְ
וּבִלְשׁוֹן חֲסִידִים תִּתְקַדָּשׁ.
וּבְקֶרֶב קְדוֹשִׁים תִּתְהַלָּל.

"In truth," said the Shomer Emunim to his chasidim, "they did have an answer. But out of respect for R' Yisrael they chose not to reply.

"For *R' Shlomo of Karlin* said, 'In the prayers we find: **and the ofanim and the holy chayos — with a great noise, raising themselves*. Because they sing with great voice they raise themselves and are uplifted. This shows us that the most worthy praise is the very loud praise. It is beautiful and pleasant; it lifts the worshiper to a lofty level' " (*Porah Mateh Aharon* 115).

בָּרְכִי נַפְשִׁי אֶת ה' / *Bless Hashem, O my soul*

Fiery Angel of Strelisk

When *R' Gershon of Kolomei* visited *R' Yisrael of Ruzhin*, the Rebbe of Ruzhin asked him if he had been in the presence of *tzaddikim*. R' Gershon said that he often traveled to *R' Uri the Fiery Angel of Strelisk*. The Rebbe of Ruzhin asked R' Gershon to tell him something of the Fiery Angel.

---

* *and the ofanim etc.* וְהָאוֹפַנִּים וְחַיּוֹת הַקֹּדֶשׁ בְּרַעַשׁ גָּדוֹל מִתְנַשְּׂאִים. This is in the first blessing of the *Shema* of the morning prayers. It refers to the *ofanim* and *chayos* who are the angels that bear the Divine Chariot.

Who is equal to You? Who can be compared to You? O great, mighty, and awesome God, the supreme God, Creator of heaven and earth. We shall laud, praise, and glorify You and bless Your holy Name, as it is said 'Of David: Bless HASHEM, O my soul, and let all my innermost being bless His holy Name!'

O God, in the omnipotence of Your strength, great in the glory of Your Name, mighty forever and awesome through Your awesome deeds, O King enthroned upon a high and lofty throne!

He Who abides forever, exalted and holy is His Name. And it is written: 'Sing joyfully, O righteous, before HASHEM; for the upright, praise is fitting.' By the mouth of the upright shall You be exalted; by the lips of the righteous shall You be blessed; by the tongue of the devout shall You be sanctified; and amid the holy shall You be lauded.

"Once," said R' Gershon, "the Fiery Angel asked me to write the title page for a manuscript. I told him that great patience was required and it would be preferable to do it after prayer. He told me that it was not a manuscript of his, and when he stood before his Creator, he was ready to hand over his soul. He could not, therefore, be certain that he would return home after prayer. And then, it would be thought that the manuscript contained his own original Torah insights. That is why he begged me to write up the title page, containing the author's name, immediately" (*Eser Tzachtzachos* 6).

הַמֶּלֶךְ / *O King*

R' Aharon of Karlin

The *Maggid of Mezritch* chose his disciple, *R' Aharon the Great of Karlin*, to lead the prayers on Rosh Hashanah. R' Aharon was accustomed to pray with sound and fury; bolts of lightning would burst forth from his lips. But when he reached the phrase "O King," *HaMelech*, he was struck silent, blanched and almost fainted.

When asked for an explanation afterwards, he replied, "When I said '*HaMelech*,' I remembered what the *gemara* (*Gemara* 56a) tells us of the meeting between Rabban Yochanan ben Zakkai and the Roman general besieging *Yerushalayim*. R' Yochanan ben Zakkai said, 'Peace to you, O king!

וּבְמַקְהֲלוֹת רִבְבוֹת עַמְּךָ בֵּית יִשְׂרָאֵל בְּרִנָּה יִתְפָּאַר שִׁמְךָ מַלְכֵּנוּ בְּכָל דּוֹר וָדוֹר שֶׁכֵּן חוֹבַת כָּל הַיְצוּרִים לְפָנֶיךָ יהוה אֱלֹהֵינוּ וֵאלֹהֵי אֲבוֹתֵינוּ לְהוֹדוֹת לְהַלֵּל לְשַׁבֵּחַ לְפָאֵר

To which the general commented, 'If I *am* a king, why did you not come until now?' " (*Beis Karlin-Stolin* 40).

יְשָׁרִים / *The upright*

R' Tzvi Elimelech of Dinov

When *R' Tzvi Elimelech of Dinov* passed away, *R' Sar Shalom of Belz* sighed and said, "What a pity! We have lost an upright Jew" (Yiddish: עֶרְלִיכֶער איד).

"An upright Jew only?" exclaimed his wife. "He was among the greatest rebbes of our age."

"Rebbes we have in plenty," replied her husband, "but upright Jews are few and far between" (*Admorei Belz* I 173).

R' David of Kishinev

R' David of Kishinev gave the following parable concerning those who imagine they have become elevated souls simply by lifting up their voices loudly, in prayer:

A man had gone mad and imagined himself to be a rooster. He hopped about the barnyard and pecked for kernels of grain; flapped his "wings"; went up on the roof before dawn and crowed his cock-a-doodle-doo.

His family saw that his physical health was being impaired, too, and asked a clever man to persuade him to eat and sleep normally. This would make it at least possible for him to return to himself sometime in the future.

One morning before dawn, the would-be rooster went aloft on the roof to crow in the day and, lo and behold, he found someone there before him. He barely stretched out his neck to let loose his halloo when the other sent forth, beforehand, a clarion-clear cock-a-doodle-doo which aroused his envy.

"Are you a rooster, too?" asked the "rooster", suspiciously.

"What do you think?" said the clever man, for it was he. "Do you call *yourself* a rooster? Your voice is weak and thin. You are a disgrace to our species. If you wish to be a credit to the rooster tribe, you should eat three meals a day and sleep eight hours a day. Then you shall have a true rooster's voice."

"But," said the confused "rooster," "if I eat like a human being and sleep like one, how can I be called a rooster?"

"Let me tell you a secret," said the clever man. "Once upon a time a

And in the assemblies of the myriads of Your people, the House of Israel, with joyous song shall Your Name be glorified, our King, throughout every generation. For such is the duty of all creatures — before You, HASHEM, our God, God of our forefathers, to thank, laud, praise, glorify,

---

rooster was a rooster. But today, it's enough just to crow!'' (*Rabbeinu HaKadosh MiSanz* III 218).

Maggid of Mezritch After the *Maggid of Mezritch* had passed away, his disciples gathered together and spoke among themselves of the deeds and modes of behavior of their great master. The *Ba'al HaTanya* asked, ''Does anyone know why our teacher would walk each day at dawn along the lakeshore?''

When no answer was forthcoming, he said, ''He went there to hear the songs of praise that the frogs offer up to the Holy One and learn from them a chapter in the service to Hashem'' (*Sipurei Chasidim; Va'erah*).

R' Nachman of Breslav A man of Zlotipola told the following about *R' Nachman of Breslav*:

''When R' Nachman lived in Zlotipola he once asked me to accompany him on a walk. We left the city and strolled in the meadows. The Rebbe said to me, 'If you would be fortunate enough to hear the songs of praise of the blades of grass, you would hear how each sings to Hashem without any self-interest, without any foreign thoughts. They look forward to no reward. How lovely it is to hear their song! How good it is to devote oneself to, and feel fear of, Hashem among them!'

''And he sat down on the earth, took a *Sha'arei Zion* in his hand and read aloud from it, with great weeping and without a halt, until the sun began to set'' (*Sichos HaRan* 164).

כָּל הַיְצוּרִים לְפָנֶיךָ / *Of all creatures — before You*

Fiery Angel of Kotzk The *Fiery Angel of Kotzk* arose and began to say the *Modeh Ani*, the praise and thanks that every Jew says upon arising. But he broke off when he had said three words — *modeh ani lefanecha* (מוֹדֶה אֲנִי לְפָנֶיךָ — I give thanks before You). *''Who am *'I'* (אֲנִי) and who is the *'before You'* (לְפָנֶיךָ)?'' he said. And in his trembling and fear, he was unable to complete the short prayer (*Siach Sarfei Kodesh* V, p. 23).

[**Who am I etc.* He was overwhelmed and experienced dread when he contemplated the infinite abyss that separated his human ''*I*'' from the Divine ''*You*'' and could not possibly envision a standing ''before You'' without overpowering awe.]

לְרוֹמֵם לְהַדֵּר וּלְנַצֵּחַ לְבָרֵךְ לְעַלֵּה וּלְקַלֵּס עַל כָּל דִּבְרֵי שִׁירוֹת וְתִשְׁבְּחוֹת דָּוִד בֶּן יִשַׁי עַבְדְּךָ מְשִׁיחֶךָ:

וּבְכֵן יִשְׁתַּבַּח שִׁמְךָ לָעַד מַלְכֵּנוּ הָאֵל הַמֶּלֶךְ הַגָּדוֹל וְהַקָּדוֹשׁ בַּשָּׁמַיִם וּבָאָרֶץ כִּי לְךָ נָאֶה יהוה אֱלֹהֵינוּ וֵאלֹהֵי אֲבוֹתֵינוּ שִׁיר וּשְׁבָחָה הַלֵּל וְזִמְרָה עֹז וּמֶמְשָׁלָה נֶצַח גְּדֻלָּה וּגְבוּרָה תְּהִלָּה וְתִפְאֶרֶת קְדֻשָּׁה וּמַלְכוּת בְּרָכוֹת וְהוֹדָאוֹת לְשִׁמְךָ הַגָּדוֹל וְהַקָּדוֹשׁ וּמֵעוֹלָם וְעַד עוֹלָם אַתָּה אֵל.

וְתִשְׁבְּחוֹת דָּוִד בֶּן יִשַׁי

Praises of David the son of Yishai

Sainted Yehudi of Pshischa

The *Sainted Yehudi of Pshischa* was a phenomenally brilliant and diligent scholar. It was said that his master, the *Chozeh of Lublin*, concealed his true personality behind the overt wonders (מוֹפְתִים) which he worked, while the Sainted Yehudi hid himself by incisive Talmudic discourses (פִּלְפּוּלִים). Nevertheless, before he prayed, he would occupy himself, in particular, with the saying of *Tehillim*.

"Wouldn't it be better to learn a number of pages of the Talmud before prayer?" asked his disciple, *R' Yeshaya of Pshedburz*. "True, David begged that the utterance of his songs of *Tehillim* be viewed like the learning of the *mishnayos* of 'Plagues' (נְגָעִים) and 'Tents' (אָהֲלוֹת) which contain the most difficult matters in the Order of Purities (סֵדֶר טְהָרוֹת). But that very plea shows that the study of *mishnah* is preferable to saying *Tehillim*."

"There is a profound meaning hidden within David *HaMelech's* plea," said the Rebbe. "He hoped that, by giving utterance to *Tehillim*, man would see the 'plagues,' the spiritual maladies, which afflict him personally, and this would bring him to dwell in the 'tents' of Hashem. Nothing can be more important as a preparatory step to prayer than these thoughts" (*Nifleos HaYehudi* II 6).

Ba'al Shem Tov

But there is the saying of *Tehillim* and the saying of *Tehillim*:

exalt, adore, render triumphant, bless, raise high, and sing praises — even beyond all expressions of the songs and praises of David the son of Yishai, Your servant, Your anointed.

And thus may Your Name be praised forever — our King, the God, the great and holy King — in heaven and on earth. Because for You is fitting — O HASHEM, our God, and the God of our forefathers — song and praise, lauding and hymns, power and dominion, triumph, greatness and strength, praise and splendor, holiness and sovereignty, blessings and thanksgivings to Your Great and Holy Name; from This World to the World-to-Come You are God.

In the days of the *Ba'al Shem Tov* there was a man who found a passage in holy works which stated that the Divine spirit (*ruach hakodesh*) would rest upon man, if he refrained from idle speech (דְּבָרִים בְּטֵלִים) for forty days consecutively. He did so. However, at the end of the fortieth day he felt no sense of the Divine spirit. He went to the Ba'al Shem Tov to discover what had happened.

"Were you careful about every word that passed your lips?" asked the Ba'al Shem Tov.

"Indeed, yes, Rebbe!" said the man. "I didn't say a word."

"Did you say *Tehillim*?"

"That, yes! With great ease!"

"Well, then," said the Ba'al Shem Tov, "Now we've solved the problem. There is your idle talk" (*Sipurei Chasidim, Parashas Noach*).

R' Yisrael of Ruzhin

A man who had assiduously guarded his tongue from speech for forty days found that, nevertheless, the Divine spirit had not come to rest upon him. He went to *R' Yisrael of Ruzhin* for an explanation.

The Rebbe of Ruzhin conducted a court in royal fashion. The man was dazzled by the splendor and the majesty. His eyes could not have enough of the grandeur of the palatial residence and the king-like deportment of the Rebbe. "This is a singular way of devoting oneself to Hashem," he thought.

The Rebbe left the mansion and made his way to the stables. There his carriage had been harnessed to four noble steeds. He approached the first

יְהַלְלוּךָ יהוה אֱלֹהֵינוּ (עַל) כָּל מַעֲשֶׂיךָ, וַחֲסִידֶיךָ צַדִּיקִים עוֹשֵׂי רְצוֹנֶךָ, וְכָל עַמְּךָ בֵּית יִשְׂרָאֵל בְּרִנָּה יוֹדוּ וִיבָרְכוּ וִישַׁבְּחוּ וִיפָאֲרוּ וִישׁוֹרְרוּ וִירוֹמְמוּ וְיַעֲרִיצוּ וְיַקְדִּישׁוּ וְיַמְלִיכוּ אֶת שִׁמְךָ מַלְכֵּנוּ, תָּמִיד כִּי לְךָ טוֹב לְהוֹדוֹת וּלְשִׁמְךָ נָאֶה לְזַמֵּר, כִּי מֵעוֹלָם וְעַד עוֹלָם אַתָּה אֵל. בָּרוּךְ אַתָּה יהוה מֶלֶךְ מְהֻלָּל בַּתִּשְׁבָּחוֹת.

The blessing over wine is recited and the fourth cup is drunk while reclining on the left side. It is preferable that the entire cup be drunk.

הֲרֵינִי מוּכָן וּמְזוּמָן לְקַיֵּם מִצְוַת כּוֹס רְבִיעִי שֶׁל אַרְבַּע כּוֹסוֹת. לְשֵׁם יִחוּד קֻדְשָׁא בְּרִיךְ הוּא וּשְׁכִינְתֵּיהּ, עַל יְדֵי הַהוּא טָמִיר וְנֶעְלָם, בְּשֵׁם כָּל יִשְׂרָאֵל. וִיהִי נֹעַם אֲדֹנָי אֱלֹהֵינוּ עָלֵינוּ, וּמַעֲשֵׂה יָדֵינוּ כּוֹנְנָה עָלֵינוּ, וּמַעֲשֵׂה יָדֵינוּ כּוֹנְנֵהוּ:

בָּרוּךְ אַתָּה יהוה אֱלֹהֵינוּ מֶלֶךְ הָעוֹלָם בּוֹרֵא פְּרִי הַגָּפֶן:

After drinking the fourth cup, the concluding blessing is recited. On Shabbos include the passage in parentheses.

בָּרוּךְ אַתָּה יהוה אֱלֹהֵינוּ מֶלֶךְ הָעוֹלָם עַל הַגֶּפֶן וְעַל פְּרִי הַגֶּפֶן וְעַל תְּנוּבַת הַשָּׂדֶה וְעַל אֶרֶץ חֶמְדָּה טוֹבָה וּרְחָבָה שֶׁרָצִיתָ וְהִנְחַלְתָּ לַאֲבוֹתֵינוּ לֶאֱכוֹל מִפִּרְיָהּ וְלִשְׂבּוֹעַ מִטּוּבָהּ. רַחֵם נָא יהוה אֱלֹהֵינוּ עַל יִשְׂרָאֵל עַמֶּךָ וְעַל יְרוּשָׁלַיִם עִירֶךָ וְעַל צִיּוֹן מִשְׁכַּן כְּבוֹדֶךָ וְעַל מִזְבְּחֶךָ וְעַל הֵיכָלֶךָ. וּבְנֵה יְרוּשָׁלַיִם עִיר הַקֹּדֶשׁ בִּמְהֵרָה בְיָמֵינוּ

---

and patted its neck. The man, who had followed the Rebbe, could not contain himself. "Begging your pardon, our master," he said, "but of what devotion to Hashem is there in the patting of horses?"

"Know," said the Rebbe "that this horse has not said an idle word for

All Your works shall praise You, Hashem our God. And Your devout ones, the righteous, who do Your will, and Your entire people, the House of Israel, with glad song will thank, bless, praise, glorify, sing about exalt, extol, sanctify, and proclaim the sovereignty of Your Name, our King, continuously. For to You it is fitting to give thanks, and unto Your Name it is proper to sing praises, for from This World to the World-to-Come You are God. Blessed are You, Hashem, the King Who is lauded with praises.

The blessing over wine is recited and the fourth cup is drunk while reclining on the left side. It is preferable that the entire cup be drunk.

Behold, I am prepared and ready to fulfill the mitzvah of the fourth of the Four Cups. For the sake of the unification of the Holy One, Blessed is He, and His Presence, through Him Who is hidden and inscrutable — [I pray] in the name of all Israel. May the pleasantness of my Lord, our God, be upon us — may He establish our handiwork for us; our handiwork may He establish.

Blessed are You, Hashem, our God, King of the universe, Who creates the fruit of the vine.

After drinking the fourth cup, the concluding blessing is recited.
On Shabbos include the passage in parentheses.

Blessed are You, Hashem, our God, King of the universe, for the vine and the fruit of the vine, and for the produce of the field. For the desirable, good, and spacious land that You were pleased to give our forefathers as a heritage, to eat of its fruit and to be satisfied with its goodness. Have mercy, we beg You, Hashem, our God, on Israel Your people; on Jerusalem, Your city; on Zion, resting place of Your glory; Your Altar, and Your Temple. Rebuild Jerusalem the city of holiness, speedily in our days. Bring us up into it and glad-

---

more than forty days."

The man understood that it is not enough to be silent; one must know *how* to be silent (*Ateres Yisrael*).

וְהַעֲלֵנוּ לְתוֹכָהּ וְשַׂמְּחֵנוּ בְּבִנְיָנָהּ וְנֹאכַל מִפִּרְיָהּ וְנִשְׂבַּע מִטּוּבָהּ וּנְבָרֶכְךָ עָלֶיהָ בִּקְדֻשָּׁה וּבְטָהֳרָה. [וּרְצֵה וְהַחֲלִיצֵנוּ בְּיוֹם הַשַּׁבָּת הַזֶּה] וְשַׂמְּחֵנוּ בְּיוֹם חַג הַמַּצּוֹת הַזֶּה. כִּי אַתָּה יהוה טוֹב וּמֵטִיב לַכֹּל וְנוֹדֶה לְּךָ עַל הָאָרֶץ וְעַל פְּרִי הַגָּפֶן: בָּרוּךְ אַתָּה יהוה עַל הָאָרֶץ וְעַל פְּרִי הַגָּפֶן:

נרצה

חֲסַל סִדּוּר פֶּסַח כְּהִלְכָתוֹ. כְּכָל מִשְׁפָּטוֹ וְחֻקָּתוֹ. כַּאֲשֶׁר זָכִינוּ לְסַדֵּר אוֹתוֹ. כֵּן נִזְכֶּה לַעֲשׂוֹתוֹ: זָךְ שׁוֹכֵן מְעוֹנָה. קוֹמֵם קְהַל עֲדַת מִי מָנָה. בְּקָרוֹב נַהֵל נִטְעֵי כַנָּה. פְּדוּיִם לְצִיּוֹן בְּרִנָּה:

לְשָׁנָה הַבָּאָה בִּירוּשָׁלָיִם:

On the first night recite the following.
On the second night continue on page 178.

וּבְכֵן וַיְהִי בַּחֲצִי הַלַּיְלָה:

אָז רוֹב נִסִּים הִפְלֵאתָ בַּלַּיְלָה.
בְּרֹאשׁ אַשְׁמוֹרֶת זֶה הַלַּיְלָה.
גֵּר צֶדֶק נִצַּחְתּוֹ כְּנֶחֱלַק לוֹ לַיְלָה.
וַיְהִי בַּחֲצִי הַלַּיְלָה.

נִרְצָה / *Nirtzah (Acceptance)*

Ahavas Yisrael of Vizhnitz

At the close of the Seder, *Nirtzah,* the *Ahavas Yisrael of Vizhnitz* sighed and said, "We have eaten the proper measure of matzah and of *maror*. How can we now find a proper measure of *nirtzah* (acceptance) so that our acts be acceptable to our Creator?" (*Kedosh Yisrael* I, ch. 14, 29).

den us in its rebuilding and let us eat from its fruit and be satisfied with its goodness and bless You upon it in holiness and purity. (Favor us and strengthen us on this Shabbos day) and grant us happiness on this Festival of Matzos; for You, HASHEM, are good and do good to all, and we thank You for the land and for the fruit of the vine. Blessed are You, HASHEM, for the land and for the fruit of the vine.

NIRTZAH

The Seder is now concluded in accordance with its laws, with all its ordinances and statutes. Just as we were privileged to arrange it, so may we merit to perform it. O Pure One, Who dwells on high, raise up the countless congregation, soon — guide the offshoots of Your plants, redeemed, to Zion with glad song.

NEXT YEAR IN JERUSALEM

On the first night recite the following.
On the second night continue on page 179.

It came to pass at midnight.

You have, of old, performed many wonders by night.
At the head of the watches of this night.
To the righteous convert (Avraham),
You gave triumph by dividing for him the night.
It came to pass at midnight.

Divrei Chaim Once, after the Seder, the *Divrei Chaim* reclined on the couch, put his hand on his stomach and said, "Be happy, my innards, be happy! Think how much holiness there is in matzah, in *maror*, in *afikoman*, in *karpas*, in *korech*, in the Four Cups, in the festival meal. And, at one and the same time, it has all descended into my innards. Be happy!" And his eyes shed tears of joy (*Mekor Chaim* 99).

דַּנְתָּ מֶלֶךְ גְּרָר בַּחֲלוֹם הַלַּיְלָה.
הִפְחַדְתָּ אֲרַמִּי בְּאֶמֶשׁ לַיְלָה.
וַיָּשַׂר יִשְׂרָאֵל לְמַלְאָךְ וַיּוּכַל לוֹ לַיְלָה.
וַיְהִי בַּחֲצִי הַלַּיְלָה.

זֶרַע בְּכוֹרֵי פַתְרוֹס מָחַצְתָּ בַּחֲצִי הַלַּיְלָה.
חֵילָם לֹא מָצְאוּ בְּקוּמָם בַּלַּיְלָה.
טִיסַת נְגִיד חֲרוֹשֶׁת סִלִּיתָ בְּכוֹכְבֵי לַיְלָה.
וַיְהִי בַּחֲצִי הַלַּיְלָה.

יָעַץ מְחָרֵף לְנוֹפֵף אִוּוּי הוֹבַשְׁתָּ פְגָרָיו בַּלַּיְלָה.
כָּרַע בֵּל וּמַצָּבוֹ בְּאִישׁוֹן לַיְלָה.
לְאִישׁ חֲמוּדוֹת נִגְלָה רָז חֲזוֹת לַיְלָה.
וַיְהִי בַּחֲצִי הַלַּיְלָה.

מִשְׁתַּכֵּר בִּכְלֵי קֹדֶשׁ נֶהֱרַג בּוֹ בַּלַּיְלָה.
נוֹשַׁע מִבּוֹר אֲרָיוֹת פּוֹתֵר בִּעֲתוּתֵי לַיְלָה.
שִׂנְאָה נָטַר אֲגָגִי וְכָתַב סְפָרִים בַּלַּיְלָה.
וַיְהִי בַּחֲצִי הַלַּיְלָה.

עוֹרַרְתָּ נִצְחֲךָ עָלָיו בְּנֶדֶד שְׁנַת לַיְלָה.
פּוּרָה תִדְרוֹךְ לְשֹׁמֵר מַה מִּלַּיְלָה.
צָרַח כַּשּׁוֹמֵר וְשָׂח אָתָא בֹקֶר וְגַם לַיְלָה.
וַיְהִי בַּחֲצִי הַלַּיְלָה.

קָרֵב יוֹם אֲשֶׁר הוּא לֹא יוֹם וְלֹא לַיְלָה.

קָרֵב יוֹם

Hasten the day (of Mashiach)

R' Shlomo of Bobov

Once, at the close of Yom Kippur, *R' Shlomo of Bobov* spoke to a simple youth and asked him, "Tell me, what did you think of during the prayers?"

You judged the king of Gerar (Avimelech),
in a dream by night.
You frightened the Aramean (Lavan), in the dark
of night.
Israel (Yaakov) fought with an angel
and overcame him by night.
It came to pass at midnight.

Egypt's first-born You crushed at midnight.
Their host they found not upon arising at night.
The army of the prince of Charoshes (Sisera)
You swept away with stars of the night.
It came to pass at midnight.

The blasphemer (Sennacherib) planned to raise his
hand against Jerusalem —
but You withered his corpses by night.
Bel was overturned with its pedestal,
in the darkness of night.
To the man of Your delights (Daniel),
was revealed the mystery of the visions of night.
It came to pass at midnight.

He (Belshazzar) who caroused from the holy vessels
was killed that very night.
From the lion's den was rescued he (Daniel)
who interpreted the 'terrors' of the night.
The Aggagite (Haman) nursed hatred
and wrote decrees at night.
It came to pass at midnight.

You began Your triumph over him
when You disturbed (Ahaseurus') sleep at night.
Trample the wine-press to help those who ask the
watchman, 'What of the long night?'
He will shout, like a watchman, and say:
'Morning shall come after night.'
It came to pass at midnight.

Hasten the day (of Mashiach),
that is neither day nor night.

"I thought about the approaching night; I awaited the dark, so that I would be able to eat already."

"Young man," said the Rebbe, "you waited for night to fall; I prayed that the morning would come, the morning when the light of the *Mashiach* would be revealed" (*Kerem HaChasidus* III 147).

רָם הוֹדַע כִּי לְךָ הַיּוֹם אַף לְךָ הַלַּיְלָה.
שׁוֹמְרִים הַפְקֵד לְעִירְךָ כָּל הַיּוֹם וְכָל הַלַּיְלָה.
תָּאִיר כְּאוֹר יוֹם חֶשְׁכַּת לַיְלָה.

וַיְהִי בַּחֲצִי הַלַּיְלָה.

On the second night recite the following.
On the first night continue on page 182.

וּבְכֵן וַאֲמַרְתֶּם זֶבַח פֶּסַח:

אֹמֶץ גְּבוּרוֹתֶיךָ הִפְלֵאתָ בַּפֶּסַח.
בְּרֹאשׁ כָּל מוֹעֲדוֹת נִשֵּׂאתָ פֶּסַח.
גִּלִּיתָ לְאֶזְרָחִי חֲצוֹת לֵיל פֶּסַח.

וַאֲמַרְתֶּם זֶבַח פֶּסַח.

דְּלָתָיו דָּפַקְתָּ כְּחֹם הַיּוֹם בַּפֶּסַח.
הִסְעִיד נוֹצְצִים עֻגוֹת מַצּוֹת בַּפֶּסַח.
וְאֶל הַבָּקָר רָץ זֵכֶר לְשׁוֹר עֵרֶךְ פֶּסַח.

וַאֲמַרְתֶּם זֶבַח פֶּסַח.

זוֹעֲמוּ סְדוֹמִים וְלוֹהֲטוּ בָּאֵשׁ בַּפֶּסַח.
חֻלַּץ לוֹט מֵהֶם וּמַצּוֹת אָפָה בְּקֵץ פֶּסַח.

הִסְעִיד נוֹצְצִים / *He satiated the angels*

R' Avraham David of Botshash

R' Avraham David of Botshash ate very sparingly. He would often say, "Eating makes a man unspiritual: Adam sinned through eating; the angels maintain their lofty spiritual heights because they need not eat. That is why Avraham told the angels who were his guests, 'I will take some bread and you will nourish your hearts; after *that* you will pass on' (*Bereishis* 18:5) — let us see how you will act after you have eaten" (*Da'as Kedoshim*).

R' Yoel Teitelbaum of Satmar

The angels asked of the Holy One, "Put Your grandeur on the heavens" (*Tehillim* 8:2) — "leave the Torah among us." To which the Holy One replied, "When you descended to earth, as guests of Avraham, you ate milk and meat in a

Most High — make known that Yours
are day and night.
Appoint guards for Your city,
all the day and all the night.
Brighten like the light of day the darkness of night.
It came to pass at midnight.

On the second night recite the following.
On the first night continue on page 183.

And you shall say: This is the feast of Passover.

You displayed wondrously Your mighty powers
on Passover.
Above all festivals You elevated Passover.
To the Oriental (Avraham) You revealed
the future midnight of Passover.
And you shall say: This is the feast of Passover.

At his door You knocked in the heat of the day
on Passover;
He satiated the angels with matzah-cakes
on Passover.
And he ran to the herd — symbolic of
the sacrificial beast of Passover.
And you shall say: This is the feast of Passover.

The Sodomites provoked (God) and were devoured
by fire on Passover;
Lot was withdrawn from them — he had baked
matzos at the time of Passover.

---

single meal."

"This shows us," said the *Satmar Rav*, R' Yoel Teitelbaum, "that one can forfeit the entire Torah because of a single non-kosher meal" (*Beis D'li*, p. 25).

R' Yitzchak of Vurka

When *R' Yitzchak of Vurka* visited Kintzk, a well-known wealthy man, R' Yechiel, invited him to his home and prepared a banquet-like repast in his honor. When the Rebbe reached the house he saw that the chandeliers were all ablaze and the steps were strewn with carpets. "If you promise me," said the Rebbe, "that you will light all these lights and spread the carpets for every other guest, too, I will agree that you may do it for me. The laws of the *mitzvah* of receiving guests (הַכְנָסַת אוֹרְחִים) make no distinction between one guest and another,

טְאטֵאתָ אַדְמַת מוֹף וְנוֹף בְּעָבְרְךָ בַּפֶּסַח.

וַאֲמַרְתֶּם זֶבַח פֶּסַח.

יָהּ רֹאשׁ כָּל אוֹן מָחַצְתָּ בְּלֵיל שִׁמּוּר פֶּסַח.

כַּבִּיר עַל בֵּן בְּכוֹר פָּסַחְתָּ בְּדַם פֶּסַח.

לְבִלְתִּי תֵּת מַשְׁחִית לָבֹא בִּפְתָחַי בַּפֶּסַח.

וַאֲמַרְתֶּם זֶבַח פֶּסַח.

מְסֻגֶּרֶת סֻגָּרָה בְּעִתּוֹתֵי פֶּסַח.

נִשְׁמְדָה מִדְיָן בִּצְלִיל שְׂעוֹרֵי עֹמֶר פֶּסַח.

שׂוֹרְפוּ מִשְׁמַנֵּי פּוּל וְלוּד בִּיקַד יְקוֹד פֶּסַח.

וַאֲמַרְתֶּם זֶבַח פֶּסַח.

עוֹד הַיּוֹם בְּנֹב לַעֲמוֹד עַד גָּעָה עוֹנַת פֶּסַח.

פַּס יַד כָּתְבָה לְקַעֲקֵעַ צוּל בַּפֶּסַח.

צָפֹה הַצָּפִית עָרוֹךְ הַשֻּׁלְחָן בַּפֶּסַח.

וַאֲמַרְתֶּם זֶבַח פֶּסַח.

קָהָל כִּנְּסָה הֲדַסָּה צוֹם לְשַׁלֵּשׁ בַּפֶּסַח.

רֹאשׁ מִבֵּית רָשָׁע מָחַצְתָּ בְּעֵץ חֲמִשִּׁים בַּפֶּסַח.

שְׁתֵּי אֵלֶּה רֶגַע תָּבִיא לְעוּצִית בַּפֶּסַח.

תָּעֹז יָדְךָ וְתָרוּם יְמִינְךָ כְּלֵיל הִתְקַדֵּשׁ חַג פֶּסַח.

וַאֲמַרְתֶּם זֶבַח פֶּסַח.

---

just as there is no distinction between one *shofar* and another in the *mitzvah* of blowing the *shofar*."

R' Yechiel had no choice but to extinguish the lights and roll up the carpets (*Zikkukin DeNura* 28).

You swept clean the soil of Moph and Noph (in
Egypt) when You passed through on Passover.
And you shall say: This is the feast of Passover.

God, You crushed every firstborn of On (in Egypt)
on the watchful night of Passover.
But Master — Your own firstborn, You skipped
by merit of the blood of Passover,
Not to allow the Destroyer to enter my doors
on Passover.
And you shall say: This is the feast of Passover.

The beleaguered (Jericho) was besieged
on Passover.
Midian was destroyed with a barley cake,
from the Omer of Passover.
The mighty nobles of Pul and Lud (Assyria) were
consumed in a great conflagration on Passover.
And you shall say: This is the feast of Passover.

He (Sennacherib) would have stood that day at Nob,
but for the advent of Passover.
A hand inscribed the destruction of Zul (Babylon)
on Passover.
As the watch was set, and the royal table decked
on Passover.
And you shall say: This is the feast of Passover.

Hadassah (Esther) gathered a congregation
for a three-day fast on Passover.
You caused the head of the evil clan (Haman) to be
hanged on a fifty-cubit gallows on Passover.
Doubly, will You bring in an instant
upon Utsis (Edom) on Passover.
Let Your hand be strong, and Your right arm exalted,
as on that night when You hallowed the festival
of Passover.
And you shall say: This is the feast of Passover.

On both nights continue here:

כִּי לוֹ נָאֶה, כִּי לוֹ יָאֶה:

אַדִּיר בִּמְלוּכָה, **בָּחוּר** כַּהֲלָכָה, **גְּדוּדָיו** יֹאמְרוּ לוֹ, לְךָ וּלְךָ, לְךָ כִּי לְךָ, לְךָ אַף לְךָ, לְךָ יהוה הַמַּמְלָכָה, כִּי לוֹ נָאֶה, כִּי לוֹ יָאֶה.

דָּגוּל בִּמְלוּכָה, **הָדוּר** כַּהֲלָכָה, **וָתִיקָיו** יֹאמְרוּ לוֹ, לְךָ וּלְךָ, לְךָ כִּי לְךָ, לְךָ אַף לְךָ, לְךָ יהוה הַמַּמְלָכָה, כִּי לוֹ נָאֶה, כִּי לוֹ יָאֶה.

זַכַּאי בִּמְלוּכָה, **חָסִין** כַּהֲלָכָה, **טַפְסְרָיו** יֹאמְרוּ לוֹ, לְךָ וּלְךָ, לְךָ כִּי לְךָ, לְךָ אַף לְךָ, לְךָ יהוה הַמַּמְלָכָה, כִּי לוֹ נָאֶה, כִּי לוֹ יָאֶה.

יָחִיד בִּמְלוּכָה, **כַּבִּיר** כַּהֲלָכָה, **לִמּוּדָיו** יֹאמְרוּ לוֹ, לְךָ וּלְךָ, לְךָ כִּי לְךָ, לְךָ אַף לְךָ, לְךָ יהוה הַמַּמְלָכָה, כִּי לוֹ נָאֶה, כִּי לוֹ יָאֶה.

מוֹשֵׁל בִּמְלוּכָה, **נוֹרָא** כַּהֲלָכָה, **סְבִיבָיו** יֹאמְרוּ לוֹ, לְךָ וּלְךָ, לְךָ כִּי לְךָ, לְךָ אַף לְךָ, לְךָ יהוה הַמַּמְלָכָה, כִּי לוֹ נָאֶה, כִּי לוֹ יָאֶה.

עָנָיו בִּמְלוּכָה, **פּוֹדֶה** כַּהֲלָכָה, **צַדִּיקָיו** יֹאמְרוּ לוֹ, לְךָ וּלְךָ, לְךָ כִּי לְךָ, לְךָ אַף לְךָ, לְךָ יהוה הַמַּמְלָכָה, כִּי לוֹ נָאֶה, כִּי לוֹ יָאֶה.

כִּי לוֹ נָאֶה / *To Him praise is due*

R' Shlomo of Bobov

Once *R' Shlomo of Bobov* received a perfect, beautiful *esrog*. Its shape was lovely, the color gold, proper ridges and grooves, the stem sunken into its cavity, a "belted" waist and not a speck of an imperfection, not a scar, be it ever so slight, of leaf or thorn. The *esrog* was an object of wonder and became the talk of the town.

On both nights continue here:

To Him praise is due! To Him praise is fitting!

Powerful in majesty, perfectly distinguished, His companies of angels say to Him: Yours and only Yours; Yours, yes Yours; Yours, surely Yours; Yours, HASHEM, is the sovereignty. To Him praise is due! To Him praise is fitting!

Supreme in kingship, perfectly glorious, His faithful say to Him: Yours and only Yours; Yours, yes Yours; Yours, surely Yours; Yours, HASHEM, is the sovereignty. To Him praise is due! To Him praise is fitting!

Pure in kingship, perfectly mighty, His angels say to Him: Yours and only Yours; Yours, yes Yours; Yours, surely Yours; Yours, HASHEM, is the sovereignty. To Him praise is due! To Him praise is fitting!

Alone in kingship, perfectly omnipotent, His scholars say to Him: Yours and only Yours; Yours, yes Yours; Yours, surely Yours; Yours, HASHEM, is the sovereignty. To Him praise is due! To Him praise is fitting!

Commanding in kingship, perfectly wondrous, His surrounding (angels) say to Him: Yours and only Yours; Yours, yes Yours; Yours, surely Yours; Yours, HASHEM, is the sovereignty. To Him praise is due! To Him praise is fitting!

Gentle in Kingship, perfectly the Redeemer, His righteous say to Him: Yours and only Yours; Yours, yes Yours; Yours, surely Yours; Yours, HASHEM, is the sovereignty. To Him praise is due! To Him praise is fitting!

However, when the time came for performing the *mitzvah* of *lulav* and *esrog*, to everyone's astonishment the Rebbe made his blessing over another *esrog* which did not approach the marvelous *esrog* in beauty. Yet no one dared to say a word to him.

Meanwhile, a youth, bitten by curiosity, went up to the Rebbe's *succah* to

קָדוֹשׁ בִּמְלוּכָה, רַחוּם כַּהֲלָכָה, שִׁנְאַנָּיו יֹאמְרוּ לוֹ, לְךָ וּלְךָ, לְךָ כִּי לְךָ, לְךָ אַף לְךָ, לְךָ יהוה הַמַּמְלָכָה, כִּי לוֹ נָאֶה, כִּי לוֹ יָאֶה.

תַּקִּיף בִּמְלוּכָה, תּוֹמֵךְ כַּהֲלָכָה, תְּמִימָיו יֹאמְרוּ לוֹ, לְךָ וּלְךָ, לְךָ כִּי לְךָ, לְךָ אַף לְךָ, לְךָ יהוה הַמַּמְלָכָה, כִּי לוֹ נָאֶה, כִּי לוֹ יָאֶה.

אַדִּיר הוּא יִבְנֶה בֵיתוֹ בְּקָרוֹב, בִּמְהֵרָה, בִּמְהֵרָה, בְּיָמֵינוּ בְּקָרוֹב. אֵל בְּנֵה, אֵל בְּנֵה, בְּנֵה בֵיתְךָ בְּקָרוֹב.

בָּחוּר הוּא. גָּדוֹל הוּא. דָּגוּל הוּא. יִבְנֶה בֵיתוֹ בְּקָרוֹב, בִּמְהֵרָה, בִּמְהֵרָה, בְּיָמֵינוּ בְּקָרוֹב. אֵל בְּנֵה, אֵל בְּנֵה, בְּנֵה בֵיתְךָ בְּקָרוֹב.

הָדוּר הוּא. וָתִיק הוּא. זַכַּאי הוּא. חָסִיד הוּא. יִבְנֶה בֵיתוֹ בְּקָרוֹב, בִּמְהֵרָה, בִּמְהֵרָה, בְּיָמֵינוּ בְּקָרוֹב. אֵל בְּנֵה, אֵל בְּנֵה, בְּנֵה בֵיתְךָ בְּקָרוֹב.

טָהוֹר הוּא. יָחִיד הוּא. כַּבִּיר הוּא. לָמוּד הוּא. מֶלֶךְ הוּא. נוֹרָא הוּא. סַגִּיב הוּא. עִזּוּז הוּא. פּוֹדֶה הוּא. צַדִּיק הוּא. יִבְנֶה בֵיתוֹ בְּקָרוֹב, בִּמְהֵרָה,

---

look at the fabled *esrog* from up close. As he raised it, his hand trembled in fright lest he be caught in the act, and the *esrog* dropped. In hurried confusion, he picked it up, put it back into its box and quickly slipped out of the *succah*.

When the Rebbe entered his *succah*, he sensed that someone had touched the *esrog* box. He removed the *esrog* and saw that the *pittam* (tip) was fastened to the *esrog* by a needle. Previously, the needle had gone undetected, but the fall had disturbed the joint and now the needle was clearly visible.

"When I saw the *esrog*," said the Rebbe with a smile, "I saw perfection

Holy in kingship, perfectly merciful, His troops of angels say to Him: Yours and only Yours; Yours, yes Yours; Yours, surely Yours; Yours, HASHEM, is the sovereignty. To Him praise is due! To Him praise is fitting.

Almighty in kingship, perfectly sustaining, His perfect ones say to Him: Yours and only Yours; Yours, yes Yours; Yours, surely Yours; Yours, HASHEM, is the sovereignty. To Him praise is due! To Him praise is fitting!

He is most mighty. May He soon rebuild His House, speedily, yes speedily, in our days, soon. God, rebuild, God, rebuild, rebuild Your House soon!

He is distinguished, He is great, He is exalted. May He soon rebuild His House, speedily, yes speedily, in our days, soon. God, rebuild, God, rebuild, rebuild Your House soon!

He is all glorious, He is faithful, He is faultless, He is righteous. May He soon rebuild His House, speedily, yes speedily, in our days, soon. God, rebuild, God, rebuild, rebuild Your House soon!

He is pure, He is unique, He is powerful, He is all-wise, He is King, He is awesome, He is sublime, He is all-powerful, He is the Redeemer, He is the all-righteous. May He soon rebuild His House,

---

and beauty come true. But, specifically because of that I refrained from pronouncing a blessing over it. For perfection without a fault can only be attributed to the Master of the universe. 'To Him praise is due! To Him praise is fitting!' Other than He, there is nothing that does not have its fault. And it is now clear that the beautiful *esrog* was impaired and not fit for a blessing!" (*Kerem HaChasidus* III 139).

לְךָ אַף לְךָ / *Yours, surely Yours*

R' David Moshe of Kretchnif

R' Yisrael of Ruzhin once lamented to a *tzaddik*, "When will that time come when

בִּמְהֵרָה, בְּיָמֵינוּ בְּקָרוֹב. אֵל בְּנֵה, אֵל בְּנֵה, בְּנֵה בֵיתְךָ בְּקָרוֹב.

קָדוֹשׁ הוּא. רַחוּם הוּא. שַׁדַּי הוּא. תַּקִּיף הוּא. יִבְנֶה בֵיתוֹ בְּקָרוֹב, בִּמְהֵרָה, בִּמְהֵרָה, בְּיָמֵינוּ בְּקָרוֹב. אֵל בְּנֵה, אֵל בְּנֵה, בְּנֵה בֵיתְךָ בְּקָרוֹב.

אֶחָד מִי יוֹדֵעַ? אֶחָד אֲנִי יוֹדֵעַ. אֶחָד אֱלֹהֵינוּ שֶׁבַּשָּׁמַיִם וּבָאָרֶץ.

שְׁנַיִם מִי יוֹדֵעַ? שְׁנַיִם אֲנִי יוֹדֵעַ. שְׁנֵי לֻחוֹת הַבְּרִית, אֶחָד אֱלֹהֵינוּ שֶׁבַּשָּׁמַיִם וּבָאָרֶץ.

שְׁלֹשָׁה מִי יוֹדֵעַ? שְׁלֹשָׁה אֲנִי יוֹדֵעַ. שְׁלֹשָׁה אָבוֹת, שְׁנֵי לֻחוֹת הַבְּרִית, אֶחָד אֱלֹהֵינוּ שֶׁבַּשָּׁמַיִם וּבָאָרֶץ.

אַרְבַּע מִי יוֹדֵעַ? אַרְבַּע אֲנִי יוֹדֵעַ. אַרְבַּע אִמָּהוֹת, שְׁלֹשָׁה אָבוֹת, שְׁנֵי לֻחוֹת הַבְּרִית, אֶחָד אֱלֹהֵינוּ שֶׁבַּשָּׁמַיִם וּבָאָרֶץ.

חֲמִשָּׁה מִי יוֹדֵעַ? חֲמִשָּׁה אֲנִי יוֹדֵעַ. חֲמִשָּׁה חֻמְשֵׁי תוֹרָה, אַרְבַּע אִמָּהוֹת, שְׁלֹשָׁה אָבוֹת,

---

we will truly be able to serve Hashem, without any personal interests, 'except to Hashem only' (*Shemos* 22:19)?"

"It is difficult," replied the *tzaddik*, "to find devotion directed solely to Hashem, 'Yours, yes Yours' (לְךָ כִּי לְךָ). But we can easily reach a level where the service is *also* for the sake of Hashem (לְךָ אַף לְךָ)" [אַף is to be understood as *also*] (*Arba'ah Arazim* 100).

אֶחָד מִי יוֹדֵעַ / *Who knows one?*

R' Yissachar Dov of Belz

Why do we say, "Who knows one," specifically on the evening of the Seder? Is this not a

speedily, yes speedily, in our days, soon. God, rebuild, God, rebuild, rebuild Your House soon!

He is holy, He is compassionate, He is Almighty, He is omnipotent. May He soon rebuild His House, speedily, yes speedily, in our days, soon. God, rebuild, God, rebuild, rebuild Your House soon!

Who knows one? I know one: One is our God, in heaven and on earth.

Who knows two? I know two: two are the Tablets of the Covenant; One is our God, in heaven and on earth.

Who knows three? I know three: three are the Patriarchs; two are the Tablets of the Covenant; One is our God, in heaven and on earth.

Who knows four? I know four: four are the Matriarchs; three are the Patriarchs; two are the Tablets of the Covenant; One is our God, in heaven and on earth.

Who knows five? I know five: five are the Books of Torah; four are the Matriarchs; three are the Patri-

---

subject that is constantly with us, day in day out?

Let us draw a parallel. A rich man does not reveal his assets to the world at large. But when he has had too much too drink, "the wine goes in and the secrets are let out"; then, he holds forth on what he possesses. So, too, at the end of the evening of the Seder, after we have drunk four cups of wine, we count up our treasure: *One is our God*; *two are the Tablets of the Covenant*; *three are the Patriarchs* . . . (*Admorei Belz* III 100).

שְׁנַיִם מִי יוֹדֵעַ . . . אֶחָד אֱלֹקֵינוּ / *Who knows two? . . . One is our God*

R' Yitzchak of Vurka

We may speak of "two", of "three", of "four." But the end result is always: "One is our God, in heaven and on earth" (*Siach Sarfei Kodesh* v. 59).

[The *Rebbe of Vurka* extracted an important thought from the very form of the song.]

שְׁנֵי לֻחוֹת הַבְּרִית, אֶחָד אֱלֹהֵינוּ שֶׁבַּשָּׁמַיִם וּבָאָרֶץ.

שִׁשָּׁה מִי יוֹדֵעַ? שִׁשָּׁה אֲנִי יוֹדֵעַ. שִׁשָּׁה סִדְרֵי מִשְׁנָה, חֲמִשָּׁה חֻמְשֵׁי תוֹרָה, אַרְבַּע אִמָּהוֹת, שְׁלֹשָׁה אָבוֹת, שְׁנֵי לֻחוֹת הַבְּרִית, אֶחָד אֱלֹהֵינוּ שֶׁבַּשָּׁמַיִם וּבָאָרֶץ.

שִׁבְעָה מִי יוֹדֵעַ? שִׁבְעָה אֲנִי יוֹדֵעַ. שִׁבְעָה יְמֵי שַׁבַּתָּא, שִׁשָּׁה סִדְרֵי מִשְׁנָה, חֲמִשָּׁה חֻמְשֵׁי תוֹרָה, אַרְבַּע אִמָּהוֹת, שְׁלֹשָׁה אָבוֹת, שְׁנֵי לֻחוֹת הַבְּרִית, אֶחָד אֱלֹהֵינוּ שֶׁבַּשָּׁמַיִם וּבָאָרֶץ.

שְׁמוֹנָה מִי יוֹדֵעַ? שְׁמוֹנָה אֲנִי יוֹדֵעַ. שְׁמוֹנָה יְמֵי מִילָה, שִׁבְעָה יְמֵי שַׁבַּתָּא, שִׁשָּׁה סִדְרֵי מִשְׁנָה, חֲמִשָּׁה חֻמְשֵׁי תוֹרָה, אַרְבַּע אִמָּהוֹת, שְׁלֹשָׁה אָבוֹת, שְׁנֵי לֻחוֹת הַבְּרִית, אֶחָד אֱלֹהֵינוּ שֶׁבַּשָּׁמַיִם וּבָאָרֶץ.

שִׁשָּׁה סִדְרֵי מִשְׁנָה / *Six are the Orders of the Mishnah*

R' Tzvi Elimelech of Bluzhov

One of the elder chasidim entered the chamber of *R' Tzvi Elimelech of Bluzhov* in the last winter of the Rebbe's life and found him reciting *mishnayos* from memory, in the manner of a schoolboy. The chasid's face expressed obvious astonishment, and the Rebbe felt that he should explain his behavior.

"Behold the day is coming, that terrible day," said the Rebbe, and smote himself on his lips, as if he had just passed on bad news, "that day on which we see the awesome angel, studded with eyes, whose stature fills the height from earth until the heavens. And he attempts to seduce a man in the last moment of life." The Rebbe did not leave off striking his lips. "Know that none of the fears that a man experiences in his life comes close to the fear he feels at that moment! At that moment whoever knows ten chapters of *mishnayos* by heart need not fear the angel at all!" (*Uvda D'Aharon*, p. 80).

archs; two are the Tablets of the Covenant; One is our God, in heaven and on earth.

Who knows six? I know six: six are the Orders of the Mishnah; five are the Books of the Torah; four are the Matriarchs; three are the Patriarchs; two are the Tablets of the Covenant; One is our God, in heaven and on earth.

Who knows seven? I know seven: seven are the days of the week; six are the Orders of the Mishnah; five are the Books of the Torah; four are the Matriarchs; three are the Patriarchs; two are the Tablets of the Covenant; One is our God, in heaven and on earth.

Who knows eight? I know eight: eight are the days of circumcision; seven are the days of the week; six are the Orders of the Mishnah; five are the Books of the Torah; four are the Matriarchs; three are the Patriarchs; two are the Tablets of the Covenant; One is our God, in heaven and on earth.

שְׁמוֹנָה יְמֵי מִילָה / *Eight are the days of circumcision*

R' David of Lelov

R' Isaac had come to visit his brother *R' David of Lelov*. Shortly after his arrival his brother, the Rebbe, turned to him and said, "Although it is not mannerly to tell a guest — and a brother — to return home, nevertheless, I'm telling you to go home immediately."

R' Isaac was frightened and wondered what had happened at home, what tragedy, that his brother should pack him off in such haste. He didn't walk; he ran — as quickly as he could. Upon reaching home, he found everyone in the family whole and healthy. He thanked the Holy One, but could not help but be puzzled by his brother's conduct.

He was still trying to overcome his wonder, when the door burst open and a stranger fell into the room in a faint. R' Isaac hurried over, carried him to a couch and helped him recover. "What happened?" asked R' Isaac.

"Today is the eighth day after the birth of my son," said the man. "I've been running around all day searching for a *mohel*. Wherever I asked, I was told that the *mohel* was away. I thought I would go out of my mind. Would the child be circumcised after the eighth day? I traveled from town to town;

תִּשְׁעָה מִי יוֹדֵעַ? תִּשְׁעָה אֲנִי יוֹדֵעַ. תִּשְׁעָה יַרְחֵי לֵדָה, שְׁמוֹנָה יְמֵי מִילָה, שִׁבְעָה יְמֵי שַׁבַּתָּא, שִׁשָּׁה סִדְרֵי מִשְׁנָה, חֲמִשָּׁה חֻמְשֵׁי תוֹרָה, אַרְבַּע אִמָּהוֹת, שְׁלֹשָׁה אָבוֹת, שְׁנֵי לֻחוֹת הַבְּרִית, אֶחָד אֱלֹהֵינוּ שֶׁבַּשָּׁמַיִם וּבָאָרֶץ.

עֲשָׂרָה מִי יוֹדֵעַ? עֲשָׂרָה אֲנִי יוֹדֵעַ. עֲשָׂרָה דִבְּרַיָּא, תִּשְׁעָה יַרְחֵי לֵדָה, שְׁמוֹנָה יְמֵי מִילָה, שִׁבְעָה יְמֵי שַׁבַּתָּא, שִׁשָּׁה סִדְרֵי מִשְׁנָה, חֲמִשָּׁה חֻמְשֵׁי תוֹרָה, אַרְבַּע אִמָּהוֹת, שְׁלֹשָׁה אָבוֹת, שְׁנֵי לֻחוֹת הַבְּרִית, אֶחָד אֱלֹהֵינוּ שֶׁבַּשָּׁמַיִם וּבָאָרֶץ.

I was finally told to come here. I ran all the way; my strength gave out and I fainted."

R' Isaac quickly took up the circumcision knife and, following the lead of the stranger, arrived at the man's home before sundown. R' Isaac performed the circumcision in its due time.

Now, he understood why his brother had dismissed him so abruptly (*Pri Kodesh Hillulim,* p. 24).

R' Yisrael of Bluzhov When I was in the concentration camp, working at forced labor, a woman suddenly ran up to me and asked in disturbed tones, "Rebbe, perhaps you have a knife?"

I was not allowed to lift my head to answer, for the guards had orders to shoot to kill for daring to speak while working. But I understood that the unfortunate woman could no longer bear living and wished to commit suicide. I felt I must say something to her. "Listen, my daughter," I said, "Our life is a valuable object of safekeeping which the Creator has deposited with us. We have no right to cut it short by our own hand. He gave us life; it is He Who will take it from us."

I was still speaking when the Nazi guard caught sight of her. "What did she want?" he screamed.

I kept silent, but the woman said, "I asked him for a knife."

The German laughed a satanic laugh and said, "You wish to kill yourself? Let me help you!" And he drew his knife from his belt and handed it to her.

The woman snatched up the knife eagerly and ran to a corner where a bundle of cloth was lying. She loosened the tie, and behold, there was a tiny infant.

Who knows nine? I know nine: nine are the months of pregnancy; eight are the days of circumcision; seven are the days of the week; six are the Orders of the Mishnah; five are the Books of the Torah; four are the Matriarchs; three are the Patriarchs; two are the Tablets of the Covenant; One is our God, in heaven and on earth.

Who knows ten? I know ten: ten are the Ten Commandments; nine are the months of pregnancy; eight are the days of circumcision; seven are the days of the week; six are the Orders of the Mishnah; five are the Books of the Torah; four are the Matriarchs; three are the Patriarchs; two are the Tablets of the Covenant; One is our God, in heaven and on earth.

"Master of the universe," cried the woman, "I know what fate is in store for us here! But eight days ago You granted me an infant. His circumcision should take place today. I wish to return him to You as a circumcised proper Jew." With that she bent down and circumcised the child.

She returned and handed the cruel guard his knife. He was so shocked that he took it without a word.

עֲשָׂרָה דִּבְּרַיָּא / *The Ten Commandments*

R' Elimelech of Lizensk

R' Shmelke of Nikolsburg spoke before his community incisive words conveying lofty thoughts. When he had ended, *R' Elimelech of Lizensk* rose and said, "There was once a king's horse which took ill. They summoned the greatest of doctors; they dosed the horse with all sorts of medicines; they bandaged him. Nothing helped, until they finally brought a veterinarian. He cured the animal. For a horse, you need a horse doctor.

"Your saintly *rav* has given you dainty medicines that one administers to refined patients — deep discourses, noble ideas. But I'll speak to you in your tongue. Keep the Ten Commandments — 'You shall not kill,' 'You shall not steal!' " (*Siach Sarfei Kodesh* V, p. 26).

בַּשָּׁמַיִם וּבָאָרֶץ / *In heaven and on earth*

Fiery Angel of Kotzk

When the great Torah sages of the generation were once assembled, the *Fiery Angel of Kotzk* asked suddenly, "Tell me! Where does the Holy One abide?"

אַחַד עָשָׂר מִי יוֹדֵעַ? אַחַד עָשָׂר אֲנִי יוֹדֵעַ. אַחַד עָשָׂר כּוֹכְבַיָּא, עֲשָׂרָה דִבְּרַיָּא, תִּשְׁעָה יַרְחֵי לֵדָה, שְׁמוֹנָה יְמֵי מִילָה, שִׁבְעָה יְמֵי שַׁבַּתָּא, שִׁשָּׁה סִדְרֵי מִשְׁנָה, חֲמִשָּׁה חֻמְשֵׁי תוֹרָה, אַרְבַּע אִמָּהוֹת, שְׁלשָׁה אָבוֹת, שְׁנֵי לֻחוֹת הַבְּרִית, אֶחָד אֱלֹהֵינוּ שֶׁבַּשָּׁמַיִם וּבָאָרֶץ.

שְׁנֵים עָשָׂר מִי יוֹדֵעַ? שְׁנֵים עָשָׂר אֲנִי יוֹדֵעַ. שְׁנֵים עָשָׂר שִׁבְטַיָּא, אַחַד עָשָׂר כּוֹכְבַיָּא, עֲשָׂרָה דִבְּרַיָּא, תִּשְׁעָה יַרְחֵי לֵדָה, שְׁמוֹנָה יְמֵי מִילָה, שִׁבְעָה יְמֵי שַׁבַּתָּא, שִׁשָּׁה סִדְרֵי מִשְׁנָה, חֲמִשָּׁה חֻמְשֵׁי תוֹרָה, אַרְבַּע אִמָּהוֹת, שְׁלשָׁה אָבוֹת, שְׁנֵי לֻחוֹת הַבְּרִית, אֶחָד אֱלֹהֵינוּ שֶׁבַּשָּׁמַיִם וּבָאָרֶץ.

שְׁלשָׁה עָשָׂר מִי יוֹדֵעַ? שְׁלשָׁה עָשָׂר אֲנִי יוֹדֵעַ. שְׁלשָׁה עָשָׂר מִדַּיָּא, שְׁנֵים עָשָׂר שִׁבְטַיָּא, אַחַד עָשָׂר כּוֹכְבַיָּא, עֲשָׂרָה דִבְּרַיָּא, תִּשְׁעָה יַרְחֵי לֵדָה, שְׁמוֹנָה יְמֵי מִילָה, שִׁבְעָה יְמֵי שַׁבַּתָּא, שִׁשָּׁה סִדְרֵי מִשְׁנָה, חֲמִשָּׁה חֻמְשֵׁי תוֹרָה, אַרְבַּע אִמָּהוֹת, שְׁלשָׁה אָבוֹת, שְׁנֵי לֻחוֹת הַבְּרִית, אֶחָד אֱלֹהֵינוּ שֶׁבַּשָּׁמַיִם וּבָאָרֶץ.

All smiled, for who does not know that "all the world is filled with His glory" (מְלֹא כָל הָאָרֶץ כְּבוֹדוֹ; *Yeshayahu* 6:3)?

"The Holy One abides," said the Rebbe of Kotzk, in a thundering voice, "wherever He is allowed in!"

No one smiled any longer (*Siach Sarfei Kodesh* I 357).

Who knows eleven? I know eleven: eleven are the stars (in Yosef's dream); ten are the Ten Commandments; nine are the months of pregnancy; eight are the days of circumcision; seven are the days of the week; six are the Orders of the Mishnah; five are the Books of the Torah; four are the Matriarchs; three are the Patriarchs; two are the Tablets of the Covenant; One is our God, in heaven and on earth.

Who knows twelve? I know twelve: twelve are the tribes; eleven are the stars (in Yosef's dream); ten are the Ten Commandments; nine are the months of pregnancy; eight are the days of circumcision; seven are the days of the week; six are the Orders of the Mishnah; five are the Books of the Torah; four are the Matriarchs; three are the Patriarchs; two are the Tablets of the Covenant; One is our God, in heaven and on earth.

Who knows thirteen? I know thirteen: thirteen are the attributes of God; twelve are the tribes; eleven are the stars (in Yosef's dream); ten are the Ten Commandments; nine are the months of pregnancy; eight are the days of circumcision; seven are the days of the week; six are the Orders of the Mishnah; five are the Books of the Torah; four are the Matriarchs; three are the Patriarchs; two are the Tablets of the Covenant; One is our God, in heaven and on earth.

Chidushei HaRim

When the *Chidushei HaRim of Gur* was three years old, he was already known as a prodigy. One day someone who liked to jest said to him, "I'll give you a gold coin if you will tell me where the Holy One resides."

Without hesitation the youngster answered, "And I shall give you two gold coins if you will tell me where He doesn't!"

He received the gold coin (*HaMa'or HaGadol*, p.31).

חַד גַּדְיָא, חַד גַּדְיָא, דְּזַבִּין אַבָּא בִּתְרֵי זוּזֵי, חַד גַּדְיָא חַד גַּדְיָא.

וְאָתָא **שׁוּנְרָא** וְאָכְלָה לְגַדְיָא, דְּזַבִּין אַבָּא בִּתְרֵי זוּזֵי, חַד גַּדְיָא חַד גַּדְיָא.

וְאָתָא **כַלְבָּא** וְנָשַׁךְ לְשׁוּנְרָא, דְּאָכְלָא לְגַדְיָא, דְּזַבִּין אַבָּא בִּתְרֵי זוּזֵי, חַד גַּדְיָא חַד גַּדְיָא.

וְאָתָא **חוּטְרָא** וְהִכָּה לְכַלְבָּא, דְּנָשַׁךְ לְשׁוּנְרָא, דְּאָכְלָה לְגַדְיָא, דְּזַבִּין אַבָּא בִּתְרֵי זוּזֵי, חַד גַּדְיָא חַד גַּדְיָא.

וְאָתָא **נוּרָא** וְשָׂרַף לְחוּטְרָא, דְּהִכָּה לְכַלְבָּא, דְּנָשַׁךְ לְשׁוּנְרָא, דְּאָכְלָה לְגַדְיָא, דְּזַבִּין אַבָּא בִּתְרֵי זוּזֵי, חַד גַּדְיָא חַד גַּדְיָא.

וְאָתָא **מַיָּא** וְכָבָה לְנוּרָא, דְּשָׂרַף לְחוּטְרָא, דְּהִכָּה לְכַלְבָּא, דְּנָשַׁךְ לְשׁוּנְרָא, דְּאָכְלָה לְגַדְיָא, דְּזַבִּין אַבָּא בִּתְרֵי זוּזֵי, חַד גַּדְיָא חַד גַּדְיָא.

חַד גַּדְיָא / *A kid*

R' Nasan Adler

When Frankfurt became embroiled in a fire of controversy which surrounded the conduct of the pious *R' Nasan Adler*, R' Nasan retired to a town where he was unknown. There, he heard men who were strangers to him speaking critically about him.

"Gentlemen," he said, "I've had a question about the *Chad Gadya* poem that has bothered me for a long while.

"The cat which ate the kid did a dastardly deed. If so, the dog which bit the cat acted justly. It follows that the staff which beat the dog was unjust and the fire which burned the staff acted properly; the water should not have extinguished the fire and the ox justly punished the water by drinking it; the ox should not have been slaughtered and the Angel of Death was acting correctly in taking revenge on the slaughterer. And there we have the problem. Why did *Hashem* punish the Angel of Death?"

The audience could find no solution. They asked R' Nasan if he could solve the problem.

A kid, a kid, that father bought for two zuzim, a kid, a kid.

A cat then came and devoured the kid, that father bought for two zuzim, a kid, a kid.

A dog then came and bit the cat, that devoured the kid, that father bought for two zuzim, a kid, a kid.

A stick then came and beat the dog, that bit the cat, that devoured the kid, that father bought for two zuzim, a kid, a kid.

A fire then came and burnt the stick, that beat the dog, that bit the cat, that devoured the kid, that father bought for two zuzim, a kid, a kid.

Water then came and quenched the fire, that burnt the stick, that beat the dog, that bit the cat, that devoured the kid, that father bought for two zuzim, a kid, a kid.

"Indeed, yes," he said. "True, the cat had acted unjustly in devouring the kid. And the father, certainly, had good reason to be angry and punish it. But, although there was a controversy between the father and the cat, what business was it of the dog's? Who asked the dog to get involved? The dogs who involve themselves in a quarrel in which they have no part and fan the fires of controversy are the most guilty of all.

"And thus, the staff was just in beating the dog; the fire which burned it was unjust. The water was just; the ox unjust. The slaughterer was just; the Angel of Death unjust. And the Holy One, Blessed is He, Who slaughtered the Angel of Death, acted in justice" (*Sichos Chachamim* 8).

וְאָתָא נוּרָא / *A fire then came*

Maggid of Kozhnitz

When the armies of Napoleon swept across Europe on their way to invade Russia, one of the divisions camped in the city of Kozhnitz.

A fire broke out and the wooden houses went up in flame. The fire traveled with lightning speed from one thatched roof to the next. The frightened townsmen stood by helplessly, nor were the soldiers able to render aid. The townsmen cried out to the sainted *Maggid of Kozhnitz*. He hurried to the site of the fire, at the head of his chasidim, looked at the

וְאָתָא **תוֹרָא** וְשָׁתָה לְמַיָּא, דְּכָבָה לְנוּרָא, דְּשָׂרַף לְחוּטְרָא, דְּהִכָּה לְכַלְבָּא, דְּנָשַׁךְ לְשׁוּנְרָא, דְּאָכְלָה לְגַדְיָא, דְּזַבִּין אַבָּא בִּתְרֵי זוּזֵי, חַד גַּדְיָא חַד גַּדְיָא.

וְאָתָא **הַשּׁוֹחֵט** וְשָׁחַט לְתוֹרָא, דְּשָׁתָא לְמַיָּא, דְּכָבָה לְנוּרָא, דְּשָׂרַף לְחוּטְרָא, דְּהִכָּה לְכַלְבָּא, דְּנָשַׁךְ לְשׁוּנְרָא, דְּאָכְלָה לְגַדְיָא, דְּזַבִּין אַבָּא בִּתְרֵי זוּזֵי, חַד גַּדְיָא חַד גַּדְיָא.

וְאָתָא **מַלְאַךְ הַמָּוֶת** וְשָׁחַט לְשׁוֹחֵט, דְּשָׁחַט לְתוֹרָא, דְּשָׁתָה לְמַיָּא, דְּכָבָה לְנוּרָא, דְּשָׂרַף לְחוּטְרָא, דְּהִכָּה לְכַלְבָּא, דְּנָשַׁךְ לְשׁוּנְרָא, דְּאָכְלָה לְגַדְיָא, דְּזַבִּין אַבָּא בִּתְרֵי זוּזֵי, חַד גַּדְיָא חַד גַּדְיָא.

וְאָתָא **הַקָּדוֹשׁ בָּרוּךְ הוּא** וְשָׁחַט לְמַלְאַךְ הַמָּוֶת, דְּשָׁחַט לְשׁוֹחֵט, דְּשָׁחַט לְתוֹרָא, דְּשָׁתָה לְמַיָּא, דְּכָבָה לְנוּרָא, דְּשָׂרַף לְחוּטְרָא, דְּהִכָּה לְכַלְבָּא, דְּנָשַׁךְ לְשׁוּנְרָא, דְּאָכְלָה לְגַדְיָא, דְּזַבִּין אַבָּא בִּתְרֵי זוּזֵי, חַד גַּדְיָא חַד גַּדְיָא.

Although the *Haggadah* formally ends at this point, one should continue to occupy himself with the story of the Exodus, and the laws of Pesach, until sleep overtakes him.

---

flames and, wonder of wonders, they began to die down and the fire was extinguished of its own accord.

The division broke camp, participated in the invasion, was beaten and retreated from Russia with the other remnants of the French army. It passed through a town in Germany. And there, once again, the soldiers encountered a fire. The commander of the division hurried to the site of the fire and ordered that the local rabbi be summoned. The rabbi was a

An ox then came and drank the water, that quenched the fire, that burnt the stick, that beat the dog, that bit the cat, that devoured the kid, that father bought for two zuzim, a kid, a kid.

A slaughterer then came and slaughtered the ox, that drank the water, that quenched the fire, that burnt the stick, that beat the dog, that bit the cat, that devoured the kid, that father bought for two zuzim, a kid, a kid.

The angel of death then came and killed the slaughterer, who slaughtered the ox, that drank the water, that quenched the fire, that burnt the stick, that beat the dog, that bit the cat, that devoured the kid, that father bought for two zuzim, a kid, a kid.

The Holy One, Blessed is He, then came and slew the angel of death, who killed the slaughterer, who slaughtered the ox, that drank the water, that quenched the fire, that burnt the stick, that beat the dog, that bit the cat, that devoured the kid, that father bought for two zuzim, a kid, a kid.

Although the *Haggadah* formally ends at this point, one should continue to occupy himself with the story of the Exodus, and the laws of Pesach, until sleep overtakes him.

"modern" one of the Reform stripe and appeared in his clerical garb. The officer ordered him to "look at the fire and let it be extinguished." The rabbi was astonished at the strange command and explained that it was not in his power to extinguish fires by looking at them. The officer became angry and shouted, "Take him away and flog him! What sort of rabbi is this who can't put out a fire by looking at it? He's not a true rabbi; he's an impostor" (*Sipurei Chasidim*).

Many recite שִׁיר הַשִּׁירִים, *Song of Songs,* after the *Haggadah.*

שיר השירים

א

א **שִׁיר הַשִּׁירִים** אֲשֶׁר לִשְׁלֹמֹה. ב יִשָּׁקֵנִי מִנְּשִׁיקוֹת
פִּיהוּ, כִּי טוֹבִים דֹּדֶיךָ מִיָּיִן. ג לְרֵיחַ
שְׁמָנֶיךָ טוֹבִים, שֶׁמֶן תּוּרַק שְׁמֶךָ, עַל כֵּן עֲלָמוֹת אֲהֵבוּךָ.
ד מָשְׁכֵנִי אַחֲרֶיךָ נָּרוּצָה, הֱבִיאַנִי הַמֶּלֶךְ חֲדָרָיו, נָגִילָה
וְנִשְׂמְחָה בָּךְ. נַזְכִּירָה דֹדֶיךָ מִיַּיִן, מֵישָׁרִים אֲהֵבוּךָ. ה שְׁחוֹרָה
אֲנִי וְנָאוָה, בְּנוֹת יְרוּשָׁלָיִם, כְּאָהֳלֵי קֵדָר, כִּירִיעוֹת שְׁלֹמֹה.
ו אַל תִּרְאוּנִי שֶׁאֲנִי שְׁחַרְחֹרֶת, שֶׁשֱּׁזָפַתְנִי הַשָּׁמֶשׁ, בְּנֵי אִמִּי
נִחֲרוּ בִי, שָׂמֻנִי נֹטֵרָה אֶת הַכְּרָמִים, כַּרְמִי שֶׁלִּי לֹא נָטָרְתִּי.
ז הַגִּידָה לִּי, שֶׁאָהֲבָה נַפְשִׁי, אֵיכָה תִרְעֶה, אֵיכָה תַּרְבִּיץ
בַּצָּהֳרָיִם, שַׁלָּמָה אֶהְיֶה כְּעֹטְיָה עַל עֶדְרֵי חֲבֵרֶיךָ. ח אִם לֹא
תֵדְעִי לָךְ, הַיָּפָה בַּנָּשִׁים, צְאִי לָךְ בְּעִקְבֵי הַצֹּאן, וּרְעִי אֶת
גְּדִיֹּתַיִךְ עַל מִשְׁכְּנוֹת הָרֹעִים. ט לְסֻסָתִי בְּרִכְבֵי פַרְעֹה
דִּמִּיתִיךְ, רַעְיָתִי. י נָאווּ לְחָיַיִךְ בַּתֹּרִים, צַוָּארֵךְ בַּחֲרוּזִים.
יא תּוֹרֵי זָהָב נַעֲשֶׂה לָּךְ, עִם נְקֻדּוֹת הַכָּסֶף. יב עַד שֶׁהַמֶּלֶךְ
בִּמְסִבּוֹ, נִרְדִּי נָתַן רֵיחוֹ. יג צְרוֹר הַמֹּר דּוֹדִי לִי, בֵּין שָׁדַי
יָלִין. יד אֶשְׁכֹּל הַכֹּפֶר דּוֹדִי לִי, בְּכַרְמֵי עֵין גֶּדִי. טו הִנָּךְ יָפָה,
רַעְיָתִי, הִנָּךְ יָפָה, עֵינַיִךְ יוֹנִים. טז הִנְּךָ יָפֶה, דוֹדִי, אַף נָעִים,
אַף עַרְשֵׂנוּ רַעֲנָנָה. יז קֹרוֹת בָּתֵּינוּ אֲרָזִים, רַהִיטֵנוּ בְּרוֹתִים.

ב

א אֲנִי חֲבַצֶּלֶת הַשָּׁרוֹן, שׁוֹשַׁנַּת הָעֲמָקִים. ב כְּשׁוֹשַׁנָּה בֵּין
הַחוֹחִים, כֵּן רַעְיָתִי בֵּין הַבָּנוֹת. ג כְּתַפּוּחַ בַּעֲצֵי הַיַּעַר, כֵּן
דּוֹדִי בֵּין הַבָּנִים, בְּצִלּוֹ חִמַּדְתִּי וְיָשַׁבְתִּי, וּפִרְיוֹ מָתוֹק
לְחִכִּי. ד הֱבִיאַנִי אֶל בֵּית הַיָּיִן, וְדִגְלוֹ עָלַי אַהֲבָה. ה סַמְּכוּנִי
בָּאֲשִׁישׁוֹת, רַפְּדוּנִי בַּתַּפּוּחִים, כִּי חוֹלַת אַהֲבָה אָנִי.
ו שְׂמֹאלוֹ תַּחַת לְרֹאשִׁי, וִימִינוֹ תְּחַבְּקֵנִי. ז הִשְׁבַּעְתִּי אֶתְכֶם,

בְּנוֹת יְרוּשָׁלָםִ, בִּצְבָאוֹת אוֹ בְּאַיְלוֹת הַשָּׂדֶה, אִם תָּעִירוּ
וְאִם תְּעוֹרְרוּ אֶת הָאַהֲבָה עַד שֶׁתֶּחְפָּץ. ח קוֹל דּוֹדִי הִנֵּה זֶה
בָּא, מְדַלֵּג עַל הֶהָרִים, מְקַפֵּץ עַל הַגְּבָעוֹת. ט דּוֹמֶה דוֹדִי
לִצְבִי, אוֹ לְעֹפֶר הָאַיָּלִים, הִנֵּה זֶה עוֹמֵד אַחַר כָּתְלֵנוּ,
מַשְׁגִּיחַ מִן הַחַלֹּנוֹת, מֵצִיץ מִן הַחֲרַכִּים. י עָנָה דוֹדִי וְאָמַר
לִי, קוּמִי לָךְ, רַעְיָתִי, יָפָתִי, וּלְכִי לָךְ. יא כִּי הִנֵּה הַסְּתָו
עָבָר, הַגֶּשֶׁם חָלַף הָלַךְ לוֹ. יב הַנִּצָּנִים נִרְאוּ בָאָרֶץ, עֵת
הַזָּמִיר הִגִּיעַ, וְקוֹל הַתּוֹר נִשְׁמַע בְּאַרְצֵנוּ. יג הַתְּאֵנָה חָנְטָה
פַגֶּיהָ, וְהַגְּפָנִים סְמָדַר נָתְנוּ רֵיחַ, קוּמִי לָךְ, רַעְיָתִי, יָפָתִי,
וּלְכִי לָךְ. יד יוֹנָתִי, בְּחַגְוֵי הַסֶּלַע, בְּסֵתֶר הַמַּדְרֵגָה, הַרְאִינִי
אֶת מַרְאַיִךְ, הַשְׁמִיעִנִי אֶת קוֹלֵךְ, כִּי קוֹלֵךְ עָרֵב, וּמַרְאֵיךְ
נָאוֶה. טו אֶחֱזוּ לָנוּ שׁוּעָלִים, שֻׁעָלִים קְטַנִּים, מְחַבְּלִים
כְּרָמִים, וּכְרָמֵינוּ סְמָדַר. טז דּוֹדִי לִי, וַאֲנִי לוֹ, הָרֹעֶה
בַּשּׁוֹשַׁנִּים. יז עַד שֶׁיָּפוּחַ הַיּוֹם, וְנָסוּ הַצְּלָלִים, סֹב דְּמֵה לְךָ,
דוֹדִי, לִצְבִי אוֹ לְעֹפֶר הָאַיָּלִים, עַל הָרֵי בָתֶר.

ג

א עַל מִשְׁכָּבִי בַּלֵּילוֹת בִּקַּשְׁתִּי אֵת שֶׁאָהֲבָה נַפְשִׁי, בִּקַּשְׁתִּיו
וְלֹא מְצָאתִיו. ב אָקוּמָה נָּא וַאֲסוֹבְבָה בָעִיר, בַּשְּׁוָקִים
וּבָרְחֹבוֹת, אֲבַקְשָׁה אֵת שֶׁאָהֲבָה נַפְשִׁי, בִּקַּשְׁתִּיו וְלֹא
מְצָאתִיו. ג מְצָאוּנִי הַשֹּׁמְרִים הַסֹּבְבִים בָּעִיר, אֵת שֶׁאָהֲבָה
נַפְשִׁי רְאִיתֶם. ד כִּמְעַט שֶׁעָבַרְתִּי מֵהֶם, עַד שֶׁמָּצָאתִי אֵת
שֶׁאָהֲבָה נַפְשִׁי, אֲחַזְתִּיו וְלֹא אַרְפֶּנּוּ, עַד שֶׁהֲבֵיאתִיו אֶל
בֵּית אִמִּי, וְאֶל חֶדֶר הוֹרָתִי. ה הִשְׁבַּעְתִּי אֶתְכֶם, בְּנוֹת
יְרוּשָׁלָםִ, בִּצְבָאוֹת אוֹ בְּאַיְלוֹת הַשָּׂדֶה, אִם תָּעִירוּ וְאִם
תְּעוֹרְרוּ אֶת הָאַהֲבָה עַד שֶׁתֶּחְפָּץ. ו מִי זֹאת עֹלָה מִן
הַמִּדְבָּר, כְּתִימְרוֹת עָשָׁן, מְקֻטֶּרֶת מֹר וּלְבוֹנָה, מִכֹּל אַבְקַת
רוֹכֵל. ז הִנֵּה מִטָּתוֹ שֶׁלִּשְׁלֹמֹה, שִׁשִּׁים גִּבֹּרִים סָבִיב לָהּ,
מִגִּבֹּרֵי יִשְׂרָאֵל. ח כֻּלָּם אֲחֻזֵי חֶרֶב, מְלֻמְּדֵי מִלְחָמָה, אִישׁ

חַרְבּוֹ עַל יְרֵכוֹ, מִפַּחַד בַּלֵּילוֹת. ט אַפִּרְיוֹן עָשָׂה לוֹ הַמֶּלֶךְ
שְׁלֹמֹה מֵעֲצֵי הַלְּבָנוֹן. י עַמּוּדָיו עָשָׂה כֶסֶף, רְפִידָתוֹ זָהָב,
מֶרְכָּבוֹ אַרְגָּמָן, תּוֹכוֹ רָצוּף אַהֲבָה מִבְּנוֹת יְרוּשָׁלָיִם.
יא צְאֶינָה וּרְאֶינָה, בְּנוֹת צִיּוֹן, בַּמֶּלֶךְ שְׁלֹמֹה, בַּעֲטָרָה
שֶׁעִטְּרָה לּוֹ אִמּוֹ, בְּיוֹם חֲתֻנָּתוֹ, וּבְיוֹם שִׂמְחַת לִבּוֹ.

ד

א הִנָּךְ יָפָה, רַעְיָתִי, הִנָּךְ יָפָה, עֵינַיִךְ יוֹנִים, מִבַּעַד לְצַמָּתֵךְ,
שַׂעְרֵךְ כְּעֵדֶר הָעִזִּים, שֶׁגָּלְשׁוּ מֵהַר גִּלְעָד. ב שִׁנַּיִךְ כְּעֵדֶר
הַקְּצוּבוֹת שֶׁעָלוּ מִן הָרַחְצָה, שֶׁכֻּלָּם מַתְאִימוֹת, וְשַׁכֻּלָה
אֵין בָּהֶם. ג כְּחוּט הַשָּׁנִי שִׂפְתוֹתַיִךְ, וּמִדְבָּרֵךְ נָאוֶה, כְּפֶלַח
הָרִמּוֹן רַקָּתֵךְ, מִבַּעַד לְצַמָּתֵךְ. ד כְּמִגְדַּל דָּוִיד צַוָּארֵךְ, בָּנוּי
לְתַלְפִּיּוֹת, אֶלֶף הַמָּגֵן תָּלוּי עָלָיו, כֹּל שִׁלְטֵי הַגִּבּוֹרִים.
ה שְׁנֵי שָׁדַיִךְ כִּשְׁנֵי עֳפָרִים, תְּאוֹמֵי צְבִיָּה, הָרוֹעִים בַּשּׁוֹשַׁנִּים.
ו עַד שֶׁיָּפוּחַ הַיּוֹם, וְנָסוּ הַצְּלָלִים, אֵלֶךְ לִי אֶל הַר הַמּוֹר,
וְאֶל גִּבְעַת הַלְּבוֹנָה. ז כֻּלָּךְ יָפָה, רַעְיָתִי, וּמוּם אֵין בָּךְ.
ח אִתִּי מִלְּבָנוֹן, כַּלָּה, אִתִּי מִלְּבָנוֹן תָּבוֹאִי, תָּשׁוּרִי מֵרֹאשׁ
אֲמָנָה, מֵרֹאשׁ שְׂנִיר וְחֶרְמוֹן, מִמְּעֹנוֹת אֲרָיוֹת, מֵהַרְרֵי
נְמֵרִים. ט לִבַּבְתִּנִי, אֲחֹתִי כַלָּה, לִבַּבְתִּנִי בְּאַחַת מֵעֵינַיִךְ,
בְּאַחַד עֲנָק מִצַּוְּרֹנָיִךְ. י מַה יָּפוּ דֹדַיִךְ, אֲחֹתִי כַלָּה, מַה
טֹּבוּ דֹדַיִךְ מִיַּיִן, וְרֵיחַ שְׁמָנַיִךְ מִכָּל בְּשָׂמִים. יא נֹפֶת
תִּטֹּפְנָה שִׂפְתוֹתַיִךְ, כַּלָּה, דְּבַשׁ וְחָלָב תַּחַת לְשׁוֹנֵךְ, וְרֵיחַ
שַׂלְמֹתַיִךְ כְּרֵיחַ לְבָנוֹן. יב גַּן נָעוּל אֲחֹתִי כַלָּה, גַּל נָעוּל,
מַעְיָן חָתוּם. יג שְׁלָחַיִךְ פַּרְדֵּס רִמּוֹנִים, עִם פְּרִי מְגָדִים,
כְּפָרִים עִם נְרָדִים. יד נֵרְדְּ וְכַרְכֹּם, קָנֶה וְקִנָּמוֹן, עִם כָּל עֲצֵי
לְבוֹנָה, מֹר וַאֲהָלוֹת, עִם כָּל רָאשֵׁי בְשָׂמִים. טו מַעְיַן גַּנִּים,
בְּאֵר מַיִם חַיִּים, וְנֹזְלִים מִן לְבָנוֹן. טז עוּרִי צָפוֹן, וּבוֹאִי
תֵימָן, הָפִיחִי גַנִּי, יִזְּלוּ בְשָׂמָיו, יָבֹא דוֹדִי לְגַנּוֹ, וְיֹאכַל פְּרִי
מְגָדָיו.

ה

א בָּאתִי לְגַנִּי, אֲחֹתִי כַלָּה, אָרִיתִי מוֹרִי עִם בְּשָׂמִי, אָכַלְתִּי
יַעְרִי עִם דִּבְשִׁי, שָׁתִיתִי יֵינִי עִם חֲלָבִי, אִכְלוּ רֵעִים, שְׁתוּ
וְשִׁכְרוּ דּוֹדִים. ב אֲנִי יְשֵׁנָה וְלִבִּי עֵר, קוֹל דּוֹדִי דוֹפֵק,
פִּתְחִי לִי, אֲחֹתִי, רַעְיָתִי, יוֹנָתִי, תַמָּתִי, שֶׁרֹּאשִׁי נִמְלָא
טָל, קְוֻצּוֹתַי רְסִיסֵי לָיְלָה. ג פָּשַׁטְתִּי אֶת כֻּתָּנְתִּי, אֵיכָכָה
אֶלְבָּשֶׁנָּה, רָחַצְתִּי אֶת רַגְלַי, אֵיכָכָה אֲטַנְּפֵם. ד דּוֹדִי שָׁלַח
יָדוֹ מִן הַחוֹר, וּמֵעַי הָמוּ עָלָיו. ה קַמְתִּי אֲנִי לִפְתֹּחַ לְדוֹדִי,
וְיָדַי נָטְפוּ מוֹר, וְאֶצְבְּעֹתַי מוֹר עֹבֵר, עַל כַּפּוֹת הַמַּנְעוּל.
ו פָּתַחְתִּי אֲנִי לְדוֹדִי, וְדוֹדִי חָמַק עָבָר, נַפְשִׁי יָצְאָה בְדַבְּרוֹ,
בִּקַּשְׁתִּיהוּ וְלֹא מְצָאתִיהוּ, קְרָאתִיו וְלֹא עָנָנִי. ז מְצָאֻנִי
הַשֹּׁמְרִים הַסֹּבְבִים בָּעִיר, הִכּוּנִי פְצָעוּנִי, נָשְׂאוּ אֶת רְדִידִי
מֵעָלַי שֹׁמְרֵי הַחֹמוֹת. ח הִשְׁבַּעְתִּי אֶתְכֶם, בְּנוֹת יְרוּשָׁלָיִם,
אִם תִּמְצְאוּ אֶת דּוֹדִי, מַה תַּגִּידוּ לוֹ שֶׁחוֹלַת אַהֲבָה אָנִי.
ט מַה דּוֹדֵךְ מִדּוֹד, הַיָּפָה בַּנָּשִׁים, מַה דּוֹדֵךְ מִדּוֹד, שֶׁכָּכָה
הִשְׁבַּעְתָּנוּ. י דּוֹדִי צַח וְאָדוֹם, דָּגוּל מֵרְבָבָה. יא רֹאשׁוֹ כֶּתֶם
פָּז, קְוֻצּוֹתָיו תַּלְתַּלִּים, שְׁחֹרוֹת כָּעוֹרֵב. יב עֵינָיו כְּיוֹנִים עַל
אֲפִיקֵי מָיִם, רֹחֲצוֹת בֶּחָלָב, יֹשְׁבוֹת עַל מִלֵּאת. יג לְחָיָו
כַּעֲרוּגַת הַבֹּשֶׂם, מִגְדְּלוֹת מֶרְקָחִים, שִׂפְתוֹתָיו שׁוֹשַׁנִּים,
נֹטְפוֹת מוֹר עֹבֵר. יד יָדָיו גְּלִילֵי זָהָב, מְמֻלָּאִים בַּתַּרְשִׁישׁ,
מֵעָיו עֶשֶׁת שֵׁן, מְעֻלֶּפֶת סַפִּירִים. טו שׁוֹקָיו עַמּוּדֵי שֵׁשׁ,
מְיֻסָּדִים עַל אַדְנֵי פָז, מַרְאֵהוּ כַּלְּבָנוֹן, בָּחוּר כָּאֲרָזִים.
טז חִכּוֹ מַמְתַקִּים, וְכֻלּוֹ מַחֲמַדִּים, זֶה דוֹדִי וְזֶה רֵעִי, בְּנוֹת
יְרוּשָׁלָיִם.

ו

א אָנָה הָלַךְ דּוֹדֵךְ, הַיָּפָה בַּנָּשִׁים, אָנָה פָּנָה דוֹדֵךְ, וּנְבַקְשֶׁנּוּ
עִמָּךְ. ב דּוֹדִי יָרַד לְגַנּוֹ, לַעֲרֻגוֹת הַבֹּשֶׂם, לִרְעוֹת בַּגַּנִּים

וְלִלְקֹט שׁוֹשַׁנִּים. ג אֲנִי לְדוֹדִי, וְדוֹדִי לִי, הָרוֹעֶה בַּשּׁוֹשַׁנִּים.
ד יָפָה אַתְּ רַעְיָתִי כְּתִרְצָה, נָאוָה כִּירוּשָׁלָיִם, אֲיֻמָּה
כַּנִּדְגָּלוֹת. ה הָסֵבִּי עֵינַיִךְ מִנֶּגְדִּי, שֶׁהֵם הִרְהִיבֻנִי, שַׂעְרֵךְ
כְּעֵדֶר הָעִזִּים, שֶׁגָּלְשׁוּ מִן הַגִּלְעָד. ו שִׁנַּיִךְ כְּעֵדֶר הָרְחֵלִים,
שֶׁעָלוּ מִן הָרַחְצָה, שֶׁכֻּלָּם מַתְאִימוֹת, וְשַׁכֻּלָה אֵין בָּהֶם.
ז כְּפֶלַח הָרִמּוֹן רַקָּתֵךְ, מִבַּעַד לְצַמָּתֵךְ. ח שִׁשִּׁים הֵמָּה
מְלָכוֹת, וּשְׁמֹנִים פִּילַגְשִׁים, וַעֲלָמוֹת אֵין מִסְפָּר. ט אַחַת
הִיא יוֹנָתִי תַמָּתִי, אַחַת הִיא לְאִמָּהּ, בָּרָה הִיא לְיוֹלַדְתָּהּ,
רָאוּהָ בָנוֹת וַיְאַשְּׁרוּהָ, מְלָכוֹת וּפִילַגְשִׁים, וַיְהַלְלוּהָ. י מִי
זֹאת הַנִּשְׁקָפָה כְּמוֹ שָׁחַר, יָפָה כַלְּבָנָה, בָּרָה כַּחַמָּה, אֲיֻמָּה
כַּנִּדְגָּלוֹת. יא אֶל גִּנַּת אֱגוֹז יָרַדְתִּי לִרְאוֹת בְּאִבֵּי הַנָּחַל,
לִרְאוֹת הֲפָרְחָה הַגֶּפֶן, הֵנֵצוּ הָרִמֹּנִים. יב לֹא יָדַעְתִּי, נַפְשִׁי
שָׂמַתְנִי, מַרְכְּבוֹת עַמִּי נָדִיב.

ז

א שׁוּבִי שׁוּבִי, הַשּׁוּלַמִּית, שׁוּבִי שׁוּבִי וְנֶחֱזֶה בָּךְ, מַה תֶּחֱזוּ
בַּשּׁוּלַמִּית, כִּמְחֹלַת הַמַּחֲנָיִם. ב מַה יָּפוּ פְעָמַיִךְ בַּנְּעָלִים, בַּת
נָדִיב, חַמּוּקֵי יְרֵכַיִךְ כְּמוֹ חֲלָאִים, מַעֲשֵׂה יְדֵי אָמָּן. ג שָׁרְרֵךְ
אַגַּן הַסַּהַר, אַל יֶחְסַר הַמָּזֶג, בִּטְנֵךְ עֲרֵמַת חִטִּים, סוּגָה
בַּשּׁוֹשַׁנִּים. ד שְׁנֵי שָׁדַיִךְ כִּשְׁנֵי עֳפָרִים, תָּאֳמֵי צְבִיָּה. ה צַוָּארֵךְ
כְּמִגְדַּל הַשֵּׁן, עֵינַיִךְ בְּרֵכוֹת בְּחֶשְׁבּוֹן, עַל שַׁעַר בַּת רַבִּים,
אַפֵּךְ כְּמִגְדַּל הַלְּבָנוֹן, צוֹפֶה פְּנֵי דַמָּשֶׂק. ו רֹאשֵׁךְ עָלַיִךְ
כַּכַּרְמֶל, וְדַלַּת רֹאשֵׁךְ כָּאַרְגָּמָן, מֶלֶךְ אָסוּר בָּרְהָטִים. ז מַה
יָּפִית וּמַה נָּעַמְתְּ, אַהֲבָה בַּתַּעֲנוּגִים. ח זֹאת קוֹמָתֵךְ דָּמְתָה
לְתָמָר, וְשָׁדַיִךְ לְאַשְׁכֹּלוֹת. ט אָמַרְתִּי, אֶעֱלֶה בְתָמָר, אֹחֲזָה
בְּסַנְסִנָּיו, וְיִהְיוּ נָא שָׁדַיִךְ כְּאֶשְׁכְּלוֹת הַגֶּפֶן, וְרֵיחַ אַפֵּךְ
כַּתַּפּוּחִים. י וְחִכֵּךְ כְּיֵין הַטּוֹב, הוֹלֵךְ לְדוֹדִי לְמֵישָׁרִים, דּוֹבֵב
שִׂפְתֵי יְשֵׁנִים. יא אֲנִי לְדוֹדִי, וְעָלַי תְּשׁוּקָתוֹ. יב לְכָה דוֹדִי,
נֵצֵא הַשָּׂדֶה, נָלִינָה בַּכְּפָרִים. יג נַשְׁכִּימָה לַכְּרָמִים, נִרְאֶה אִם

פָּרְחָה הַגֶּפֶן, פִּתַּח הַסְּמָדַר, הֵנֵצוּ הָרִמּוֹנִים, שָׁם אֶתֵּן אֶת
דֹּדַי לָךְ. יד הַדּוּדָאִים נָתְנוּ רֵיחַ, וְעַל פְּתָחֵינוּ כָּל מְגָדִים,
חֲדָשִׁים גַּם יְשָׁנִים, דּוֹדִי, צָפַנְתִּי לָךְ.

ח

א מִי יִתֶּנְךָ כְּאָח לִי, יוֹנֵק שְׁדֵי אִמִּי, אֶמְצָאֲךָ בַחוּץ אֶשָּׁקְךָ,
גַּם לֹא יָבֻזוּ לִי. ב אֶנְהָגְךָ, אֲבִיאֲךָ אֶל בֵּית אִמִּי, תְּלַמְּדֵנִי,
אַשְׁקְךָ מִיַּיִן הָרֶקַח, מֵעֲסִיס רִמֹּנִי. ג שְׂמֹאלוֹ תַּחַת רֹאשִׁי,
וִימִינוֹ תְּחַבְּקֵנִי. ד הִשְׁבַּעְתִּי אֶתְכֶם, בְּנוֹת יְרוּשָׁלָיִם, מַה
תָּעִירוּ וּמַה תְּעֹרְרוּ אֶת הָאַהֲבָה עַד שֶׁתֶּחְפָּץ. ה מִי זֹאת
עֹלָה מִן הַמִּדְבָּר, מִתְרַפֶּקֶת עַל דּוֹדָהּ, תַּחַת הַתַּפּוּחַ
עוֹרַרְתִּיךָ, שָׁמָּה חִבְּלַתְךָ אִמֶּךָ, שָׁמָּה חִבְּלָה יְלָדַתְךָ.
ו שִׂימֵנִי כַחוֹתָם עַל לִבֶּךָ, כַּחוֹתָם עַל זְרוֹעֶךָ, כִּי עַזָּה כַמָּוֶת
אַהֲבָה, קָשָׁה כִשְׁאוֹל קִנְאָה, רְשָׁפֶיהָ רִשְׁפֵּי אֵשׁ,
שַׁלְהֶבֶתְיָה. ז מַיִם רַבִּים לֹא יוּכְלוּ לְכַבּוֹת אֶת הָאַהֲבָה,
וּנְהָרוֹת לֹא יִשְׁטְפוּהָ, אִם יִתֵּן אִישׁ אֶת כָּל הוֹן בֵּיתוֹ
בָּאַהֲבָה, בּוֹז יָבוּזוּ לוֹ. ח אָחוֹת לָנוּ קְטַנָּה, וְשָׁדַיִם אֵין לָהּ,
מַה נַּעֲשֶׂה לַאֲחוֹתֵנוּ בַּיּוֹם שֶׁיְּדֻבַּר בָּהּ. ט אִם חוֹמָה הִיא,
נִבְנֶה עָלֶיהָ טִירַת כָּסֶף, וְאִם דֶּלֶת הִיא, נָצוּר עָלֶיהָ לוּחַ
אָרֶז. י אֲנִי חוֹמָה, וְשָׁדַי כַּמִּגְדָּלוֹת, אָז הָיִיתִי בְעֵינָיו
כְּמוֹצְאֵת שָׁלוֹם. יא כֶּרֶם הָיָה לִשְׁלֹמֹה בְּבַעַל הָמוֹן, נָתַן אֶת
הַכֶּרֶם לַנֹּטְרִים, אִישׁ יָבִא בְּפִרְיוֹ אֶלֶף כָּסֶף. יב כַּרְמִי שֶׁלִּי
לְפָנָי, הָאֶלֶף לְךָ שְׁלֹמֹה, וּמָאתַיִם לְנֹטְרִים אֶת פִּרְיוֹ.
יג הַיּוֹשֶׁבֶת בַּגַּנִּים, חֲבֵרִים מַקְשִׁיבִים לְקוֹלֵךְ, הַשְׁמִיעִנִי.
יד בְּרַח דּוֹדִי, וּדְמֵה לְךָ לִצְבִי, אוֹ לְעֹפֶר הָאַיָּלִים, עַל הָרֵי
בְשָׂמִים.

Chassidic Insights: Stories about Tzaddikim

The Shabbos HaGadol Sermon

R' Tzvi Hirsch of Liska

R' Mordechai of Nadvorna to a chasid of *R' Tzvi Hirsch of Liska*:

When you visit your rebbe give him my warm regards and tell him the following:

The author of the *Shulchan Aruch* writes that one should inquire about, and give discourses on, the laws of Pesach thirty days before Pesach *(Orach Chaim* 429). The *Rama* adds: "*and* it is the custom to buy wheat and distribute it among the poor for their Pesach needs. Why has the *Rama* chosen to place his comment about buying wheat as an addendum to speaking on the topics of Pesach, even to the point of joining it to the above with an "*and*"? The *Rama* implies to rabbis that it is more important for them to supply the poor with their Pesach needs than to spend time on their Pesach sermons.

The chasid reached Liska and passed on the thought to his rebbe. A few days later, as the Rebbe sat in his study preparing his *Shabbos HaGadol* talk, a woman entered, weeping, and told him she had no *matzos* for the festival. The Rebbe remembered the words of R' Mordechai of Nadvorna, closed his books, called his sons-in-law and together they left to bake *matzos* for the woman. And when the members of the community saw them on their way, who could refrain from joining them? Everyone left his work and went along, and in a short while the *matzos* had been baked and they together with all the other Pesach provisions were brought to the house of the unfortunate woman (*Sipurim Niflaim* 14).

Preparations for Pesach

R' Simchah Bunim of Psishcha

Before Pesach, all of Israel scrubs and scours it pots and pans; soaks and scalds them. This is exceptionally important. But those who possess understanding should realize that this is the way to spiritual redemption, too. Before we are judged worthy of deliverance we must remove the stains of our soul by a cleansing, a soaking, a scalding of the spirit. The verse says (about choosing the Pesach sacrifice in Egypt): "Draw forth and take [sheep or goats] to yourselves" (*Shemos* 12:21). *Chazal* comment to this: "Draw your hand away from idol worship and take a *Pesach* sacrifice" (*Shemos Rabbah* 16:2) "Draw away from idol worship"; that is what is involved in the pre-Pesach cleaning and scouring. It is a condition which we must fill to be worthy of the deliverance on Pesach (*Siach Sarfei Kodesh* I :53).

Ahavas Yisrael of Vizhnitz

A man once came before the *Ahavas Yisrael of Vizhnitz* and poured his heart out. He had arranged a match for his son some time before, but he had no funds with which to meet the many wedding expenses. The Rebbe asked if they had already set a date for the wedding. "No," replied the man, "I have no wherewithal to pay for anything. How could I set a date?"

"Look," said the Rebbe, "our Torah has demanded of us that not a particle of *chametz* be found in our home on Pesach, and Pesach expenses are large. Now, imagine that the Torah had not set a date for Pesach and that we would only celebrate it when we had completed our preparations; we would never celebrate it. But since the Torah has established a specific date, a great wonder takes place. All the women manage to clean their homes; all the needs of Pesach are filled. Take a lesson from the Torah. Set the wedding date, and you will see that you will succeed in acquiring whatever you need by then" (*Kedosh Yisrael* I, ch. 15,12).

Drawing Water for Matzos

R' Yechiel Meir of Ovstrovtza

Two times a year, Israel goes down to the river. On Rosh Hashanah they go to cast away their sins (תַּשְׁלִיךְ). And before Pesach they go to draw water for the baking of *matzos*. The actions and the times are significant.

On Rosh Hashanah we repent because of fear, fear of the imminent judgment, and we throw our sins from us. But on Pesach we were chosen as an elect nation against a background of miracles. Then is the time for repentance (*teshuvah*) because of love. And when one does *teshuvah* from love, "the intentional sins" are changed into worthy acts in his favor (*Yoma* 86b). Then we return to the river to gather up the sins which we had cast away and transform them into shining deeds of merit (*Bircas Chaim* II, p. 114).

Maggid of Osteroha

Rav Yeiv'i, the Maggid of Osteroha rode towards the river in his carriage, on his way to draw water for the baking of *matzos*. He caught sight of the sage the *Meir Nesivim*, rabbi of the town and one of the important disciples of the *Ba'al Shem Tov*, trudging along on foot. R' Yeiv'i halted the carriage and said, "Would the honored Rabbi please join me? Why dirty your feet in the mud?"

The Rabbi smiled and replied, "I have a chance to do this precious *mitzvah*, which comes but once a year. Shall I hand it over to the horses?"

When R' Yeiv'i heard this, he hurriedly descended from the carriage and accompanied the Rabbi on foot (*Dor De'ah*).

The Search for Chametz

Ahavas Yisrael of Vizhnitz

The preparations of the *Ahavas Yisrael of Vizhnitz* for the search for *chametz* were lengthy and he approached the act with great feeling. He made the blessing on the removal of *chametz* with great fervor while wearing his tall fur hat (*spodek*). He would search the cracks and crannies by candlelight, constantly beating his chest and calling out, "Oy, oy, oy!" All who heard him trembled, and their hearts broke to the sound of his groans.

When he had completed the search, he turned to his faithful chasid, R' Mordechai Chaneh, and standing before him, he tore open his shirt, baring his chest and said, "Now, search out the *chametz* in my heart."

R' Mordechai did not lose his presence of mind and replied, "Rebbe, the *halachah* instructs us that we need not search a place where *chametz* has not entered" (*Kedosh Yisrael* I, ch. 14, 28).

"Put what is left (of the chametz) in a hidden place lest a rat take it up" (Pesachim 9).

Imrei Chaim of Vizhnitz

Chametz signifies pride; it rises and we must be rid of it. But as with *chametz*, we must leave something of it. As *Chazal* have put it: a wise man should have an eighth of an eighth of pride. Pride is at times needed in our service to Hashem, as it is stated: "And his heart *rose up* in the ways of Hashem" (II *Divrei HaYamim* 17:6). Yet, man must take care that the small measure of pride which he leaves over be in a hidden place; he should take great care lest a rat come and spread it about — lest the evil desire (*yetzer hara*) not persuade him to make his pride public (*Likutei Imrei Chaim* 142).

The Burning of the Chametz

Beis Aharon of Karlin

We are to search for *chametz* in all places "where the hand can reach." We must rid ourselves of the *yetzer hara* to the limit of our powers and "proclaim the rest non-existent". That we do with our heart — with the burning, passion of the heart. For there is no removal of *chametz* but through burning, through the flame and fervor of our clinging to the Creator (*Beis Karlin-Stolin* 225).

Even a Particle of Chametz is Forbidden

R' Menachem Mendel of Kotzk

Since the Torah was so concerned about our putting distance between ourselves and *chametz* and was so harsh in the punishment meted out to those who violate the prohibition of *chametz*, would it not have been preferable to completely forbid the eating of grain products on Pesach, including *matzah*? Why then, are we instructed to eat *matzah*?

The answer is that it is not much of an accomplishment to swear off eating. The feat is to eat and avoid the forbidden (*Siach Sarfei Kodesh* I 387).

R' Levi Yitzchak of Berditchov

Once, on the day before Pesach, after noon, *R' Levi Yitzchak of Berditchov* went to the marketplace, called over a gentile, gave him a coin, and said, "Bring me some foreign-made snuff." The man was back in a moment with the contraband merchandise. The Rebbe thanked him and, turning to a nearby Jew, said, "Here, take this coin and buy me a loaf of bread from a Jew." The man was shaken and cried out, "Rebbe, it is the day before Pesach and the possession of *chametz* is already forbidden at this hour!"

R' Levi Yitzchak lifted his eyes on high and said, "Behold, Master of the world, who is like Your nation Israel? The czar has forbidden the sale of this snuff and appointed thousands of guards and inspectors to maintain his decree; he has punished offenders with fines and prison. Yet, nevertheless, huge quantities of the forbidden product are smuggled in. You have written in Your Torah: 'And *chametz* shall not be seen by you' (*Shemos* 13:7). You have not appointed a single guard or inspector and, nevertheless, one cannot even get a smidgen of *chametz* from a Jewish home" (*Toledos Kedushas Levi* 67).

מַצָּה שְׁמוּרָה — *'Guarded' Matzah*

R' Avraham of Tchechinov

Year after year, *R' Avraham of Tchechinov* would go out to the fields with his chasidim to stand over the reapers and keep a watchful eye over the wheat as it was harvested. When the sheaves were loaded onto the wagon, he would walk behind it, with a hand on its side. Once, the wagon passed through a puddle. The Rebbe went around the puddle and returned to his position behind the wagon. The wheat was threshed, winnowed, and sifted under his observant care, then stored in the granary to be used for *matzos* of *mitzvah*.

When Pesach drew near, the Rebbe asked his son *R' Yaakov of Yezov* to write to his chasidim in Poltosk asking that they send wheat for the baking of *matzos*.

"We have wheat of our own which we guarded carefully," said a puzzled R' Yaakov.

"Those moments when my hand left the wagon, when I skirted the puddle, were moments when my attention shifted away from the wheat and it lost its status of being under watch."

"And do you think that the chasid in Poltosk did not allow his attention to wander for even a moment?" asked his son.

"In matters of the forbidden and permitted we accept the testimony of a single witness. A man who says that his wheat was under watch is presumed to be telling the truth. But I — I know that my mind wandered for a moment" (*Sipurim Niflaim*).

Beis Aharon of Karlin Not only *what* we do is important, but also *how* we do it and *why*.

For example, if water spills on flour designated for the special *sh'mura matzah*, everyone strikes his hands together in sorrow. Yet what is the normal order of things? In the end, we deliberately pour water on the flour to bake *matzos* and we accompany the pouring with a song of praise. It may be the very same flour, the very same water. But the intention and purpose make all the difference (*Darchei Aharon* 22).

R' Yitzchak of Neschiz A chasid poured out his trouble before *R' Yitzchak of Neschiz*. The wheat he had guarded for *matzos* had become *chametz* and he would be forced to eat the simple "unguarded" *matzos* on Pesach.

"The eating of *matzah sh'mura* ("guarded" *matzos)* is only an adornment to the *mitzvah*" said the Rebbe, "but the commandment to rejoice on the festival is itself given in the Torah. It is preferable to eat the simple *matzah* in joy rather than the "guarded" *matzah* in sadness" (*Chasidim Mesaprim* I 637).

The Baking of Matzos

R' Pinchas of Radvanka Becoming angry is more serious than violating the prohibition against *chametz* in one respect. *Chametz*, even a particle, is forbidden for one week of the year; anger, even a smidgen, is forbidden throughout the entire year (*Uvda D'Aharon*, p. 32).

R' Tzvi Elimelech of Dinov Once, the *Chozeh of Lublin* asked his disciples to bake the *matzos*. They agreed to assemble at a given hour and chose *R' Tzvi Elimelech of Dinov* to be their leader.

Noon came and went, and there was no R' Tzvi Elimelech. They searched the Rebbe's *beis midrash* and R' Tzvi Elimelech's lodgings, without success.

"We know," said *R' Chaim of Sanz*, the youngest among them, "that R' Tzvi Elimelech does not perform a *mitzvah* before he has studied all that *Chazal* have said on the matter and all that is found in *kabbalah* and *chasidus* pertaining to it. I am certain that he is sitting in the *beis midrash* of the *Maharshal* which has many books."

They went there immediately and, sure enough, there was R' Tzvi Elimelech, immersed in study, books piled high on either side of him (*Rabbeinu HaKadosh of Sanz* I p. 25).